Mastering First Amendment Law

Carolina Academic Press Mastering Series

Russell Weaver, Series Editor

Mastering Administrative Law, Second Edition
Linda D. Jellum

Mastering Adoption Law and Policy
Cynthia Hawkins DeBose

Mastering Alternative Dispute Resolution
Kelly M. Feeley, James A. Sheehan

Mastering American Indian Law
Angelique Wambdi EagleWoman, Stacy L. Leeds

Mastering Appellate Advocacy and Process, Revised Printing
Donna C. Looper, George W. Kuney

Mastering Art Law
Herbert Lazerow

Mastering Bankruptcy
George W. Kuney

Mastering Civil Procedure, Third Edition
David Charles Hricik

Mastering Constitutional Law, Second Edition
John C. Knechtle, Christopher J. Roederer

Mastering Contract Law
Irma S. Russell, Barbara K. Bucholtz

Mastering Corporate Tax, Second Edition
Gail Levin Richmond, Reginald Mombrun, Felicia Branch

Mastering Corporations and Other Business Entities, Second Edition
Lee Harris

Mastering Criminal Law, Second Edition
Ellen S. Podgor, Peter J. Henning, Neil P. Cohen

Mastering Criminal Procedure, Volume 1: The Investigative Stage, Second Edition
Peter J. Henning, Andrew Taslitz, Margaret L. Paris, Cynthia E. Jones, Ellen S. Podgor

Mastering Criminal Procedure, Volume 2: The Adjudicatory Stage, Second Edition
Peter J. Henning, Andrew Taslitz, Margaret L. Paris, Cynthia E. Jones, Ellen S. Podgor

Mastering Elder Law, Second Edition
Ralph C. Brashier

Mastering Employment Discrimination Law, Second Edition
Paul M. Secunda, Jeffrey M. Hirsch, Joseph A. Seiner

Mastering Evidence
Ronald W. Eades

Mastering Family Law
Janet Leach Richards

Mastering First Amendment Law
John C. Knechtle

Mastering Income Tax
Christopher M. Pietruszkiewicz, Gail Levin Richmond

Mastering Intellectual Property
George W. Kuney, Donna C. Looper

Mastering Labor Law
Paul M. Secunda, Anne Marie Lofaso, Joseph E. Slater, Jeffrey M. Hirsch

Mastering Legal Analysis and Communication
David T. Ritchie

Mastering Legal Analysis and Drafting
George W. Kuney, Donna C. Looper

Mastering Negotiable Instruments (UCC Articles 3 and 4) and Other Payment Systems, Second Edition
Michael D. Floyd

Mastering Negotiation
Michael R. Fowler

Mastering Partnership Taxation
Stuart Lazar

Mastering Products Liability
Ronald W. Eades

Mastering Professional Responsibility, Second Edition
Grace M. Giesel

Mastering Property Law, Revised Printing
Darryl C. Wilson, Cynthia Hawkins DeBose

Mastering Secured Transactions: UCC Article 9, Second Edition
Richard H. Nowka

Mastering Statutory Interpretation, Second Edition
Linda D. Jellum

Mastering Tort Law, Second Edition
Russell L. Weaver, Edward C. Martin, Andrew R. Klein, Paul J. Zwier, II, John H. Bauman

Mastering Trademark and Unfair Competition Law
Lars S. Smith, Llewellyn Joseph Gibbons

Mastering Trusts and Estates
Gail Levin Richmond, Don Castleman

Mastering First Amendment Law

John C. Knechtle
Senior Lecturer, Faculty of Law
The University of the West Indies, St. Augustine

Carolina Academic Press
Durham, North Carolina

Library of Congress Cataloging-in-Publication

Names: Knechtle, John C., author.
Title: Mastering First Amendment law / John C. Knechtle.
Description: Durham, North Carolina : Carolina Academic Press, LLC, 2016. | Series: Mastering series | Includes bibliographical references and index.
Identifiers: LCCN 2016044627 | ISBN 9781594605819 (alk. paper)
Subjects: LCSH: United States. Constitution. 1st Amendment. | Freedom of expression--United States.
Classification: LCC KF4770 .K66 2016 | DDC 342.7308/5--dc23
LC record available at https://lccn.loc.gov/2016044627

eISBN: 978-1-5310-1153-6

Carolina Academic Press, LLC
700 Kent Street
Durham, North Carolina 27701
Telephone (919) 489-7486
Fax (919) 493-5668
www.cap-press.com

Printed in the United States of America

To Heather:

"The minute I heard my first love story, I started looking for you,
not knowing how blind that was.
Lovers don't finally meet somewhere.
They're in each other all along."
—*Rumi*

To Lily, Matthew, Blake and Lucy:

"Freedom of speech does not protect you from the aftermath."
—*JCK*

"Believe in truth. To abandon facts is to abandon freedom. If nothing is true, then no one can criticize power, because there is no basis upon which to do so. If nothing is true, then all is spectacle. The biggest wallet pays for the most blinding lights."
—*Timothy Snyder*

To students of the First Amendment:

"We should be eternally vigilant against attempts to check the expression of opinions that we loathe and believe to be fraught with death, unless they so imminently threaten immediate interference with the lawful and pressing purposes of the law that an immediate check is required to save the country."
—*Oliver Wendell Holmes dissent, Abrams v. United States (1919)*

"Speech is often provocative and challenging. It may strike at prejudices and preconceptions and have profound unsettling effects as it presses for acceptance of an idea. That is why freedom of speech, though not absolute, is nevertheless protected against censorship or punishment . . . There is no room under our Constitution for a more restrictive view. For the alternative would lead to standardization of ideas either by legislatures, courts, or dominant political or community groups."
—*William O. Douglas, Terminiello v. City of Chicago (1949)*

"If there is any fixed star in our constitutional constellation, it is that no official, high or petty, can prescribe what shall be orthodox in politics, nationalism, religion, or other matters of opinion or force citizens to confess by word or act their faith therein."
—*Robert H. Jackson, West Virginia State Board of Education v. Barnette (1943)*

Contents

Table of Cases

Series Editor's Foreword

The Carolina Academic Press Mastering Series is designed to provide you with a tool that will enable you to easily and efficiently "master" the substance and content of law school courses. Throughout the series, the focus is on quality writing that makes legal concepts understandable. As a result, the series is designed to be easy to read and is not unduly cluttered with footnotes or cites to secondary sources.

In order to facilitate student mastery of topics, the Mastering Series includes a number of pedagogical features designed to improve learning and retention. At the beginning of each chapter, you will find a "Roadmap" that tells you about the chapter and provides you with a sense of the material that you will cover. A "Checkpoint" at the end of each chapter encourages you to stop and review the key concepts, reiterating what you have learned. Throughout the book, key terms are explained and emphasized. Finally, a "Master Checklist" at the end of each book reinforces what you have learned and helps you identify any areas that need review or further study.

We hope that you will enjoy studying with, and learning from, the Mastering Series.

Russell L. Weaver
Professor of Law & Distinguished University Scholar
University of Louisville, Louis D. Brandeis School of Law

Mastering First Amendment Law

Introduction

The First Amendment expressly protects six freedoms:

> Congress shall make no law [1] respecting an establishment of religion or [2] prohibiting the free exercise thereof; or [3] abridging the freedom of speech, or [4] of the press; or [5] the right of the people peaceably to assemble, and [6] to petition the Government for a redress of grievances.

Although courts and commentators often merge establishment and free exercise into freedom of religion, absorb free press into free speech, dissolve freedom to peaceably assemble into freedom of association and free speech, and relegate the right to petition to the dustbin of history, the founders thought it important to identify each freedom separately. In fact, the history of these rights shows that although related, each freedom is a distinct and separate right.

The Supreme Court has added freedom of association as a fundamental right protected by the First Amendment, despite not being mentioned in the text. The court grounds this right "to engage in association for the advancement of beliefs and ideas" in the First Amendment's right to assemble peaceably and right to free speech, as well as the "liberty" interest in the 14th Amendment's due process clause. Because the Supreme Court recognized this right long after the adoption of the First Amendment, its context will be examined under freedom to peaceably assemble and in Chapter 5.

I. A Brief History of the First Amendment

The drafters of the First Amendment incorporated substantially broader views regarding the freedoms of religion, speech, press, assembly and petition than English common law of 1790. However, those views were still much more restrictive, both in to whom they applied and in scope, than today's Supreme Court jurisprudence and popularly held views. This ability of First

Amendment "rights" to evolve over time may be the secret to the Amendment's longevity and deep support.

This growth in First Amendment rights tracks the historical devolution of power from concentrated central authority to group and individual rights. Every minority group, whether based on religion, race, ethnicity, gender, age, disability, sexual orientation or some other characteristic, gained rights only after fighting long and tenacious battles. The rights King John agreed to recognize under Magna Carta were based upon the demands of a small group of powerful barons, and initially only applied to them. Over time as the desire and demand for freedom grew, the rights expanded both in their coverage and understanding.

The most obvious example from the nation's founding was the institution of slavery. The first draft of the Declaration of Independence by Thomas Jefferson condemned King George for allowing the slave trade in the colonies, labeling it "a cruel war against human nature." Yet in order to assemble all thirteen colonies to form the new republic, Jefferson's outrage was removed from the Constitution as a concession to the delegates from South Carolina and Georgia. Thus the founding fathers never maintained the moral high ground in the push for independence and many saw the hypocrisy of demanding freedom for themselves, but not for the slaves in the southern colonies. Dr. Samuel Johnson, immortalized by James Boswell's biography, asked "How is it that we hear the loudest yelps for liberty from the drivers of Negroes?" Yet Thomas Jefferson's soaring rhetoric in the Declaration of Independence, "*We hold these truths to be self-evident, that all men are created equal, that they are endowed by their Creator with certain unalienable Rights*" continued to inspire. It wasn't until the struggle of slaves for freedom, the Abolitionist Movement, Civil War, Emancipation Proclamation and the adoption of the 13th, 14th, and 15th Amendments, and the Civil Rights Movement that Jefferson's words and the first words of the Constitution, "*We the People of the United States,*" began to have meaning for African Americans.

Another example is the right to vote and hold office, the essence of who participates in democracy. At the time of independence, typically white, male, property owners, twenty-one or older could vote and run for office if they paid poll taxes. It wasn't until the Women's Suffrage Movement, Civil Rights Movement, Vietnam War and the adoption of the 19th, 24th and 26th Amendments, that all races, both genders, and those 18 and over, regardless of property ownership and payment of poll taxes, could vote and run for office.

First Amendment rights also began with narrow application and expanded with time. After the adoption of the First Amendment in 1791, state governments taxed their residents to support the established church and openly discriminated on the basis of religion in government jobs. Through the Alien and Sedition Acts of 1798, the federal government criminalized speech that criticized government leaders. Matthew Lyon, a member of Congress from Vermont, was convicted of seditious libel and imprisoned for writing in a letter that President John Adams had "unbounded thirst for ridiculous pomp, foolish adulation, and self avarice." Today the Supreme Court would unanimously strike down such state and federal acts as unconstitutional under the First Amendment. Martin Luther King Jr. characterized this evolution of rights when stating, "the arc of the moral universe is long, but it bends toward justice."

The first ten amendments to the Constitution protect many of the fundamental freedoms that today are considered basic international human rights. They were not included with the original text of the constitution when ratified by the states. However, they were essential to the ratification of the Constitution. Many Americans were afraid of a strong central government because of their perceived mistreatment by the English government. Those Americans saw the proposed Constitution as placing too much power in the hands of the federal government and felt they needed written guarantees of rights that the federal government could not take away without their permission. Many who supported the adoption of the Constitution without the amendments argued that the new federal government possessed only specifically delegated powers and because the text did not grant powers over speech, press and religion, the federal government had no power to regulate them.

One delegate at the Constitutional Convention, George Mason, who helped draft Virginia's Declaration of Rights, proposed adding a bill of rights to the Constitution which would protect civil liberties. Other delegates, including future Bill of Rights drafter James Madison, disagreed, arguing that existing state guarantees of civil liberties were sufficient and that any attempt to enumerate individual rights risked the implication that other, unnamed rights were unprotected. After a brief debate, Mason's proposal was defeated by a unanimous vote of the state delegations.

The Constitution was adopted and signed in September 1787 and then brought to the states for ratification. The Constitution had to be ratified by nine of the 13 states to become binding. That happened when New Hampshire ratified it on June 21, 1788. During the constitutional ratification debates, the Anti-Federalist's opposition to ratification was partly based on the Constitution's lack of adequate guarantees for civil liberties, including liberty of conscience. The last five original states to ratify the constitution, New Hampshire, Virginia, New York, North Carolina, and Rhode Island, requested an amendment to the constitution protecting religious liberty. The Virginia

Convention, in its ratification statement, expressed its understanding that the Federal Government could not limit religious liberty: "Among other essential rights, the liberty of conscience, and of the press, cannot be cancelled, abridged, restrained, or modified, by any authority of the United States."

In 1789, James Madison, fulfilling a campaign promise and meeting the demands of the ratifying bodies of five states, began working on a Bill of Rights. Drawing on the Magna Carta of 1215, English Bill of Rights of 1689, Virginia's Declaration of Rights (written by George Mason in 1776) and state constitutions, Madison introduced 39 amendments in the House. The House passed seventeen, the Senate passed twelve, and the states ratified ten. These ten amendments became known as the Bill of Rights.

The groundwork for these ten amendments was laid in the state constitutions. All of the rights contained in the Bill of Rights could be found in at least one of the state constitutions adopted between 1776 and 1780. Although Connecticut and Rhode Island chose to retain their colonial charters and just delete references to the monarchy, the other eleven wrote constitutions that included common law rights and newly articulated natural law rights. Seven of the eleven wrote a separate Declaration of Rights and in Virginia and Delaware, these bill of rights were written chronologically and conceptually prior to the constitution.

An important conceptual shift in separation of powers occurred between the newly adopted state constitutions (1776–1780) and the adoption of the Bill of Rights in 1791. The shift moved power from the legislature to the judiciary. State constitutions created a weak executive, an independent judiciary, and a dominant legislature with the bill of rights thought to protect the people from an unreasonable executive. By 1791 the federal Bill of Rights was viewed as protecting minority groups from an unreasonable Congressional majority and with this shift, the courts instead of the legislatures, were viewed as the protector and enforcer of these rights. This conceptual shift lay the foundation for Marbury v. Madison's (1803) assertion of judicial review of legislative and administrative acts, and the application of the Bill of Rights to states through the 14th Amendment beginning in Gitlow v. New York (1925). This shift of emphasis from legislative to judicial protection of rights did not occur in European democracies until after World War II.

A. Freedom from an Established Religion and Freedom to Practice Religion

The First Amendment has two clauses regarding religion: the first, freedom from an established religion, referred to as the establishment clause, and the second, freedom to practice religion, referred to as the free exercise clause. The establishment clause prohibits the government from establishing a particular religion because this would force non-adherents to practice or support a religion in which they do not believe, and from giving preferential treatment to a particular religion which could cause division. The free exercise clause prohibits the government from interfering with an individual or group's religious practice. Most of the colonies had established religions and interfered with the free practice of minority religions. This continued after the adoption of the First Amendment so religious liberty by today's standards was quite limited at the founding.

Escaping religious persecution was one motivation for European immigrants to uproot their families and sail across the Atlantic Ocean to the New World. However, it took more experience before they would support the religious freedom principles embedded in the First Amendment. Typically, the dominant religious group in a settler community used political power to continue the theocratic approach to government, only the roles were reversed. The once religiously oppressed became the religious oppressors as they discriminated against those who believed differently. One way colonies sought to protect the religious sensibilities of the community was to criminalize blasphemy (irreverence, insult or rudeness towards God or sacred things). However, the crime of blasphemy was often coupled or conflated with heresy (any belief or theory strongly at variance with established beliefs or customs), treason (numerous offences against the King, Queen, eldest son, eldest daughter, high officials, etc.) and sedition (speech or conduct that tends toward insurrection against the established order). Until the late 18th century, convicted blasphemers were punished by death, banishment or whipping. Although religious discrimination involved all religions, the overwhelming majority of European settlers belonged at least nominally to some strain of Christianity, so most of the settler victims of this intolerance were other Christians.

The journey to religious freedom in the colonies was largely the story of the dominant religion, Christianity, adapting to the growing religious diversity which immigrants brought to the shores of the New World. This occurred in overlapping stages with the first stage, Protestant denominations tolerating other Protestant denominations, and Protestants tolerating Catholics, the focus during the 17th and 18th centuries. The next two stages, Christians tolerating Jews, Muslims and other major religious groups, and finally Christians tolerating the more esoteric minority religions, atheism and unbelief, did not occur until migrants and adherents of these groups reached sufficient numbers in the 19th and 20th centuries. This journey to religious freedom benefitted other freedoms because once people could tolerate other religious thought and practices (often the most deeply held views), it laid a path to tolerate other views and practices (political, social, economic, etc). This tolerance of differences impacted understandings of free speech, freedom of association, freedom to peaceably assemble and free press.

In the early 1600s, English Puritans settled in New England and attempted to create a new, perfect union of church and state. They sought to "purify" the Church of England by getting rid of Catholic rituals, artwork, and hierarchy and instead, focus on studying the authority of the Bible. Most Puritans were "non-separating Puritans" meaning they advocated reform but not separating from the Church of England; a small minority of Puritans were "separating Puritans" who advocated breaking from the Church of England. One separatist group, the Pilgrims, after being persecuted for their religious beliefs in England migrated to Holland where they experienced religious tolerance. There they found it difficult to maintain their English identity and make a living. After King James I of England gave them a charter to settle in Virginia where they thought they would have their own "English" community, a better life financially, and religious freedom, they set off for the New World. They were blown off course and landed at Plymouth Rock, Massachusetts in 1620. Many died the first year due to the harshness of the climate and they may not have survived if not for the support of the Native American tribes. However, the Pilgrims failed to achieve lasting economic success and several prominent members left to found other communities. The Massachusetts Bay Colony absorbed Plymouth in 1692.

In 1630 about 1,000 non-separating Puritans under the leadership of John Winthrop established the Massachusetts Bay Colony, which later became the most populous and prosperous colony in New England. The Puritans started the Congregational Church, a distinguishing feature being the complete autonomy of the local congregation, reflecting their rejection of Anglican Church hierarchy and the acceptance of more democratic norms. The life of Puritans in New England centered on their Congregational meetinghouse, both for self-governance and for religious worship. During most of the colonial period Congregationalism was the established church in New England, outside of Rhode Island. It received all taxes for the support of religion and with the civil authorities, expelled those of other religions, including Baptists and Quakers. In 1658 Massachusetts decided on the gruesome penalty of cutting off the ears of offending Quakers, before banishing them. Between 1658 and 1661, four Quakers were convicted of blasphemy and hung on the Boston Common for returning to the colony after being expelled for proclaiming their Quaker beliefs. With the adoption of the Cart and Whip Act in 1662,

Quakers were tied to a cart, stripped to the waist (in any season), and whipped while walking behind the cart all the way to the colony border.

According to Leonard Levy, Massachusetts's execution of the four Quakers was the last death penalty imposed for a blasphemy conviction in America and blasphemy prosecutions declined. In the 1660s there were eleven prosecutions, all in New England, five in Connecticut, four in Plymouth, and two in Maine. There were four cases in the 1670s and six in the 1680s.

In 1635 Roger Williams, Cambridge educated and of Welsh descent, became the minister of a church in Salem, Massachusetts. Shortly thereafter he was brought before a General Court of the Massachusetts Bay Colony and charged with teaching four false doctrines: that the true owners of the land were the Indians; that one should not pray with the unregenerate; that communion could not be had with the ministers of the Church of England; and that civil power could not be used to enforce religious opinions. After he admitted the truth of these charges the court ordered him to leave the colony. In the middle of January 1636 Williams fled from Salem and moved south to Narragansett Bay (what is today part of Rhode Island) where he purchased land from the Indians. In 1638, he along with 12 followers, signed a social compact in which they agreed to submit themselves "to all such orders or agreements as shall be made for the public good of the body, in an orderly way, by the major consent of the present inhabitants ... *only in civil things*."

In order to resist encroachment from the Puritans to his north, Roger Williams returned to England in 1644 to obtain a patent from parliament recognizing the Providence Plantation's legal title to the land. While there he published his classic defense of religious freedom, *The Bloudy Tenent of Persecution for the Cause of Conscience Discussed* in the same year, 1644, that John Milton wrote his great plea for freedom of conscience, *Areopagitica*. William's views influenced the Portsmouth assembly when it met in 1647 to draft and sign a governing instrument for the Commonwealth of Rhode Island and Providence Plantation. The founding document stated, "All men may walk as their consciences persuade them, everyone in the name of his God." The doctrine of religious freedom and the separation of church and state were officially recognized. Conceived out of Puritan heresy, Rhode Island became a seat for religious pluralism and freedom, remarkable for its day. The First Baptist Church at Providence formed by Roger Williams and his followers is generally called the first Baptist church in America. Quakers, Anglicans, and Congregationalists also flourished. Later it was a colonial center for Judaism, and eventually it would have more Roman Catholics, in proportion to its population, than any state in the Union.

In 1634, Anne Hutchinson and her husband left England to follow Anglican Minister John Cotton to the Massachusetts Bay Colony. As the daughter of a discredited Anglican minister, she questioned authority and was an independent thinker. She was particularly drawn to John Cotton's theology of absolute grace, which pointed her life in the direction of study and interpreting the Bible. Taking Cotton's doctrine of the Holy Ghost dwelling within a "justified person", Hutchinson "saw herself as a mystic participant in the transcendent power of the Almighty." This theology empowered women and gave them a voice in a society where the status of a woman was determined by the husband or father. Hutchinson's theology of a personal continuing revelation stood in opposition to the dominant Reformed doctrine of a closed canon of biblical revelation. Concerned about maintaining order in their community and protecting their exclusive position as sole interpreters of the Bible, the magistrates quickly confronted any deviance from their strict doctrine. Governor John Winthrop charged Hutchinson with sedition and heresy. At her trial in November 1637, Winthrop interrogated her and claimed that she had defamed the ministers by questioning their Bible teachings. Toward the end of the trial, Hutchinson claimed her revelations came directly from God, which was a clear case of heresy in Puritan Massachusetts because they believed God spoke only through the Bible. As a result, she was excommunicated from the Church of Boston and banished from the colony. With her husband, she travelled to and established the settlement of Portsmouth (which later became part of the Colony of Rhode Island), where she and a group of followers drafted and signed the Portsmouth Compact on March 7, 1638. This was the first document in colonial history that severed both political and religious ties with mother England.

Over time, the Massachusetts puritans found it increasingly difficult to maintain the exclusivity of their "City on a Hill" because of pressure from England and to splits among the puritans. After the Glorious Revolution of 1688 when William and Mary assumed the throne of England, the colony lost its charter. Its renewal in 1692 was subject to parliament's *English Act of Toleration of 1689* which granted freedom of worship to Nonconformists who had taken the oaths of Allegiance and Supremacy and rejected transubstantiation. This included certain Protestants who dissented from the Church of England (i.e. Baptists and Congregationalists) but not Catholics, nontrinitarians, atheists or those who practiced other religions. This Act demonstrated that the idea of a "comprehensive" Church of England had been abandoned and that hope lay only in toleration of division among certain Protestants. So William and Mary's second Charter to the Massachusetts Bay Colony required granting a degree of religious toleration to Protestants. Although the Act and second Charter did not include Catholicism or any other religion, recognizing that no Protestant denomination could maintain a government-enforced monopoly on religious worship and practice, constituted an important step in the evolution of religious freedom.

In 1636, Connecticut separated from Massachusetts and became its own colony. The Congregational Church was the established, tax-supported church and laws compelled attendance. However, in the late 1700s, John Leyland, an itinerant Baptist preacher, became a famous proponent of religious liberty in Connecticut (as well as in Virginia). Baptists were an oppressed religious minority in most of the colonies, and like most Baptists of the time, he advocated strict separation between church and state. He opposed the use of tax money to support any church or Congressional or army chaplains and advocated religious freedom for all, not just Christians. He said, "The notion of a Christian commonwealth should be exploded forever ... Government should protect every man in thinking and speaking freely, and see that one does not abuse another ... all should be equally free, Jews, Turks, Pagans and Christians."

Roman Catholics were even less welcomed in the colonies than fellow Protestants. Although Spanish Catholic Missions in Florida supported trips into Georgia, Carolina, and as far north as the Chesapeake Bay, they did not create a lasting presence in the 13 colonies (Spanish Catholic missions in California developed later: 1760–1833). The same was true about Missions from New France that approached the colonies from the north (present day Canada and parts of Maine). Protestant Britain's long wars with Catholic France starting in 1688 and culminating in the French and Indian Wars (1756–1763) only heightened anti-Catholic sentiment in the colonies.

"Mary-land" was carved out of the existing crown colony of Virginia under unusual circumstances. George Calvert, first Lord Baltimore, was secretary of state of England when, due to his conversion to the Catholic faith in 1625, he was forced to resign. However, he remained in Royal favor and shortly after his death in 1632, Charles I delivered the Maryland charter to his son, Cecilius Calvert who allowed freedom of religion to all Christians who settled in Maryland. Despite this auspicious beginning—at least for Christians—Maryland soon reverted to intolerance. At the time of the American Revolution, only 1.2% of the 2.5 million white population of the thirteen seaboard colonies was Catholic.

The modest success of Quaker colonization in western New Jersey stimulated one of its leaders, William Penn (1644–1718), to lay plans for a larger colony based upon religious freedom, representative government, cheap land, and feudal proprietary. The colony would be a haven for poor and oppressed peoples, an example of enlightened government, and a source of income for his family. In 1661 he persuaded Charles II to discharge a substantial financial obligation to him by making him owner and governor of what was to become Pennsylvania. William Penn's "Holy Experiment" became the "Keystone State" of American religious history, first among Christian denominations and then for all religions. In addition to becoming a world center of Quaker influence, the country's first Presbyterian church was organized in Philadelphia, the Episcopal Church in the U.S. was constituted in Philadelphia, the Roman Catholic Church laid foundations there upon which later immigration built, the Moravians, Mennonites, Amish, and other German groups flourished there, and the African Methodist Episcopal church—the first independent African American denomination—had its origins there. As the chief residence of Benjamin Franklin, it was the seat of the American Philosophical Society and the birthplace of both the Declaration of Independence and the Constitution. Penn's experiment, while showing the possibilities, also encountered difficulty. In 1705, after hearing reports of the public celebration of Mass in Pennsylvania (circulated to embarrass Penn), Queen Anne required the colony to enforce laws that prevented Roman Catholics from voting or holding office. The 1790 Pennsylvania Constitution eliminated this bar from holding public office.

Virginia was named after Queen Elizabeth. On May 24, 1607, four years after her death, the *Susan Constant*, the *Godspeed*, and the *Discovery* landed on the shores of the James River, starting an English colony that finally took root. The Church of England was the established church though religion was hardly the primary motive of the London merchants who funded the trip. The religious motives included halting the advance of popery and evangelizing the Indians, the latter obligation recognized in their (and every subsequent) colonial charter. In 1629, Virginia ejected Lord Baltimore and his Roman Catholic followers after they refused to take the Oath of Supremacy. The Oath of Supremacy required any person taking public or church office to swear allegiance to the monarch as Head of the Church of England. Roman Catholics who refused to take the Oath of Supremacy were indicted for treason.

Religious discrimination in the colonies was most severe for the Native Americans, Jews, African slaves, and other non-Christians. No founder expressed any interest in accommodating the African religions of the slaves or the Native American religions. Evangelizing the Indians for Christianity was a priority for many of the early settlers. While these Christians had considerable difficulty understanding the piety of the Jews, the animistic spiritual life of the pre-Columbian Indian was removed at another order of magnitude. Native American religion was so integrated in its culture that changing an aspect of culture also meant changing the religion. Thus the gun, trap, individual wage earning and private property were just as powerful instruments of religious change as the missionaries' theological message.

The very small Jewish population was discriminated against in all of the colonies. The first census of the United States occurred in 1790 and recorded between 1,300 and 1,500 Jewish inhabitants, out of a total population of three million (less than .5%). In Maryland, Jews were subject to blasphemy laws; in Virginia they were prohibited from employing Christian servants; in eight colonies they were taxed to pay for the established Christian church, and in all colonies they were ineligible for public office. Even North Carolina's 1835 Constitution barred any non-Christian from holding public office. The requirement of a Christian Oath prevented them from becoming lawyers in most colonies and from becoming teachers in many public schools and colleges. In Connecticut, Delaware, Maryland, Pennsylvania, Rhode Island, South Carolina, and Virginia they could not vote. Rhode Island was an especially ironic example. Roger Williams, its founder, believed in religious freedom for all, and by 1763 there were a synagogue and a Jewish community equal to about 1 percent of the population of Newport. However, Jews were denied the right to vote and to hold office. They were not emancipated until the Rhode Island Constitution of 1842.

Slaves were not allowed to worship as they pleased. Slaves worshipped what their masters and local laws required. They learned the religious doctrines their masters thought suitable and supported the churches to which their masters contributed income from their labor. Madison and Jefferson, though tireless advocates for removing external religious restraints, did not acknowledge that they had left the African slaves religiously bound.

Although religious discrimination was legal in most of the colonies, this gradually changed as immigration brought religious pluralism and a series of legal concessions. The independence movement made Loyalists and the Church of England unpopular. The five southern colonies and New York and Maryland all dis-established the Church of England during the Revolutionary War, the timing of which may reveal more political than religious freedom reasons for dis-establishment. Perhaps the most dramatic change occurred in Virginia where up until 1776, religious restrictions had been ardently enforced. With the adoption of the Virginia Statute for Religious Freedom in 1786, the Church of England was dis-established and freedom of religion was guaranteed. Written by Thomas Jefferson, the statute passed in the Virginia General Assembly on January 16, 1786, because dissenting sects (i.e. Baptists, Presbyterians, and Methodists) had petitioned strongly during the preceding decade for religious liberty, including the separation of church and state. The statute was a notable precursor to the Establishment Clause and Free Exercise Clause of the First Amendment.

As the colonies moved towards rebellion with the British Empire, the rising tide of sentiment against an established religion, advocated now by most denominations, won out, not necessarily because of a devotion to religious freedom but because practically speaking, there was no agreement on a national Church and no one wanted to live under the thumb of another denomination.

English immigrant Thomas Paine, the author of the hugely popular pamphlet *Common Sense* (over 500,000 sold), which stated that all the arguments for separation from England were based on nothing more than simple facts, plain arguments and common sense, urged the non-establishment of religion: "Persecution is not an original feature in any religion; but it is always the strongly marked feature of all law-religions, or religions established by law. Take away the law-establishment, and every religion reassumes its original benignity."

Religion was a topic of discussion during the drafting and ratifying of the constitution. At the Constitutional Convention in Philadelphia in 1787, Charles Pinckney, a delegate from South Carolina, proposed a "no religious test for public office" clause. After the wording was slightly amended, the Convention unanimously voted to add the following text to Art. VI: "But no religious test shall ever be required as a qualification to any office or public trust under the authority of the United States." Because this clause applied only to the Federal Government, many states continued with religious tests for public office. The state of Maryland retained a religious test for state and local public offices until the U.S. Supreme Court held it unconstitutional in 1961 in Torasco v. Watkins. The Court based its decision on the 1st and 14th Amendments, not on the no religious test clause of Art. VI of the Constitution because the latter applied only to the federal government.

The Constitutional Convention also made a concession to Quakers and others opposed to swearing an oath to uphold the constitution. Quakers refused to swear oaths, even in courtrooms, believing that one must speak the truth at all times, and that the act of swearing an oath implied different standards of truth with and without oaths. They saw this as contravening Jesus' teaching in the Sermon on the Mount in which he stated, "Do not swear an oath at all … All you need to say is simply 'Yes' or 'No'; anything beyond this comes from the evil one." The drafters changed the language to allow an "oath or affirmation" in the four places oaths were mentioned in the Constitution (Art. I, Art. II, Art. VI and Amendment IV). On March 4, 1853,

Franklin Pierce became the fourteenth President of the U.S. and is the only president to date, who affirmed, rather than swore to, the oath of office.

Although religious diversity in the colonies initially brought persecution and discrimination, it eventually birthed religious freedom. Thomas Jefferson recognized the strength of this diversity when he said, "difference of opinion is advantageous to religion," uniformity is not. He observed, "Millions of innocent men, women and children, since the introduction of Christianity, have been burnt, tortured, fined, imprisoned; yet we have not advanced one inch towards uniformity ... Reason and persuasion are the only practicable instruments." In a letter to Jefferson, John Adams observed that in the political and religious spheres, "checks and balances are our only security" because every religious or non-religious group, "if it had unchecked and unbalanced power ... would persecute another." He concluded, "Know thyself, human nature!"

James Madison made a similar observation: "Freedom arises from multiplicity of sects, which pervades America, and which is the best and only security for religious liberty in any society. For where there is such a variety of sects, there cannot be a majority of any one sect to oppress and persecute the rest."

There are few records on the ratification by the states of the Bill of Rights or the Congressional debate on the First Amendment. This has left judges and historians with a paucity of information about the intent of the drafters, Congressional adopters and the state legislators who ratified the amendments. The religion clauses in particular, have engendered deep searches into the historical record as the Supreme Court seeks history to justify its decisions. Perhaps this absence has served the country well as religious freedom is far more robust today than at the country's founding.

B. Freedom of Speech

The historical underpinnings of the First Amendments' protection of free speech overlap with the underpinnings of protection for a free press and freedom of religion. These underpinnings include:

1. Abolition of prior censorship in England (herein C. Freedom of the Press)
2. Emerging opposition to seditious libel (herein C. Freedom of the Press)
3. Growth of religious toleration and opposition to blasphemy and heresy convictions (herein A. Freedom from an Established Religion and Freedom to Practice Religion)

4. Crown's use of treason and constructive treason (herein II. Other Constitutional Provisions Addressing Speech)
5. Parliamentary privilege of freedom of debate (herein II. Other Constitutional Provisions Addressing Speech)
6. Theory of natural rights (herein III. Constitutional Interpretation) and Cato's Letters

These elements underscored the importance of freedom of speech as a counterbalance to what colonists considered over-reach and abuse not only by the Crown, but by earlier colonial governments.

Prior to 1776, the only mention of "freedom of speech" in a colonial charter referred to the rights of legislators to speak freely in their political deliberations. This principle of parliamentary privilege connected free speech with the political process. This right began in 1215 when King John promised to the powerful barons in Magna Carta not to levy taxes on them without their "assembled consent." When this right expanded eventually to the House of Commons, its members readily appreciated the benefits of criticism in drafting legislation and of an atmosphere that encouraged such candor and participation. When Sir Edward Coke asserted that free speech in parliament was a customary right, King James responded that it was a privilege that he was free to revoke. This dispute was not settled until the Glorious Revolution of 1689 when the English Bill of Rights, enacted in that same year, stated:

> "the freedom of speech and debates or proceedings in parliament ought not to be impeached or questioned in any court or place out of parliament."

The colonial assemblies sought the same right with the Massachusetts Declaration of Rights in 1780, stating:

> "The freedom of deliberations, speech and debate, in either house of the legislature, is so essential to the rights of the people, that it cannot be the foundation of any accusation or prosecution, action or complaint, in any other court or place whatsoever."

The first U.S. constitution, the Articles of Confederation, mirrored the English Bill of Rights language by stating:

> "Freedom of speech and debate in Congress shall not be impeached or questioned in any court or place out of Congress."

Thus the concept of parliamentary or legislative privilege established a "free speech zone" in the legislative body and the close connection between free speech, political speech and effective self-government, a foundational rationale for First Amendment analysis.

The preamble to the constitution starts with the words, "We, the people of the United States," and thereby establishes the fundamental principle that ultimate political power resides with "the people" and not the government. The already established tie between legislative privilege and free speech and democratic self-governance, soon extended to "the people." For democracy to be informed and effective, "the people" must have the right to speak freely on political issues without fear of being hauled into court. A right initially vested only in parliamentarians, was now claimed by the population as a whole.

The essays of British writers John Trenchard and Thomas Gordon under the pseudonym of Cato, the implacable foe of Julius Caesar, provided inspiration for the American Revolution as well as the First Amendment. First published from 1720 to 1723 in England, the essays were distributed widely across the thirteen colonies and, being more popular than John Locke's influential *Civil Government*, were frequently quoted in newspapers. They shared Locke's natural rights philosophy as shown in Cato's Fifty-ninth letter: "All Men are born free; Liberty is a Gift that they receive from God Himself; nor can they alienate the same by consent, though possibly they may forfeit it by Crimes." Cato's Fifteenth Letter asserted that "Freedom of Speech is the great Bulwark of Liberty; they prosper and die together: And it is the Terror of Traytors and Oppressors, and a Barrier against them," language the drafters of the 1776 Virginia Declaration of Rights employed. Benjamin Franklin published Cato's essay on Freedom of Speech after his brother was imprisoned by the Massachusetts legislature for criticizing the government. John Peter Zenger printed this essay in 1733 shortly before his criticism of the governor of New York which precipitated his infamous trial for seditious libel.

Unlike the restrictive English libel laws, Cato considered truth a complete defense to libel. Cato's Thirty-second Letter states: "The exposing therefore of publick Wickedness, as it is a Duty which every Man owes to Truth and his Country, can never be a Libel in the Nature of Things." Thus Cato viewed truthful criticism of the government not only legal, but a patriotic duty.

C. Freedom of the Press

In the age of the Internet, when newspapers are going out of business and the publishing industry is in decline, it is difficult to imagine a time when the printed word was the only form of mass communication. However, before the internet, satellites, cable, TV, radio, telephone, telegraph, and electricity, there was the printing press. The printing press was invented by Johannes Gutenberg in Mainz, Germany around 1440 and it revolutionized the European world. It spread literature to the masses for the first time, dramatically increased the flow of information, and democratized the ideas that were the driving force behind the Renaissance and Reformation. Within 50 years some 2,500 European cities had acquired presses and produced about 20 million volumes. Printing stimulated the literacy of lay people and eventually came to have a deep and lasting impact on their public and private lives. Printers typically produced newspapers, pamphlets, magazines, and books.

The Spanish colonies, settled before the British colonies, housed the first printing press in the New World. Mexico City set up a press in 1539. The first printing press to come to the British colonies arrived in the town of Cambridge in the Massachusetts Bay Colony in 1638. The press was brought by Reverend Joseph Glover, who, when deprived of his position in the Church of England, shipped his family, his possessions, and the press to the colonies. Glover also paid for the passage of the man in charge of running his press, Stephen Daye, a locksmith by profession. Daye was under financial contract to work in Glover's home in Cambridge in order to repay the cost of passage for himself, his wife, and his household — a total of around £51. Rev. Glover, however, did not survive the passage to the New World. When Daye and the press arrived, his debt was transferred to Glover's widow, Elizabeth, now owner of the printing press. Daye set to work almost immediately along with his son Matthew, an apprentice printer, perhaps more skilled than his father. Within the first year in the Massachusetts Bay Colony, they printed *The Freeman's Oath*, a broadside (a large sheet of paper printed on one side only), which is generally believed to be the first tract printed in British North America.

William Penn, the founder of Pennsylvania, brought a master printer by the name of William Bradford to Philadelphia in 1685. Bradford produced several religious publications and a small number of other printed material, but he soon found that he could not run a profitable business under the oppressive moral code that ruled Penn's colony (it prevented him from printing even the most trivial news). In 1693, Bradford moved to New York and established the *New York Gazette*, the city's first newspaper.

Newspapers were a vital part of colonial life. In a rural society where communication between towns, let alone among the 13 colonies, was limited, they provided the only means of spreading news other than by word of mouth. The importance of the press was recognized during the years preceding the War of Independence: both Colonists and British rulers employed the press to spread propaganda among the people. The newspapers announced the Declaration of Independence as well as Lord Cornwallis' surrender. They were also the forum for political discussion.

Because of the power of the printed word, freedom of the press was considered more important than freedom of speech. Prior to 1784, ten states had made some form of declaration of rights or constitutional provisions protecting liberty of the press, but only two — Pennsylvania and Vermont — also mentioned freedom of speech. In 1787, future president Thomas Jefferson made the following remark about the importance of the freedom of the press: "Were it left to me to decide whether we should have a government without newspapers or newspapers without government, I should not hesitate for a moment to prefer the latter."

This place of importance for the First Amendment's protection of a free press was undergirded by the rejection of the Crown's licensing scheme and an emerging opposition to seditious libel. The Crown and parliament's suppression of speech relied primarily on a pervasive system of printing monopolies and licensing of speech which the Church ran until the Crown and Parliament assumed control. Printers could not publish anything without a license and, of course, the Church or Crown would grant the license monopoly to its supporters and publications that gave a good opinion of the Church and government. This comprehensive system prevented the publication of any material not licensed by the government.

The colonists in America were not the only Englishmen disenchanted with the status quo. In his famous commentaries on the laws of England, William Blackstone wrote in 1765 that freedom of the press consisted not of freedom from criminal sanctions after the publication of material but in eliminating "*previous* restraints upon publication." To him, subjecting the press "to the restrictive power of a licenser" subjects all expression to the whims of, at worst, one person and makes the government the "arbitrary and infallible judge of all controverted points in learning, religion, and government." When the Crown abolished licensing in 1694, seditious libel became the primary mechanism to suppress the press.

Seditious libel is the crime of publishing material that brings the government into contempt. The logic was that no government could stay in power if people had a low opinion of it so the government must prosecute any statements, true or false, that might lower people's opinion of the leaders. The Court of the Star Chamber in England held that any public criticism of the king, church or government was forbidden and could subject someone to criminal prosecution. These prosecutions were an effective method of silencing and intimidating critics. In these cases, truth was not a defense because, as the judges saw it, the greater the truth of the criticism, the greater the damage to the reputation of those in power, and therefore the greater the seditious libel. Hence truth could actually be considered an aggravating factor in prosecutions for seditious libel. When parliament adopted Fox's Libel Act in 1792, the Act allowed jurors to decide whether a publication was defamatory and the Act made truth a defense. Over the coming years, seditious libel prosecutions dwindled in Great Britain.

In the American colonies, seditious libel was considered a breach of the peace and a criminal offense. It was defined as any criticism directed against the government or a government official, and as in England, truth was not a defense. Nonetheless, many American printers behaved as if seditious libel laws did not exist, and juries could not be counted on to convict even when they were instructed that their only responsibility was to determine whether the printer published the statement. This was illustrated in the famous trial of John Peter Zenger.

The only newspaper in the Colony of New York in 1725 was the *New York Gazette*, published by William Bradford who was supportive of Governor William Cosby. When New York's Chief Judge Lewis Morris issued a dissenting opinion in the 1733 case of Cosby v. Van Dam, Governor Cosby removed Morris from office—an obvious separation of powers and judicial independence problem. Morris and some friends then set up New York's first independent newspaper, the *New York Weekly Journal* and published articles accusing the Cosby administration of tyranny and violating people's rights.

On January 15, 1734, Governor Cosby ordered the public burning of the newspaper on Wall Street, and offered fifty pounds to whoever revealed the names of the Journal's authors. Finally, Governor Cosby decided to shut down the *New York Weekly Journal* by going after its printer, John Peter Zenger. The Governor assigned a newly-arrived English barrister to lead an examination of the newspaper for statements that constituted the crime of seditious libel (seditious libel was defined as the intentional publication, without lawful excuse or justification, of written blame of any public man or of the law, or any institution established by the law). Two separate grand juries were empaneled in 1734. Evidence of seditious libel was presented to both but neither issued an indictment against John Peter Zenger.

Next, Governor Cosby requested that the Assembly order the public hangman to ceremonially burn issues of the newspaper. The popularly-elected Assembly refused to issue the order. The Cosby administration then resolved to proceed against Zenger by an information, a legal procedure, highly unpopular in the Colony that allowed a prosecution to proceed without a grand jury indictment. On November 17, 1734, the sheriff arrested Zenger and took him to New York's Old City Jail. The court set bail at £400, an amount far in excess of Zenger's means so he returned to jail pending his trial.

Zenger's allies hired Andrew Hamilton of Philadelphia, the pre-eminent colonial attorney. Hamilton's main difficulty in defending Zenger was that the truth of the published statements was immaterial. Further, the role of the jury in a seditious libel case was limited to deciding whether the person charged was responsible for publishing the allegedly libelous statement. If the jury found in the affirmative, Judges De Lancey and Philipse, close allies of Cosby, would examine the text to determine if the statements constituted seditious libel.

Hamilton asked the jury to consider the truth of the statements published and concluded with these famous words:

> The question before the Court and you, Gentlemen of the jury, is not of small or private concern. It is not the cause of one poor printer, nor of New York alone, which you are now trying. No! It may in its consequence affect every free man that lives under a British government on the main of America. It is the best cause. It is the cause of liberty.

Immediately, Chief Judge De Lancey instructed the jury that they, the jurors, should decide only the question of whether Zenger had published the issues of the *New York Weekly Journal*. Despite the instruction, the jury, after a brief deliberation, found Zenger "not guilty" of publishing seditious libel. This jury nullification (where a jury in effect nullifies a law that it believes is either immoral, unconstitutional or wrongly applied to the defendant) demonstrated the role of the jury as a curb on executive power, but more importantly, an emerging view that seditious libel violated the right to freedom of the press.

First Amendment scholar Zechariah Chafee argued that the drafters of the First Amendment sought to eliminate the common law offense of sedition, absent any incitement to law-breaking. However, legal historian Leonard Levy effectively documented that neither the American Revolution nor the First Amendment abolished the pre-existing common law of seditious libel, which helps explain how, only seven years after the adoption of the First Amendment, the Federalist-controlled Congress passed and President John Adams signed the Alien and Sedition Acts of 1798. The Alien and Sedition Acts were four bills that made it harder for an immigrant to become a citizen (Naturalization Act), allowed the president to imprison and deport non-citizens who were deemed dangerous (Alien Friends Act) or who were from a hostile nation (Alien Enemies Act), and criminalized making false statements that were critical of the federal government (Sedition Act).

The justification for these acts were national security concerns related to an undeclared naval war with France and protests at home. As one Federalist in

Congress proclaimed, there was no need to "invite hordes of Wild Irishmen, nor the turbulent and disorderly of all the world, to come here with a basic view to distract our tranquility." Not coincidentally, non-English ethnic groups had been among the core supporters of the Democratic-Republicans in 1796.

The most controversial of the new laws was the Sedition Act, which made it illegal to:

> "write, print, utter or publish ... any false, scandalous and malicious writing or writings against the government of the United States, or either House of the Congress ... or the President ... with intent to defame ... or to bring them, or either of them, into contempt or disrepute; or to excite against them, or either or any of them, the hatred of the good people of the United States."

Based on this law, more than 20 Republican newspaper editors were arrested and some were imprisoned. James Thomson Callender, a Scottish citizen who had been expelled from Great Britain for his political writings, was living in Virginia writing for the Richmond Examiner. He wrote a book entitled *The Prospect Before Us* (read and approved by Vice President Jefferson before publication) in which he called the Adams administration a "continual tempest of malignant passions" and the President a "repulsive pedant, a gross hypocrite and an unprincipled oppressor." Callender was indicted in mid-1800 under the Sedition Act and convicted, fined $200 and sentenced to nine months in jail. His trial was presided over by Supreme Court Justice Samuel Chase.[1]

David Brown, a veteran of the Revolutionary War, was opposed to the newly formed United States federal government. In November 1798, he led a group in Dedham, Massachusetts in erecting a liberty pole with the words, "No Stamp Act, No Sedition Act, No Alien Bills, No Land Tax, downfall to the Tyrants of America; peace and retirement to the President; Long Live the Vice President". Brown was arrested in Andover, Massachusetts, but because he could not afford the $4,000 bail, he was taken to Salem for trial. Brown pled guilty but Supreme Court Justice Samuel Chase, playing the role more of a prosecutor than a judge, asked him to name others who had assisted him. Brown refused, was fined $480, and sentenced to eighteen months in prison, the most severe sentence ever imposed under the Sedition Act.

In 1800, Republican James Madison declared that "the federal government" is "destitute of every authority for restraining the licentiousness of the

1. The House of Representative later impeached Justice Samuel Chase, in part due to his handling of the Callender trial, but the Senate then acquitted him on all charges.

press," and that freedom of the press meant freedom to publish opinion as well as truth. Madison and his fellow Republicans vehemently denounced the Sedition Act as unconstitutional and expanding congressional powers. The Democratic-Republicans made the Alien and Sedition Acts an important issue in the election of 1800. Thomas Jefferson, upon assuming the Presidency, pardoned those still serving sentences under the Sedition Act, and their fines were soon repaid. Federal sedition prosecutions disappeared with the expiration of the Sedition Act in 1801.

The Alien and Sedition Acts were never appealed to the Supreme Court so the court never addressed their compatibility with the First Amendment. However, if a case had been appealed to the Supreme Court, the court may well have upheld the Act both because the framers did not intend to outlaw seditious libel and because the court's right of judicial review was not established until Marbury v. Madison in 1803. However, the public learned through this experience with the Alien and Sedition Acts that seditious libel was inconsistent with public debate, honest criticism of government, and democratic governance.

This democratic repudiation of seditious libel lasted for more than a century. However, such legislation re-emerged in a slightly different form with World War I when Congress made it a crime to cast contempt on the form of the U.S. government.

D. Freedom to Peaceably Assemble

The English monarchy often restricted the right of English citizens to assemble in public, usually out of fear that they might attempt to overthrow the government (no right to free assembly was specified in Magna Carta (1215), the Petition of Right (1628) or the English Bill of Rights (1689)). Nevertheless, Englishmen often assembled to discuss their political grievances. Such gatherings were risky propositions, however, as any such meeting was not only subject to suppression, but could also be interpreted as a treasonous act.

In religious matters, once the Church of England was established, other religious groups were prohibited from gathering in public and from using even private buildings for meetings or worship. Attempts at reform resulted in a law stipulating that no meeting of more than 50 persons could be held without gaining the permission of the king, unless a magistrate was present with the authority to arrest everyone present. The penalty for resisting the magistrate exercising this authority was death.

On August 14, 1670, William Penn along with other Quakers, attempted to worship at their meeting-house in London. This violated the 1664 Conventicle Act that forbade any Nonconformists attending a religious meeting or assembling more than five persons to attend a religious meeting without the permission of the Church of England. When soldiers stopped him from entering the meeting-house, Penn began to deliver his sermon to the Quakers who had assembled in the street. Penn was arrested and charged with leading an unlawful assembly. The jury found Penn guilty of speaking in the street but refused to add "to an unlawful assembly". The infuriated judge told the jury that "they shall not be dismissed until we have a verdict that the court will accept." The jury modified the verdict to "guilty of speaking to an assembly in the street," whereupon the judge had them locked up overnight without food, water or heat. Penn protested this and the judge ordered him bound and gagged. Finally, after a two-day fast, the jury returned a not guilty verdict. The judge fined the jury for contempt of court for returning a verdict contrary to their own findings of fact and removed them to prison until the fine was paid. Penn protested that this violated the Magna Carta and was forcibly removed from the court.

Edward Bushel, a member of the jury, refused to pay the fine and petitioned the Court of Common Pleas for a writ of *habeas corpus*. Sir John Vaughan, Chief Justice of the Court of Common Pleas, ruled that a jury could not be punished simply on account of the verdict it returned, but that individual jurors could be punished if they had acted improperly. He stated that a judge "may try to open the eyes of the jurors, but not to lead them by the nose." Bushel's case is a landmark in English legal history establishing the principle of the independence of the jury.

The jury's verdict in Penn's trial, another example of jury nullification, was the subject of Penn's pamphlet, *The People's Ancient and Just Liberties Asserted* (1670), which became one of the most popular pamphlets of the time in England and America and contributed to the discussion about the freedom to assemble.

During the years leading up to the Revolutionary War, the British army sought to restrict colonists from assembling to debate and protest the various taxes Parliament had imposed. The colonists ignored these restrictions, which only cemented the colonist's view that the right to peaceably assemble was a basic right.

On October 14, 1774, the delegates to the First Continental Congress added a statement about the right to assemble in the document they published called "Declaration and Resolves." This document listed the grievances the American people had against King George III and Parliament, their objections to the various acts passed by Parliament (known collectively as the Intolerable Acts) and stated the rights to which they believed they were entitled. The statement asserted that the people *"have a right to peaceably assemble, consider of their grievances, and petition the king."*

Several states included protections for the right to assemble in their constitutions as the new nation began to emerge. The first written guarantee of freedom of assembly was the Pennsylvania Declaration of Rights of 1776. It states: "The people have a right to assemble together, to consult for their common good."

An important change in language took place during the drafting of the First Amendment's right to assemble. When the first Congress convened to draft amendments in 1789, Virginia and North Carolina proposed the following language: "That people have a right peaceably to assemble together to consult *for the common good.*" The Senate defeated a motion to delete the reference to "the common good" but that language was still dropped in the final drafting stage. This change gave the right a broader scope because the right to peaceably assemble was no longer limited to whatever a legislature or court determined was "for the common good."

The right to assemble was central to the most important social movements in American history. However, because the First Amendment's right to peaceably assemble did not apply to states until 1931 and not all states provided that right in their state constitutions, states were free to restrict this right. After independence, the next most significant social movement was the abolitionist movement. The Southern states, well aware of how freedom of assembly could mobilize public opinion, routinely prohibited its exercise among slaves and free blacks. In South Carolina, an 1800 law forbade "slaves, free negroes, mulattoes, and the mestizos" from assembling for "mental instruction or religious worship." In 1831, the Virginia Legislature declared "all meetings of free Negroes or mulattoes at any school house, church, meeting house or other place for teaching them reading or writing, either in the day or night" to be an unlawful assembly. Nat Turner's 1831 rebellion in Virginia only intensified restrictions on assembly.

An interpretative challenge arose in the Supreme Court's 1876 decision in United States v. Cruikshank. In dicta, Chief Justice Waite wrote:

> The right of the people to peaceably assemble for the purpose of petitioning Congress for a redress of grievances, or for anything else connected with the powers or the duties of the national government, is an attribute of national citizenship, and, as such, under the protection of, and guaranteed by, the United States.

In context, it appears that Waite meant a petition was one basis or purpose for freedom of assembly; however, Justice William Woods in Presser v. Illinois (1886) concluded that Waite meant the right to freedom of assembly only applied "if the purpose of the assembly was to petition the government for redress of grievances." Presser is the only Supreme Court decision to limit the right to assembly in this way and the court has since disagreed with the view that petition and assembly comprise one right. A dissenting Justice Scalia wrote in Chisom v. Roemer (1991) that the First Amendment "has not generally been thought to protect the right peaceably to assemble only when the purpose of the assembly is to petition the Government for a redress of grievances."

In Whitney v. California (1920), Anita Whitney appealed her conviction under the 1919 California Criminal Syndicalism Act for helping to establish the Communist Labor Party of America, a group charged by the state with teaching the violent overthrow of government. Although the rights to assemble and free speech lost, Anita Whitney generated an articulate statement about the right to assemble:

> Those who won our independence ... believed that freedom to think as you will and to speak as you think are means indispensable to the discovery and spread of political truth; that without free speech and assembly discussion would be futile; that with them, discussion afford ordinarily adequate protection against the dissemination of noxious doctrine; that the greatest menace to freedom is an inert people; that public discussion is a political duty; and that this should be a fundamental principle of the American government.

In 1931, the Supreme Court held in Dejonge v. Oregon that the First Amendment's right to freedom of assembly applied to states, thereby extending this right to the local level which is where most of the restrictions of this right occurred. After this decision, all governments, federal, state and local, had to respect the First Amendment's right to peaceably assemble. The right to peaceably assemble played a key role in the suffragette movement, labor movement, civil rights and anti-Vietnam War movements, environmental movement, and more recent movements like the pro- and anti-abortion movements, and Black Lives Matter.

The right to peaceably assemble helped birth a new right; the freedom of association. Freedom of association involves the right to join or leave groups of a person's own choosing, and for the group to take collective action to pursue the interests of members (to "associate" often means "assembling," hence the overlap between the rights).

Although there were echoes of a right to freedom of association in the red scare cases of the 1950s, the right came to fruition in the civil rights case of

NAACP v. Alabama ex rel. Patterson (1958). The State of Alabama alleged that NAACP's activities were causing irreparable injury to the citizens of Alabama for which criminal prosecution and civil actions at law afforded no adequate relief. So Alabama brought an equity suit in a state court to enjoin the NAACP from conducting further activities in the state and to oust it from the State. The trial court, under a state law, ordered the NAACP to disclose its membership lists. The NAACP refused and was held in contempt. The Supreme Court held the state law unconstitutional and, in an opinion by Justice Harlan, laid the groundwork for a decision based on assembly. He described how freedom of assembly applied to the states, covered political, economic, religious and secular matters, and could be restricted only to prevent a grave and immediate danger. Then he moved away from assembly in stating, "it is beyond debate that freedom to engage in association for the advancement of beliefs and ideas is an inseparable aspect of the liberty assured by the Due Process Clause of the Fourteenth Amendment, which embraces freedom of speech." He concluded that the constitutional right of association meant that the NAACP membership could "pursue their lawful private interests privately."

This new right of association soon eclipsed the freedom of assembly. The court employed freedom of assembly only to overturn convictions of African Americans who had participated in peaceful civil rights demonstrations. The Court went on to develop its forum doctrine (what rights attach to speech in different locations) within the context of its free speech cases, making no mention of the right of assembly. This has largely removed freedom of assembly from legal discourse.

E. Right to Petition the Government

The right to petition the government is the only First Amendment right that has contracted since its adoption. Although a vibrant right during the Colonial era and post-independence, the Supreme Court has since refused to define or enforce this right despite its storied history. The English and Colonial governments recognized petitioning long before they recognized freedom of speech, press or religion, and the right to petition played a critical role in developing these related rights.

The right to petition the sovereign for redress of grievances was first recognized in the Magna Carta (1215). Section 61 states that if any chief justice, official or servant of the monarch transgresses any article of peace or security, four barons can approach the monarchy "to declare it and claim immediate redress" (i.e. petition the government). If no redress is made within 40 days, the four barons may refer the issue to the 25 barons (a governing council of barons):

> "who may distrain upon and assail us in every way possible, with the support of the whole community of the land, by seizing our castles, lands, possessions, or anything else saving only our own person and those of the queen and our children, until they have secured such redress as they have determined upon. Having secured the redress, they may then resume their normal obedience to us."

Thus, in Magna Carta, King John gave barons the authority not only the right to petition their grievances, but, if not acted upon in a timely manner, the right to seize possessions as recompense. In the 1300s, King Edward III opened each Parliament with an announcement of the King's willingness to hear petitions from the people. As Parliament's power increased, it eventually received these petitions from the people. Even today, a bag hangs on the back of the Speaker's chair in the House of Commons where members may place petitions from the people.

During the first few centuries of this practice, the King and Parliament sometimes prosecuted petitioners for seditious libel, when they considered the petitions impertinent. This prompted the English Bill of Rights of 1689 to reaffirm the right of all subjects to petition the king and declare any prosecutions or imprisonment for such petitioning, illegal.

Most colonial charters and many state constitutions included procedures and protections for petitioning. The Stamp Act Congress, which coined the phrase that later became the battle cry of the colonists, "no taxation without representation," adopted the Declaration of Rights and Grievances in 1765. Section 13 asserted: "That it is the right of the British subjects in these colonies, to petition the king, or either house of parliament."

The Journals of the Continental Congress of 1774 went even further with this process by allowing the people, without filing a petition, to retain money owing to the government until their grievances were addressed. When the colonists justified their separation from England in the Declaration of Independence in 1776, they asserted:

> "In every stage of these Oppressions We have Petitioned for Redress in the most humble terms: Our repeated Petitions have been answered only by repeated injury. A Prince whose character is thus marked by every act which may define a Tyrant, is unfit to be the ruler of a free people."

When the first Congress met in 1789, petitions began to arrive and when the trickle became a stream, Congress created a committee to respond to them. By 1795, a newspaper reported that "the principal part of Congress's time has been taken up in reading and referring petitions." When abolitionists began a petitioning campaign in the 1830s, the petitions became so numerous that Senator John C. Calhoun proposed that the Senate refuse to accept any more. This precipitated a vehement debate with many senators claiming such action would violate the First Amendment. The House implemented a "gag rule" that prevented the petitions from being read into the record or being mentioned in debate. This rule was apparently never challenged in court, and even after it was repealed in 1844, Congress no longer felt obligated to respond to the petitions. Subsequently, the common law practice that petitions required a hearing and response fell into desuetude.

The Supreme Court's discussion of the right to petition is sparse, and in the few cases where it does arise the court conflates the right to petition with other First Amendment rights. When the court merges a constitutional right with another, the right loses it distinguishing features and instead of developing, becomes a relic of history. Ignoring the distinct content of the right to petition at common law, the court has held that the right creates no obligation on the government to hear or respond to petitions. Thus, what was once considered a core constitutional right that preceded the other First Amendment rights and one that makes government responsive and accountable to the people, today bears little resemblance to its practice and understanding in the colonial and post-colonial era.

II. Other Constitutional Provisions Addressing Speech

In addition to the First Amendment, speech protections arise in the Constitution in the Speech or Debate clause (legislative, executive and judicial privilege) and the Fifth Amendment's right against self-incrimination. Speech issues were involved in the adoption of the treason clause (treason is the only crime defined in the constitution), with Congress's oversight duties, and arguably with the public's duty and right to hold the government accountable.

A. Speech or Debate Clause—Legislative Privilege

The Speech or Debate Clause has its roots in England's centuries long power struggle between the Monarchy and Parliament. It is undergirded by the idea that members of legislative assemblies must have freedom of speech so that they can freely and openly debate and govern without fear of retaliatory civil or criminal persecution. This protection is referred to as legislative privilege or legislative immunity (or, in non-U.S. jurisdictions, parliamentary immunity). The principle argument in support of this privilege is to preserve an effective and autonomous legislature and in particular, to guard against executive retribution for performance of a legislature's representative duties. The Constitution's Speech or Debate Clause (Art. I, Section 6, Clause 1) states:

> The Senators and Representative ... shall in all Cases, except Treason, Felony and Breach of the Peace, be privileged from Arrest during their attendance at the Session of their Respective Houses, and in going to and from the same; and for any Speech or Debate in either House, they shall not be questioned in any other Place.

The clause was adopted without debate or opposition at the Constitutional Convention. Founding Father James Wilson argued that, for a representative of the public to successfully discharge his public trust, he must have the fullest liberty of speech to protect him from those whom he might offend. The Supreme Court held that this privilege was clearly perceived to be indispensable and universally acknowledged. Therefore, it gave the phrase a broad interpretation (Kilbourn v. Thompson, 1880). The Court in Kilbourn held that the clause not only covered speech and debate in either House, but also matters that are "an integral part of the deliberative and communicative process." For example, defamatory statements made on the floor of the legislature or in a committee session are privileged even if they are completely irrelevant to the proceedings being conducted (Tenney v. Brandhove, 1951).

The Court also held that this privilege applied to Congressional staff. In 1971, Senator Mike Gravel (D–Alaska) received a copy of the Pentagon Papers from an editor at *The Washington Post*. Over the next several days, Gravel, who was dyslexic, was assisted by his congressional office staff in reading and analyzing the report. Gravel had the Pentagon Papers entered into the Congressional Record and arranged to have them published by a private publisher.

A federal grand jury was empaneled to investigate possible violations of federal law in the release of the report. A Gravel aide was subpoenaed to testify about his role in obtaining and arranging for publication of the Pentagon

Papers. Senator Gravel intervened and asked a court to quash the subpoena, contending that forcing his aide to testify would violate the Speech or Debate Clause. Gravel lost at the federal district and court of appeals.

In Gravel v. United States (1972), the Supreme Court held (5–4) that the privileges of the Speech or Debate Clause extend to Congressional aides. Rejecting the reasoning of the Court of Appeals, the Supreme Court held, "... the privilege available to the aide is confined to those services that would be immune legislative conduct if performed by the Senator himself," the Court declared.

The Supreme Court upheld the district court ruling regarding private publication: "[Private] publication by Senator Gravel through the cooperation of Beacon Press was in no way essential to the deliberations of the Senate; nor does questioning as to private publication threaten the integrity or independence of the Senate by impermissibly exposing its deliberations to executive influence."

The Gravel case narrowed the protections offered by the Speech or Debate Clause, as did U.S. v. Brewster (1972), which was handed down the same day as Gravel. The Court in Brewster held that the Speech or Debate Clause did not cover political activities such as constituent services and issuing press releases because they are political in nature rather than legislative.

In Hutchinson v. Proxmire (1979), Professor Ronald Hutchinson sued Senator William Proxmire for defamation after the Senator gave a "Golden Fleece" award to the agencies that funded the professor's research. The court found that the Speech or Debate Clause does not protect Members of Congress against liability for information they transmit by press releases or newsletters, only core legislative activities.

The court in Gravel made it clear that the Clause does not protect criminal conduct that is not part of the legislating process. Thus a Member of Congress can be prosecuted for bribery because this is not part of the deliberative and communicative legislative process. The distinction between legislative acts and unprotected criminal acts in Gravel meant that conduct and speech at a subcommittee hearing were protected while the issues of how he obtained the Pentagon Papers and how he arranged for private publication were not.

In May 2006, following the first FBI raid on a Congressional office, the Capital Hill office of Rep. William J. Jefferson (D–La.), many members of Congress criticized the FBI's search as an unconstitutional breach of this clause. The FBI argued that the clause did not apply to the search of Jefferson because he was alleged to have committed felonies of accepting bribes, obstructing a previous search, and storing in a freezer the money he accepted in bribery. Also, Jefferson was not arrested at the House, and the FBI investigation did not concern anything Jefferson said at Congress. The U.S. Court of Appeals for the District of Columbia Circuit ruled that the search of his office was unconstitutional, and the Supreme Court declined to review the decision.

B. Speech or Debate Clause—Executive Privilege

Executive privilege is the proposition that the president must be able to keep conversations with and memoranda to or from advisors secret in order to hear all arguments and receive candid advice. Although there is no specific provision in the Constitution that provides for executive privilege, successive administrations have claimed that the principle of executive privilege is implied by the Constitution through the structure of the separation of powers. In addition, the courts have consistently recognized the existence of such a privilege in decisions dating back to the early 19th century. In United States v. Burr (1807), for example, Aaron Burr was tried for treason and the Supreme Court did not require the Jefferson administration to turn over requested documents (though it did maintain that the courts could request such documents from the executive branch).

Executive privilege is the power claimed by the president and his or her advisors to resist certain discovery and other interventions by the legislative and judicial branches of government to access information. The rationale is that if administrative officials acting in their official capacities were subject to investigation, such a threat would have a chilling effect on speech within the White House. As Chief Justice Burger explained for a unanimous court in United States v. Nixon (1974), "a president and those who assist him must be free to explore alternatives in the process of shaping policies and making decisions, and to do so in a way many would be unwilling to express except privately." He also wrote that "the privilege is fundamental to the operation of Government, and inextricably rooted in the separation of powers under the Constitution."

Despite the Supreme Court's recognition of the principle of executive privilege, it went on to deny Nixon's privilege claim, holding that to the extent that the tapes involved neither military nor diplomatic secrets: "The President's generalized assertion of privilege must yield to the demonstrated, specific need for evidence in a pending criminal trial." The Supreme Court thus ordered that the tapes be turned over to Leon Jaworski, the special prosecutor.

In 1997, President Clinton invoked executive privilege in a civil suit in which Paula Jones, a former state employee in Arkansas while Clinton was that state's governor, alleged sexual harassment by Clinton. Lawyers representing the President argued that he should be immune to civil suits during his time in service. The Supreme Court unanimously denied Clinton's request. The following year, in a related case, the court also denied a Clinton claim of privilege regarding conversations he had had in the Oval Office with White House advisers (who received federal compensation) concerning the Jones case. The court relied heavily on the precedent set in the Nixon tapes case.

During the administration of George W. Bush (2001–09), the president and his staff invoked executive privilege several times. In one case, Vice President Dick Cheney refused to turn over to a congressional committee documents related to meetings he had had with corporate executives concerning the administration's energy policies. Congress sued Cheney in the federal courts, but the vice president prevailed. The Supreme Court found that the request for documents was overly broad and that the potential infraction did not rise to the level of criminality. In another instance, however, White House Counsel Harriet Miers and White House Chief of Staff Joshua Bolten refused to respond to a congressional subpoena concerning the firing of several federal prosecutors alleged to have been unsupportive of the Bush administration's policies. The U.S. Court of Appeals for the District of Columbia ordered Miers and Bolten to comply. (Miers was subsequently deposed by the House Judiciary Committee in a closed session after the Bush administration had left office. Bolton continued to demur.)

On June 20, 2012, President Barack Obama asserted executive privilege to withhold certain Department of Justice documents related to the ongoing Operation Fast and Furious controversy. Operation Fast and Furious dealt with "gunwalking," a tactic of the Arizona Field Office of the United States Bureau of Alcohol, Tobacco, Firearms and Explosives (ATF). The office ran a series of sting operations between 2006 and 2011 in the Tucson and Phoenix areas during which the ATF "purposely allowed licensed firearms dealers to sell weapons to illegal straw buyers, hoping to track the guns to Mexican drug cartel leaders and arrest them." However, no means were employed to track either the firearms or the traffickers once they left the United States.

Guns tracked by the ATF were found at crime scenes on both sides of the Mexico–U.S. border, and the scene where U.S. Border Patrol Agent Brian Terry was killed in December 2010. The "gunwalking" operations became public in the aftermath of Terry's murder. Dissenting ATF agents came forward to Congress in response. According to a former Mexican Attorney General, related firearms were found at numerous crime scenes in Mexico where at least 150 civilians had been maimed or killed. As a result of a dispute over the release of Department of Justice documents related to the scandal, Attorney General Eric Holder became the first sitting member of a U.S. Cabinet to be held in contempt of Congress. In November 2014, Eric Holder turned over thousands of documents in response to a federal judge court order.

With the judiciary balancing competing interests (i.e., accountability and oversight) with executive privilege and often ruling against executive privilege, the principle is intact in theory but complex in practice.

C. Speech or Debate Clause — Judicial Privilege

Although the Constitution contains no express provision for judicial privilege, the federal courts have considered it an essential part of the doctrine of separation of powers. Like legislative and executive privilege, judicial privilege protects the confidentiality of judicial communications. Courts have invoked the privilege to protect communications among judges, their law clerks and the substance of judicial deliberation (U.S. v. Nixon, 1973). The substance of judicial deliberation includes any statement made during judicial proceedings made by each attorney, judge, juror, litigant party, or witness who are a part of said legal proceedings.

The purpose of judicial privilege is to protect the judiciary from legislative or executive inquiry that would threaten judicial independence. However, federal courts have rarely attempted to define the boundaries of judicial privilege. Like executive privilege, judicial privilege is not absolute and may yield in certain judicial criminal prosecutions or investigations of judicial misconduct. In Forrester v. White (1988), a case alleging sex discrimination, the Court held that the judge did not have judicial immunity for firing the probation officer because the employment decision was an administrative function, not a judicial function.

D. Fifth Amendment Right to Remain Silent

The Fifth Amendment to the Constitution protects a person from being compelled to be a witness and provide testimony against himself or herself in a criminal case. Sometimes referred to as the "right to remain silent," the Fifth Amendment states that no person "shall be compelled in any criminal case to be a witness against himself." Not every disclosure can be the subject of a Fifth Amendment assertion — only those that the witness "reasonably believes could be used in a criminal prosecution or could lead to other evidence that might be so used" (Kastigar v. United States, 1972).

Witnesses can assert the privilege against self-incrimination in civil proceedings as well as criminal ones, despite the seemingly limiting language of the Fifth Amendment. They can assert it in state or federal court, in a wide variety of proceedings (including trials, depositions, administrative law proceedings, and investigatory proceedings like grand jury hearings). But if the witness fears exposure to prosecution in a country other than the U.S., the privilege does not apply (United States v. Balsys, 1998).

Historically, the legal protection against compelled self-incrimination was directly related to the question of torture for extracting information and confessions. In England, anyone refusing to take the oath *ex officio mero* (confessions or swearing of innocence, usually before hearing any charges) was considered guilty. Suspected Puritans were pressed to take the oath and then reveal names of other Puritans. Coercion and torture were commonly used to compel "cooperation." Puritans, who were at the time fleeing to the New World, began a practice of refusing to cooperate with interrogations. In the most famous case, John Lilburne refused to take the oath in 1637. His case and his call for "freeborn rights" was a rallying point for reforms against forced oaths, forced self-incrimination, and other kinds of coercion. Oliver Cromwell's revolution overturned the practice and incorporated protections, in response to a popular group of English citizens known as the Levellers who advocated popular sovereignty, extended suffrage, equality before the law, and religious tolerance. The Levellers presented *The Humble Petition of Many Thousands* to Parliament in 1647 with 13 demands, the third of which was the right against self-incrimination in criminal cases. These protections were brought to America by the Puritans and were later incorporated into the Fifth Amendment.

This privilege allows a witness to decline to answer questions that might incriminate him or her, without penalty. A defendant cannot be compelled to become a witness at his or her own trial, but if he or she chooses to testify, he or she has relinquished this right and inferences can be drawn from a refusal to answer a question during cross-examination.

E. Treason

One method the Crown used to control speech was through the crimes of treason and constructive treason. Most Christian theology and political thinking until after the Enlightenment considered treason and blasphemy as synonymous because they both challenged the unquestioned authority of the Monarch as head of state and the church. Treason is essentially a violation of allegiance to the country and typically required some "overt act" to overthrow the government but at different times, religious and political leaders considered criticism of the church or government as treasonous. In England, the crime of treason was ill-defined so it was widely abused until parliament adopted the Treason Act of 1351 under Edward III (1327–1377) which then listed acts that constituted treason. Even then, if someone indicted for treason did not appear at trial, he could be sentenced to death as a traitor and, upon capture, executed without further trial. Henry VIII (1509–1547) made treasonous any word that affected regal dignity, slander of Queen Anne, the belief that any of his former marriages were legal, or the acceptance of any of the children of those marriages as legitimate. The refusal to take an oath to such assertions was also treason and is what brought Sir Thomas Moore to the execution block. The punishment was to be drawn, hung and beheaded; heart, entrails and bowels torn out and burned to ashes; the body cut into four quarters with each quarter hung on a nearby tower, and the head put on a post on London Bridge. In order not to expose or mangle female bodies, women were covered in tar and placed above logs saturated in tar and then burned quickly. This punishment was abolished in 1790.

English "traitors" rarely conspired to overthrow the government in collusion with a foreign government. They were leaders of England who belonged to the wrong political faction. Under the doctrine of constructive treason, the "overt act" could consist of printed or spoken words critical of the king. In 1664, John Twyn was convicted of treason and hanged for claiming the king was accountable to the people, who had a right to revolt if he did not follow that principle.

The Treason Act of 1695 provided procedural safeguards. Two safeguards were that people accused of treason had the right of to up to two legal counsel and nobody could be convicted of treason except by the evidence of two witnesses (later incorporated into the U.S. Constitution which added that both witnesses had to have witnessed the same overt act).

By the late eighteenth century, treason had been interpreted as primarily a mental rather than a physical act. Nonviolent associations and assemblies advocating parliamentary reform could be treasonous. Only Parliament and the King had the authority to alter the Constitution so any assembly, association or "convention" that attempted to usurp this authority was guilty of treason.

The fifty-six men who signed the Declaration of Independence were fully aware that the words of that document constituted treason and that the punishment for treason was death by hanging or dismemberment. Of these signers, the five Southern delegates were captured by the British, arrested as traitors and tortured. Twelve signers had their homes ransacked, looted, burned and other property destroyed. Nine fought and died from either wounds or hardships suffered during the war. After the war, most of the surviving delegates served their new government.

This experience of treason and constructive treason influenced the drafters of the U.S. Constitution to limit treason to two species, "Treason against the United States, shall consist only in levying war against them, or in adhering to their enemies, giving them aid and comfort" and to require a high standard of proof, "No person shall be convicted of treason unless on the testimony of two witnesses to the same overt act, or on confession in open court." Art. III, Sect. 3.

Concern about potential abuse of the crime of treason was one reason some opposed the adoption of the constitution with strong federal powers without a Bill of Rights, again showing how the English methods of controlling speech motivated the drafters of the First Amendment.

F. Congressional Oversight and Access to Information

Embedded in the constitutional principles of checks and balances and separation of powers is Congress's oversight responsibilities of the executive branch. The speech implications are that Congress has the right to gain access to most information from the executive branch, investigate, and hold legislative hearings that include questioning executive officials.

Congress's oversight authority derives from its "implied" powers in the Constitution, public laws, and House and Senate rules. The "implied" powers flow from Congress's array of constitutionally enumerated powers, particularly it's broad authority "to make all laws which shall be necessary and proper for carrying into execution the foregoing powers, and all other powers vested by this Constitution in the Government of the United States, or in any Department or Officer thereof." The Supreme Court has recognized Congress's investigative power, subject to constitutional safeguards for civil liberties. In 1927, the Court found that, in investigating the Department of Justice, Congress was considering a subject "on which legislation could be had or would be materially aided by the information which the investigation was calculated to elicit."

The "necessary and proper" clause of the Constitution also allows Congress to enact laws that mandate oversight by its committees, grant relevant authority to itself and its support agencies, impose specific obligations on the executive to report to or consult with Congress, and even seek its approval for specific actions.

Disputes between the executive and legislative branches frequently focus on efforts to gain access to information. This can be an endurance test and efforts to resolve these disputes on purely legal grounds often are swayed by superior political muscle. A Congress determined to exercise the many coercive tools available to it may succeed. By the same token, a Congress that is internally divided or uncertain about its institutional powers, or unwilling to maintain pressure until the documents are delivered, will lose out in the quest for information from the executive branch. Both branches are at the mercy of political developments that can arise without warning and tilt the advantage decisively to one side.

This Congressional right to information is arguably the foundation of the public's right to information. When Americans, through the Revolutionary War, substituted the sovereignty of King George III with popular sovereignty ("We the people"), access to government information became fundamental to an informed democracy and the rule of law. For people to make informed decisions, cast informed votes and hold government accountable, freedom of expression and access to information are essential. Information is power and access to information requires the government, with very limited exceptions, to provide information to the public. Access to information is critical to freedom of expression, particularly political speech which is the most protected form of speech, because the electorate cannot debate the issues and self-govern if government withholds vital information.

Elected representatives may withhold or hide information for various reasons, particularly if it may reveal acts that are illegal, unethical, embarrassing or unpopular. Poor public access to information feeds corruption. Secrecy allows back-room deals to determine public spending in the interests of the few rather than the many. Lack of information impedes citizens' ability to assess the decisions of their leaders and make informed choices about the individuals they elect to serve as their representatives. Access to information regarding government policies on health, education, housing, public transportation and many other areas can also improve living standards and quality of life.

To support popular sovereignty and government accountability, 59 countries in the world provide a constitutional right of access to government information. This right imposes an obligation on the government to make information available to the public so that the public is informed and can hold the government accountable. This right is not enumerated in the U.S. constitution; however, in *Richmond Newspapers (1980)*, the Supreme Court concluded that the right of the public and press to attend criminal trials is guaranteed under the First and Fourteenth Amendments, absent an overriding interest articulated in findings. Justice Stevens noted the monumental nature of the decision: "This is a watershed case ... never before has [the Court] squarely held that the acquisition of newsworthy matter is entitled to any constitutional protection whatsoever."

Since 1967, when Congress passed the Freedom of Information Act (FOIA), the public has the right to request access to records from any federal agency. Federal agencies are required to disclose any information requested under the FOIA unless it falls under one of nine exemptions which protect interests such as personal privacy, national security, and law enforcement.

III. Constitutional Interpretation

After the adoption of a constitution, the next most important task is its interpretation. Constitutions, like all laws, come to life when they are interpreted and applied. A constitutional text discloses its meaning and becomes an active force in society only in concretely engaged interpretation. The founders, ratifiers and people's social contract is completed in the act of interpretation which occurs on a daily, ongoing basis. Interpretation is influenced by the challenges to interpreting the constitution, the schools of legal and political philosophy, tools of interpretation, and outside critiques of prior interpretation.

A. Challenges to Interpreting the Constitution

The Constitution is simultaneously the supreme law of the country and the fundamental political document. It turned the political choices of the founders into law. This combination of supreme law and politics has, particularly in recent times, led to a controversy about who interprets the Constitution and the way it is interpreted.

The first question is: Who interprets the Constitution, and is there a final interpreter? The President and members of the Cabinet, Congress and the Supreme Court take an oath to uphold the Constitution in carrying out their duties. All these jobs require interpreting the Constitution. A lawyer filing and a judge hearing a constitutional claim, as well as a professor or student discussing constitutional law, all interpret the Constitution. Thus a wide range of public officials and private individuals interpret the Constitution, which leads to the question: Who is the final interpreter? As a practical matter, when there is a constitutional dispute, it tends to be filed in court, giving the judiciary jurisdiction to rule. This underscores Chief Justice John Marshall's conclusion that "it is emphatically the province and duty of the judicial department to say what the law is." One hundred fifty years later, a unanimous Supreme Court declared "the basic principle that the federal judiciary is supreme in the exposition of the law of the Constitution, and that principle has ever since been respected by this Court and the Country as a permanent and indispensable feature of our constitutional system."

Certainty, efficiency, and stability are served by having one clear final interpreter. However, even the Supreme Court has developed the political question doctrine to avoid interpreting certain constitutional provisions. The political question doctrine is closely linked to the concept of justiciability which addresses whether or not the court system is an appropriate forum in which to hear a case. Under the political question doctrine, courts can hear only legal questions, not political questions so political questions are nonjusticiable. Because most legal questions of a constitutional nature also involve political questions, this doctrine is rife with inconsistencies and contradictions. However, this effort by the Supreme Court to avoid certain constitutional questions and leave them for the legislative or executive branches or the electorate to resolve, lends credence to the claim that either there is no authoritative interpreter or that a different branch of government or the electorate is the authoritative interpreter, depending on the provision. Nonetheless, despite the political question doctrine, the Supreme Court is the final interpreter of the Constitution unless it gives that authority to the president or Congress.

Constitutional interpretation is critical because no matter how detailed legal drafters are, their words must be interpreted. Differences in interpretation can be substantial. This task of interpreting is not limited to law. Many religions have Holy Scriptures (e.g., Christianity, Judaism, and Islam) and major divisions within them based on different interpretations of the same language. In theology, this is referred to as hermeneutics (Hermes was the interpreter of the messages from the Greek gods); in law, this is called constitutional interpretation.

Constitutional interpretation in the United States presents a number of challenges. First, much of the text is written in general terms that require substantial interpreting (e.g. "establishment of religion," "free exercise" of religion, "freedom of speech," freedom "of the press"). A benefit of open textured language is the flexibility it allows over time to adapt to situations that could not have been contemplated when written. However, the more general the language, the more it calls on interpretive skills.

A second challenge is that many constitutional questions are not addressed, and many principles underlying the Constitution are not mentioned in the text (e.g., separation of powers, checks and balances, federalism, limited government, protection of liberty). This raises questions of how to address such issues, and the extent to which principles should be employed as opposed to just the language of the text. This is particularly a challenge in the United States because the U.S. Constitution is short—a fraction of the length of the vast majority of the constitutions in the world today—and therefore does not expressly address numerous constitutional questions. One response to this challenge is to interpret the Constitution to the crisis of the times. Another response is to do nothing until the Constitution is amended to address the particular question. However, the position that constitutional change must wait for constitutional amendment, leads to the third challenge in constitutional interpretation.

The third challenge is that the Constitution is difficult to amend; it is rigid. Article V requires proposal of amendments from either a two-thirds majority in each chamber of Congress or by a constitutional convention called by two-thirds of the states, followed by ratification by three-quarters of the state legislatures or by constitutional conventions in three-quarters of the states. Since the adoption of the Constitution, because of the difficulty and expense of creating constitutional conventions and Congress' lack of interest in delegating them this authority, all amendments have followed the congressional and state legislature path except for the 21st Amendment (repeal of Prohibition). Congress passed the 21st Amendment in February 1933 but then had it ratified by a series of state conventions rather than by state legislatures because Congress felt that many state legislators remained loyal to pro-Prohibition interests. Because forty-nine of the fifty states have bicameral legislatures and ratification in bicameral states requires a majority of both houses, a negative vote by as few as thirteen of the country's ninety-nine state legislatures is sufficient to defeat a proposed amendment. Not only is this process lengthy and costly, but a small minority can block the adoption of a constitutional amendment, which helps explain why only seventeen amendments have been adopted since 1791. This makes the U.S. Constitution one of the most difficult to amend in the democratic world; most Western democracies have a more flexible amendment process, typically requiring only a supermajority in the national legislative body and/or national referendum.

How does a rigid constitution impact constitutional interpretation? All societies need an outlet for change, and when the amendment process makes change extraordinarily difficult, pressure builds on the other avenue for change—constitutional interpretation. Constitutional rigidity puts substantially more pressure on judges to interpret and apply the Constitution to constitutional questions that the Constitution has not expressly addressed. The opposing argument leads to the next challenge—namely, that flexible constitutional interpretation can replace constitutional amendment, and in some instances, lawmaking, clearly an overstepping of boundaries by an unelected judiciary.

The fourth challenge to constitutional interpretation in the United States is wrapped in the now well-established practice of judicial review. Under judicial review, an unelected, life-tenured federal judiciary can declare a federal or state law (adopted by a majority in a representative democracy) unconstitutional. Protecting an individual's fundamental right may require a judge to overturn the democratic majority. However, when a court so acts, it inevitably incurs the wrath of the political majority. Courts survive on political capital, and if they go too far afield of the majority, they risk losing this political support. Courts are mindful of the political nature of judicial review, which in turn impacts their interpretation. Rarely do the courts stray far ahead or behind the majority because when they do, they risk that their decisions will be ignored. Arguably, the Court was about a decade ahead of its time when it handed down its famous decision in *Brown v. Board of Education* (1954). For the next ten years, many states ignored or circumvented the decision to integrate public schools. Not until Congress adopted the Civil Rights Act of 1964, which reflected the will of the majority, did the concept of integration receive more widespread support. Today the *Brown* decision has broad support and is considered one of the Supreme Court's landmark decisions; however, it also reveals the tenuous nature of interpreting the Constitution in a way that challenges the status quo. A decision to avoid or minimize this counter majoritarian difficulty often motivates the many approaches to constitutional interpretation.

B. Schools of Legal and Political Philosophy

Although there are innumerable ways to interpret the Constitution, evidenced by the unique jurisprudence of each Supreme Court justice, schools of legal and political philosophy have played an instrumental role in influencing Constitutional interpretation. These schools, typically founded by philosophers and academics, influence the interpreters. Sometimes, the most eloquent interpreters become the leading proponents of a particular school.

During the eighteenth century, when the constitution was written, natural law was the dominant theory of law in this country (it had been the dominant theory of law since the time of Aristotle and Greek civilization). The leading proponents of natural law include Plato (427–328 B.C.), Aristotle (384–322 B.C.), Thomas Aquinas (1225–1274), Thomas Hobbes (1588–1679), John Locke (1632–1704), Jean-Jacques Rousseau (1712–1778), Lon Fuller (1902–1978), and John Finnis (1940–). Natural law asserts that law and morality are intertwined and cannot be separated. Law reflects the moral choices of its enactors. Natural law theory states that there are moral principles embedded in the nature of the universe that apply to everyone. Judges, legal theorists and others use reason, instinct, and the natural moral sense implanted in all humans to discover these basic principles of the natural law. Natural law can flow from God, conscience or nature itself, but it is the preeminent source from which all other law flows. When a human law—positive law—fails to conform to natural law, it is unjust and invalid and may be disobeyed under certain circumstances. Because natural law involves a never-ending process of discerning natural law principles and their application to changing circumstances, there is no perfect positive law and natural law represents an ongoing outside critique of positive law.

Historically, the primary source of natural law has been religion. In the Western Legal Tradition, out of which the U.S. legal system grew, the Judeo-Christian religion and its evolution, such as the Reformation and Enlightenment, impacted understandings of natural law which in turn impacted the development of the positive law, including constitutional law.

Natural law birthed the natural rights philosophy, which emphasized the fundamental nature of God-given rights which no government could legitimately remove. Legal rights are those bestowed to persons by a given law but can be modified and repealed. Natural rights do not depend on laws, customs, or beliefs of any particular legal system or government, but instead are universal and inalienable. John Locke, the political theorist who had a strong influence on the country's founders, wrote in his influential *A Letter Concerning Toleration* (1689) that equality required religious liberty: "The sum of all we drive at is, that every man enjoy the same rights that are granted to others." The Continental Congress adopted Thomas Jefferson's natural rights assertions in the Declaration of Independence, including what has been referred to as the best known sentence in the English language:

> "We hold these truths to be self-evident, that all men are created equal, that they are endowed by their Creator with certain unalienable Rights that among these are Life, Liberty, and the pursuit of Happiness."

Abraham Lincoln made this statement a centerpiece of his rhetoric (i.e., Gettysburg Address, 1863) as did Martin Luther King, Jr. (i.e., I Have a Dream Speech, 1963) and since WWII it has become a major statement for proponents of international human rights, reflecting the enduring resonance of natural rights.

One reason the Federalists and their opponents, the Jefferson-Republicans, did not debate competing theories of constitutional interpretation was that both groups accepted the English declaratory theory of law. This theory states that judges do not create law; rather they discover and declare the law that already exists within the immutable legal principles of the common law. This theory parallels natural law in many ways and holds that legal principles endure so judges simply need to re-interpret and apply the principles to the changing circumstances of the day.

Alexander Hamilton (1755–1804), first Chief Justice John Jay (1745–1829), fourth Chief Justice John Marshall (1755–1835), and Abraham Lincoln (1809–1865) were strongly influenced by the thinking of English judge and law professor Sir William Blackstone (1723–1780), another natural law theorist who wrote in his *Commentaries on the Laws of England* that judges were "depositories of the laws; the living oracles" of law who were sworn "to determine, not according to [their] own private judgment, but according to the known laws and customs of the land." This view imbued a reverence for the law because it viewed law as based on enduring natural principles, not on personal preferences.

During the nineteenth century, respect for natural law gradually diminished with the ascendancy of legal positivism. The leading proponents of legal positivism included Jeremy Bentham (1748–1832), John Austin (1790–1859), H.L.A. Hart (1907–1992), Hans Kelsen (1881–1973), and Joseph Raz (1939–). Positivist theory is defined by three characteristics: separating law and morality, declaring legal validity based on how and by whom the law is promulgated, and allowing judges to create new law in cases where no law explicitly addresses the issue. For positivists, morality is subjective or, as Jeremy Bentham said, nothing more than "private opinion in disguise." So, in an effort to objectivize the law using the scientific method, all subjectivity, such as morality, must be separated from law. Under positivism, knowledge is grounded in empirical, observable facts which can be verified. Law is definable without any presuppositions and could be identified exclusively from factual sources such as statutes and court decisions. Law is simply a command of the sovereign. Whether a society has a legal system depends on its recognition of certain structures of governance, not on the extent to which it satisfies ideals of justice, democracy, or the rule of law. Law depends on the social standards its officials recognize as authoritative (For example, legislative enactments, judicial decisions, or social customs). According to positivism, law is a matter of what has been posited (ordered, decided, practiced, tolerated, etc.); it is a social construction. When a judge faces a case where no rule is immediately applicable, he or she exercises discretion to fill the gap.

In the early twentieth century, positivism birthed American legal realism, with its leading proponents being Oliver Wendell Holmes (1841–1934), Karl Llewellyn (1893–1962) and Jerome Frank (1889–1957). Oliver Wendell Holmes dismissed natural law as "a brooding omnipresence in the sky." As far as Holmes was concerned, absolute values such as "justice", "fairness", and "equality" do not exist. He said, "I hate justice, which means that I know that if a man begins to talk about that, for one reason or another he is shirking thinking in legal terms." He also attacked the formalism of legal positivism, which asserts that judges can examine laws and court decisions and render decisions in a logical process not influenced by a judge's own values and preferences. In his words,

> The life of the law has not been logic; it has been experience. The felt necessities of the time, the prevalent moral and political theories, intuitions of public policy, avowed or unconscious, even the prejudices which judges share with their fellow men, have had a good deal more to do than the syllogism in determining the rules by which men should be governed.

Legal realists, like positivists, share the belief that law is purely a human construct. However, positivists are strict textualists, replacing metaphysics with an internally defined system and meaning, whereas realists are contextualists and thus believe that the meaning of a law consists of the meaning the interpreter brings to the text. Because the interpreter is the most important indicator and creator of the law, the way to know the law is to study the decisions of individual judges. Realism is impatient with all theory, positivist or natural law; it is concerned with law as applied by judges.

Led by Karl Llewellyn, legal realism questioned the determinacy of legal rules and argued that the Supreme Court "shaped the living Constitution to the needs of the day as it felt them." Llewellyn thought law has purposes, not values. This functionalist approach saw law as performing essential "jobs," the most important being dispute resolution.

Legal realism gave birth to sociological jurisprudence. Its leading proponents include Roscoe Pound (1870–1964), Emile Durkheim (1858–1917), Max Weber (1864–1920), Michel Foucault (1926–1984), and Jurgen Habermas (1929–). Sociological jurisprudence focuses on the nature and role of law in a society, particularly in relation to changing social forces. It focuses on social structure (legal, cultural, political, economic, etc.), social stratification (discrimination based on class, sex, race, ethnicity, age, religion, etc.) and social function (how institutions and groups function in society). It generally rejects the positivist idea that law can be free of values and instead studies a society's hierarchy of moral and ideological values. Pound encouraged judges to be social engineers, molding law to the changing needs of society. Louis Brandeis, before he became a justice, filed a brief in *Muller v. Oregon* (1908) that contained only two pages of legal argument but ninety-seven pages of statistics and social science data documenting the health risks for women working long hours. Brandeis considered social science essential to court decisions if the law was to keep pace with the developments in other fields.

Another philosophy that has played a key role in interpreting the constitution is liberalism. Liberalism's proponents include John Locke (1632–1704), Adam Smith (1723–1790), Herbert Spencer (1820–1903), William Graham Sumner (1840–1910), John Rawls (1921–2002), John Maynard Keynes (1883–1946) and Ronald Dworkin (1931–2013). Franklin Delano Roosevelt (1882–1945), among U.S. presidents, perhaps best reflects liberal values. Liberalism, situated between conservatism on the right and socialism on the left, focuses on individual rights and demands freedom from state interference except to protect others from harm. These individual rights include freedom of religion, conscience, speech, association, and, more recently, sexuality. Liberalism's roots lie in the religious wars of Europe and religious discrimination in the colonies, which proved to liberals that the only stable ground for government was the separation of church and state. Liberals extend this principle of toleration to other areas where citizens have conflicting ideas of what is right. The role of the state is not to resolve these differences but to create a neutral framework that allows its citizens to pursue their ideal of the good life. For liberals, this is the only healthy response to the demands of modern pluralistic societies. Classical liberalism emphasizes the role of liberty while social liberalism stresses the importance of equality, including social and economic rights. A key component of social liberalism is the expansion of the welfare state. Social liberalism considers the legitimate role of government to include addressing economic and social issues such as poverty, health care, education, and caring for the elderly and disabled. Socially liberal policies have been widely adopted in much of the capitalist world, particularly following World War II. The term social liberalism is used to differentiate it from classical liberalism, which dominated political and economic thought for several centuries until social liberalism branched off from it around the Great Depression.

One critique of liberalism questions why individual freedom should take priority over the community and the state's interest in preserving customs. Liberalism's response is that state coercion and paternalism produce worse results in the long run than does individual autonomy. Critics of liberalism argue that by encouraging individual pursuit of self-interest, liberalism was used to promote capitalism. Although that may be true, most liberals today agree that justice requires some regulation of the market to ensure equal opportunity.

The primary counter-balance to liberalism is conservatism. Proponents of conservatism include Richard Hooker (1554–1600), the founding father of conservatism, along with the Marquess of Halifax (1633–1695), David Hume (1711–1776) and Edmund Burke (1729–1797). British Prime Minister Margaret Thatcher (1925–2013) and President Ronald Reagan (1911–2004) reflect the revival in the past forty years of conservative values at the political level. Conservatism favors stability and continuity and seeks to preserve the status quo and reform society slowly. It supports tradition in the sense of various religious, cultural, or nationally-defined beliefs and customs. Conservatives criticize liberalism and socialism for their utopian views of human perfectibility. Conservative prescriptions are based on what they regard as experience rather than reason; for conservatives, the ideal and the practical are inseparable. Conservatism's sense of the darker side of humanity and the corrupting influence of power causes it to prefer a limited government focused on security and a legal framework to facilitate transactions. Conservatism, hostile to regulation and government planning, favors autonomous institutions and individual freedom.

Conservatism is rooted in the American Revolution and a commitment to republicanism, sovereignty of the people, and individual rights and liberties. Today, it seeks to protect Western civilization from the challenges of modernist culture and totalitarian governments. It advocates free market capitalism and the preservation of personal wealth and private ownership. It also emphasizes self-reliance and individualism. Conservatives in general are more punitive toward criminals, tend to hold more orthodox religious views, and are often nationalistic and hostile toward emerging rights of the LGBTI and other minority groups. When freedom and equality compete, conservatives pursue freedom, preferring the right of individuals to succeed or fail on their own. Conservatives emphasize property rights and traditional views of social units such as the family, organized religion, and local government.

A critique of conservatism is that it rejects modernity and does not offer a theory for accepting change. Why should a time-honored tradition continue without a rationale grounded in contemporary reality? In modern society where the pace of change is rapid, the conservative's fear of change and distrust of the new, hold society back from reaching its potential.

C. Interpretive Tools

As the British inherited common law tradition has evolved in the U.S., certain time-honored tools to judicial interpretation have developed. Although a justice may use only one tool in a particular case, justices typically employ most or all of these tools in their jurisprudence. It is important to remember that using a particular tool to constitutional interpretation is not outcome determinative. So, for example, two justices using the textualist approach may well reach different conclusions in a case.

Although the divisions in constitutional interpretation sometimes run deep, there is widespread agreement on the following aspects: The text, history, structure, and precedent are valid tools of constitutional interpretation. The differences focus on how to use these tools and whether the court can look to additional factors.

1. Textualism

Textualism finds the meaning of the Constitution in the words of the text. After a detailed examination of the words, the resulting reasoning is applied to resolve the legal problem at hand.

Pure textualists believe that judicial decisions must be based only on the text of the Constitution. This raises the question of what rules of construction should be employed in interpreting the Constitution. Should only the literal and natural meaning of words be employed? Dictionaries often provide multiple meanings of words, and choosing which meaning applies may be a subjective process.

The "original meaning" approach looks at how the words would have been commonly understood at the time they were written and adopted. Such interpreters would examine dictionaries in use at the time of the drafting.

What if the plain meaning leads to an unintended or absurd result? For example, the Court has never adopted the literal meaning of the First Amendment, which begins "Congress shall make no law" establishing religion, prohibiting free exercise, or abridging freedom of speech, press, or association. The Court has allowed Congress, as well as states, to adopt laws limiting each of these First Amendment freedoms for various reasons, including the intent of the drafters.

Should words be examined in their context? A flaw of the literal approach is the assumption that words have plain meaning apart from their context. The contextual approach focuses on words surrounding the text in question, as well as from other parts of the Constitution, to shed light on the clause under consideration.

Often, the principle or concept behind a word is more important than the wording itself. When the text is inconclusive, as is often the case, the judiciary has developed other forms of constitutional interpretation to give meaning to the general language of the Constitution.

Other textualists, sometimes called strict constructionists, interpretivists, or legal formalists, would allow judges to examine the historical record to discern what the Framers and ratifiers intended the constitutional provisions to mean.

2. *Structuralism*

The structural approach involves drawing inferences from relevant parts of the Constitution as a whole and in relationship to one another. Under this approach, the structure of the Constitution, government and institutional relationships it creates constitute an important interpretive tool. Chief Justice Marshall used a structural argument in *McCulloch v. Maryland* (1819) when addressing the reasons a state could not tax the Bank of the United States. Looking at how the union was formed as well as the relationship between the national government and states, he argued for a kind of structural supremacy clause. To contend that the First Amendment is the most important amendment because it is first, is a structural argument.

3. *History*

There are a variety of ways the Supreme Court employs history to interpret the Constitution. History as a tradition can be used to resist change by maintaining a 200-year-old understanding of a constitutional phrase such as "liberty" or "equality." Or, historical argument can guide change by tracing the arc of history and recognizing the unfolding progress of "liberty" and "equality" through constitutional amendment, legislation and court decisions.

a. Stare Decisis

The common law doctrine of *stare decisis* ("let the decision stand"), or precedent, exerts significant influence in constitutional interpretation. Under this doctrine, the decision of a higher court acts as binding authority on a lower court within that same jurisdiction because cases must be decided the same way when their material facts are the same. The ratio decidendi (reason of deciding) of a case defines the material facts of the case. The Supreme Court follows the doctrine of precedent with respect to its own decisions. Adherence to precedent constrains future courts by requiring past constitutional articulations to bind them. Of course, the greater the body of cases in an area, the less flexibility a court has to depart from the prior line of decisions.

The rationale for the doctrine of stare decisis is the desirability of stability, consistency and certainty in the law. History becomes vital to achieve these goals. Benjamin Cardozo in his treatise *The Nature of the Judicial Process* states:

> "If a group of cases involves the same point, the parties expect the same decision. It would be a gross injustice to decide alternate cases on opposite principles. If a case was decided against me yesterday when I was a defendant, I shall look for the same judgment today if I

> am plaintiff. To decide differently would raise a feeling of resentment and wrong in my breast; it would be an infringement, material and moral, of my rights."

A critic would ask why should the Supreme Court today be bound by its decision from 100 years ago when the time and circumstances were different. One response is that the Supreme Court should hold to precedent only if it provides the proper reconciliation of the competing values and interests involved.

Although *stare decisis* is part of common law tradition, the judicial philosophy of each justice determines when to overturn or otherwise weaken precedents by overruling, narrowing or distinguishing precedent (sometimes to the point of nullification).

b. Original Intent

This approach says that the Constitution should be interpreted in accordance with the original intent of the framers and ratifiers. Original intent views the meaning of the Constitution as fixed as of the time of enactment (The Framers of the Constitution are usually considered the members of the Constitutional Convention; the framers of the constitutional amendments are the members of Congress who proposed it. The ratifiers are those at the federal and state levels that voted to ratify the constitution or amendment). Establishing original intent is difficult because few Framers or ratifiers spoke to the issue, it is unclear what the intent was for the others, and a public statement of a public official may reveal multiple intents or a smokescreen for his or her true intent. Often, the best that historical research into original intent can produce is the view of "leading proponents." *The Federalist Papers*, written in 1787 and 1788 by Alexander Hamilton, James Madison, and John Jay to promote the ratification of the proposed Constitution, is an example. Although recently associated with conservative thinkers like Justice Antonin Scalia (1936–2016), Justice Clarence Thomas (1948–), and Judge Robert Bork (1927–2012), liberal thinkers have also subscribed to this approach: John Hart Ely (1938–2003), Justice Hugo Black (1886–1971), and Akhil Reed Amar (1958–).

c. Historical Context: Problem, Remedy, and Purpose

This approach seeks to understand a constitutional provision by examining the larger historical context that gave rise to its drafting. Leading proponents of the historical school, Friedrich Karl von Savigny (1779–1861) and Sir Henry Maine (1822–1888), considered law an organic part of the social fabric that emanated from the life, culture, traditions, and customs of a society.

They thought that law makes no sense without understanding its historical context, including how it developed and progressed. By understanding the social, economic, or political problems the law was designed to address, the interpreter can understand the underlying motivations and purposes. This approach allows the interpreter to go beyond the mere language and specific intent of the framers and take a more holistic perspective, examining the historical context of the problem, remedy, and general intent of the Framers. James Madison listed this approach first on his "obvious and just guides applicable to the Constitution" ("the evils & defects for curing which the Constitution was called for & introduced"). Similar to the British Mischief Rule of statutory interpretation, this inquiry focuses on what was the "mischief and defect" for which this language was drafted and what was the remedy the framers sought, thereby revealing the true reason for the constitutional language.

4. *Prudential Reasoning*

Prudential reasoning is premised on the argument that the court should consider the outcomes of its decision. Courts should be pragmatic. Prudential reasoning is also called consequentialism because the consequences of a particular ruling should form the basis for any valid evaluation of that ruling. Chief Justice Marshall argued that for the Constitution to succeed, the court must interpret it in a way that "the exigencies of the nation may require." Utilitarianism — "that action is best which procures the greatest happiness for the greatest numbers" — a form of prudential reasoning, adopts the maximization of happiness as its fundamental norm. Leading proponents of this approach include Jeremy Bentham (1748–1832), John Stuart Mill (1806–1873), Henry Sidgwick (1838–1900), and G.E. Moore (1873–1958). At its best, prudential reasoning preserves constitutional principles by moderating or delaying the pursuit of ideals when the costs are too high. At its worst, it turns constitutional interpretation into expediency, abandoning fundamental principles as it ignores an individual's rights for the benefit of the majority's happiness.

5. *Ethical or Moral Reasoning*

The ethical or moral reasoning approach offers judges another interpretative tool to interpret the constitution: the ethical or moral principles of the Constitution. This reasoning seeks to vindicate what is moral, just, or desirable in the text. This includes the natural law approach and is exemplified by the following statement in Martin Luther King, Jr.'s Letter from a Birmingham Jail: "An unjust law is no law at all." Judge Learned Hand reportedly told

Justice Oliver Wendell Holmes to "do justice" (moral reasoning approach), to which Holmes replied, "That is not my job. It is my job to apply the law" (positivist approach).

Ronald Dworkin (1931–2013), a modern leading proponent of this approach, says, "moral reading" asks an interpreter "to find the best conception of constitutional moral principles ... that fits the broad story of America's historical record. It does not ask them to follow the whisperings of their own consciences or the traditions of their own class or sect if these cannot be seen as embedded in that record."

Proponents of this position argue that moral principles undergirding the constitution are critical to understanding specific language of the text as well as the primary tool to bridge gaps in the text. Proponents argue that moral reasoning substantially influences judge's decision making (which helps explain the battles over Supreme Court nominees), so it is better to make such reasoning explicit rather than force judges to hide those moral choices behind mechanisms that pretend to avoid those choices. Critics argue that this approach is too subjective and antidemocratic and tends to entrench prejudicial beliefs.

6. *Comparative Constitutional Theory*

Comparative constitutional theory posits that the ideas, practices, and experiences of other countries can inform the Supreme Court's understanding, not as binding precedent but as persuasive authority. Although the federal courts have considered foreign sources of law since the founding of the country, this theory has recently become controversial because of the sensitivity of the cases involved (including the death penalty, rights of the LGBT community, affirmative action, and assisted suicide).

This approach raises some methodological concerns regarding which countries the court should survey and whether there is sufficient expertise about the national legal context where a foreign case originates to adequately interpret and transport the reasoning. However, in an increasingly interconnected world, the communication and sharing of ideas among judges and courts is inevitable and perhaps, as in virtually all other disciplines, beneficial.

7. *Clustering of Approaches: Originalism versus Non-originalism*

Two broad categories (also called clusterings) of approaches to interpreting the Constitution that have formed much of the recent debate are originalism and nonoriginalism, also called interpretivism and noninterpretivism. Originalism considers the text and the original intent of the drafters and ratifiers of the Constitution at the time of its adoption as authoritative for purposes of constitutional interpretation in the present. Originalists see the amendment process as the only way to change or develop the Constitution and therefore do not want the Supreme Court to recognize rights that are not expressly enumerated in the Constitution.

Nonoriginalists also examine text and original intent, but in addition interpret constitutional principles in light of contemporary understandings. Nonoriginalists see the Constitution as a living document evolving over time, which makes room for unenumerated rights, such as the right to privacy. Nonoriginalists would interpret the equal protection clause to prohibit sex discrimination even though that was not the original intent of its drafters. This example also raises the question of the level of generality (as opposed to specificity) at which the Court finds a constitutional norm. Arguably, if the original intent was the principle that no person should be denied the equal protection of the laws, than even originalists could accept its application to women despite the absence of that specific intent at the time of adoption.

D. Recent External Critiques of Constitutional Interpretation

1. *Critical Legal Studies*

Critical legal studies is more of a critique of current constitutional theory, revealing its limitations and biases, than a proposal for the way justices should analyze the Constitution. Its leading proponents include Duncan Kennedy (1942–), Peter Gabel (1947–), Karl Klare (1947–), Mark Tushnet (1945–), Mark Kelman (1951–), and Roberto Unger (1947–). Growing out of the radical political culture of the 1960s, it asserts the inescapability of commitment to values and interests and rejects any search for a value-neutral jurisprudence. It is concerned with the politics of law, particularly how legal reasoning has attempted to make a particular social order appear inevitable. It sees law as merely the assertion of power by those with power. It seeks to show that the social order is less structured and impartial and more complex and irrational than the law suggests. It hopes to overturn this legal consciousness and emancipate the individual without establishing a new orthodoxy.

Critical legal studies is united by a concern for outgroups (i.e., the poor, racial, ethnic, sexual, and other minorities) and a commitment to a more egalitarian society. Its greatest legacy may be the many off-shoots it has spawned, such as critical race theory, feminist legal theory, the LatCrit movement (examines how law treats Latina/o communities), queer jurisprudence (challenges categories of gender and sexual orientation), and other outgroup jurisprudence.

2. *Feminist Legal Theory*

Feminist legal theory states that legal theory has long ignored the position of women. Therefore, Feminist theorists examine the inequalities found in criminal law (especially rape, domestic violence and sexual harassment), family law, contract, tort, property, and other areas. There are several strands of feminist legal theory. Liberal feminism emphasizes the ways men and women are the same, rather than ways they are different, with the hope that this will break down gender-based distinctions that limit equal opportunities for women. It is reluctant to accept special treatment for women out of fear this will reinforce limiting views of women. It argues that because women and men are equally rational, they should have the same social, economic, and political opportunities that men possess. Although acknowledging the patriarchal nature of the current liberal, "rights based" legal system, it seeks to operate within this system. Similar to liberal constitutional theory, it is committed to individual autonomy and therefore tends to focus on legal rights as the avenue to secure nondiscriminatory treatment. Leading proponents include Wendy Williams (1945–), Martha Nussbaum (1947–), and Martha Minow (1954–).

Radical feminism focuses on how women are different than men. They challenge the view that, because men have historically used gender differences to discriminate against women, women can never achieve equality while recognizing differences. Radical feminists say the issue is ultimately one of power, not of sameness versus difference, so they assault the current liberal "rights based" legal system. Leading proponents include Catherine MacKinnon (1946–), Carol Smart (1948–), and Carol Gilligan (1936–). As part of MacKinnon's effort to redefine "woman" from the current phallocentric and oppressive definition, MacKinnon advocates a ban on pornography that subordinates women.

3. *Critical Race Theory*

Critical race theory includes a variety of legal theories founded on the belief that the legal system or its white-dominated social institutions do not treat racial minorities equally. Leading proponents include Derrick Bell (1930–2011), Kimberlé Williams Crenshaw (1959–), Mari Matsuda (1956–) , Richard Delgado (1939–), Patricia Williams (1951–) Neil Gotanda (1954–) and Michelle Alexander (1967–). Following in the footsteps of the critical legal studies movement, it has developed various analytical techniques to demonstrate the racial bias built into the legal system. Critical race theorists continually ask the "race question" to reveal the ways in which seemingly neutral rules adversely affect racial minorities. Critical race theorists explore how federalism, privacy, traditional values, and established property interests serve as vessels of racial subordination. This theory values experiential knowledge of people of color and critical reflection on the lived experience of racism.

After incidents of racist hate speech on college campuses in the 1980s, several critical race theorists analyzed the injuries experienced by students of color who were targets of such incidents. They drafted speech codes for regulating campus speech and defended those codes against First Amendment challenges, arguing that the speech codes, which prohibited certain language, had much in common with existing defamation and obscenity laws and the doctrines excluding fighting words and threats. They argued that the First Amendment, could be interpreted to fight subordination and respect human dignity. They also argued that the First Amendments values of self-fulfillment, knowledge, and political participation are undermined when hate speech gains legal protection. Although no court upheld the codes against First Amendment challenges, the critical race theorists' efforts altered the terms of the debate and taught many about the kinds of injuries tolerated under the First Amendment.

4. *Postmodernism*

Postmodernism, as its name suggests, implies a contrast with modernism and its commitment to Enlightenment ideas, such as reason, science, universal values (individual rights, equality and justice), and the conviction that these prove an independent reality. Instead, postmodernism turns reason on its head, asserting that reason is nothing more than social practices. Therefore, ideas about what the Constitution means are really just social constructions, not an objective reality that exists independently of the speaker. Leading proponents of postmodernism include Michael Foucault (1926–1984), Jacques Derrida (1930–2004), Charles Taylor (1931–), and Richard Rorty (1931–2007). Postmodernists doubt the possibility of objective truth or meta-narratives and reject sharp dichotomies and hierarchy.

5. *Law and Economics*

The law and economics movement, a form of utilitarianism, seeks economic efficiency and wealth maximization in the law. A leading proponent, Judge Richard Posner (1939–), argues that the free-market economy functions best when the legal system defines entitlements so as to minimize information and transaction costs. This approach ranges from changing regulatory practice to allow for efficient markets, to returning to the unregulated pre-welfare state of the early 1900s, better known as the Lochner era. Economist Vilfredo Pareto came up with one definition of efficiency. Given a set of alternative allocations of goods or services, a change from one allocation to another that can make at least one individual better off without making any other individual worse off is called a Pareto improvement (An allocation is defined as Pareto efficient or Pareto optimal when no further Pareto improvements can be made). Nicholas Kaldor and John Hicks took the Pareto efficient one step further. Under the Kaldor-Hicks efficiency, an outcome is considered more efficient if a Pareto optimal outcome can be reached by arranging some compensation from those that are made better off to those that are made worse off. Critics of law and economics argue that economic efficiency is often not the democratic ideal and can lead to inhumane results. They say that it oversimplifies assumptions about human nature, and undervalues human rights and distributive justice. Finally, they believe that it inadequately measures the economic, social and human costs of excluding those who are less efficient versus the gains of inclusion.

Bibliography

Ahlstrom, Sydney, *A Religious History of the American People*, Yale University Press, 1972.

Amar, Akhil Reed. *The Bill of Rights: Creation and Reconstruction*, New Haven: Yale University Press, 1998.

Blackstone, William, *Commentaries on the Laws of England*, (1768).

Bogan, David S. *The Origins of Freedom of Speech and Press*, 42 Md. L. Rev. 429 (1983).

Cardozo, Benjamin N., *The Nature of the Judicial Process*, Dover Publications, 2012.

Chafee, Zechariah Jr. *Free Speech in the United States*, Cambridge, Massachusetts: Harvard University Press, 1941.

Chaffee, Zechariah Jr., *Freedom of Speech in Wartime*, 32 Harv. L. Rev. 932 (1919).

Curtis, Michael Kent, *Free Speech, The People's Darling Privilege: Struggles for Freedom of Expression in American History*, Duke University Press, 2000.

Dworkin, Ronald, *Freedom's Law: The Moral Reading of the American Constitution*, Harvard University Press, 1997.

Emerson, Thomas, *The System of Freedom of Expression*, New York: Random House, 1970.

Finkelman, Paul. *A Brief Narrative of the Cast and Tryal of John Peter Zenger*. Bedford: St. Martin's, 2010.

Finkelman, Paul. *A March of Liberty: A Constitutional History of the United States.* With Melvin I. Urofsky. 2 vols. 3rd ed., Oxford University Press, 2011.

Freeman, M.D.A., *Lloyd's Introduction to Jurisprudence* 9th ed. Sweet & Maxwell, 2014.

Graber, Mark, *Transforming Free Speech,* University of California Press, 1992.

Hamburger, Philip. *The Development of the Law of Seditious Libel and Control of the Press,* Stanford Law Review 37 (1985): 661–765.

Inazu, John D. *The Forgotten Freedom of Assembly,* 84 Tulane Law Review 565–612 (2010).

Jeffries, John C., Jr., and James E. Ryan, *A Political History of the Establishment Clause,* 100 Mich. L Rev. 279, 2001.

Krotoszynski, Ronald J. *Reclaiming the Petition Clause: Seditious Libel, Offensive Protest, and the Right to Petition the Government for a Redress of Grievances,* Yale University Press, 2012.

Labunski, Richard. *James Madison and the Struggle for the Bill of Rights,* New York: Oxford University Press, 2006.

Levy, Leonard Williams. *Legacy of Suppression: Freedom of Speech and Press in Early American History,* Cambridge: Belknap Press of Harvard University Press, 1960.

Levy, Leonard Williams. *Emergence of a Free Press,* Oxford: Oxford University Press, 1985.

Levy, Leonard Williams. *Origins of the Bill of Rights,* New Haven: Yale University Press, 1999.

Levy, Leonard Williams. *Blasphemy: Verbal Offense Against the Sacred, From Moses to Salman Rushdie,* New York: Alfred A. Knopf, 1993.

Locke, John, *The Second Treatise of Government and A Letter Concerning Toleration,* Dover Publications, 2012.

Miller, Peter P. "Freedom of Expression under State Constitutions," 20 Stanford Law Review 318 (1968).

Paine, Thomas, Collected Writings: Common Sense/The American Crisis/The Rights of Man/The Age of Reason/A Letter Addressed to the Abbe Raynal, Coyote Canyon Press, 2010.

Rakove, Jack N. *Original Meanings: Politics and Ideas in the Making of the Constitution,* New York: Knopf, 1996.

Wacks, Raymond, *Understanding Jurisprudence, An Introduction to Legal Theory,* 4th ed. Oxford University Press, 2015.

Witte, John Jr. *Religion and the American Constitutional Experiment,* 2nd Ed., Boulder: Westview Press, 2005.

Chapter 1

First Amendment Theory and Methodology

Roadmap

- **Theory and Methodology of Freedom of Expression**
  - The interpretation of the First Amendment during the eighteenth, nineteenth and early twentieth centuries was highly restrictive by today's standards.
  - The Supreme Court has never adopted a literal interpretation of the First Amendment.
  - Incorporation: The Applicability of the First Amendment to State and Local Governments
  - Competing Theories of the Meaning and Application of the First Amendment
    - Enhancing Self-Government
    - Seeking Truth (the Marketplace of Ideas)
    - Self-Fulfillment and Personal Autonomy
    - Balancing Stability and Change
    - Promoting Tolerance in a Pluralistic Society
  - Defining Speech: Oral and written communication of information, ideas or emotions from one person to another is speech. Conduct and symbolic expressions can also be speech.
  - Vagueness and Overbreadth: A law can be void for vagueness or for overbreadth by a third party challenge before the law is even violated.
  - Content-Neutral Laws versus Content-Based Laws: Government regulations based on content must pass strict scrutiny.
  - Prior Restraints: The Court disfavors prior restraints of speech, and applies a very strict standard when determining their validity.
    - Finding a Definition of a Prior Restraint
    - The Evils of Prior Restraints

- Forms of Prior Restraints
    - Administrative Licensing Schemes
    - Court-Ordered Injunctions against Speech
- The First Amendment also protects the right to not speak.

I. Theory and Methodology of Freedom of Expression

The third freedom protected by the First Amendment to the U.S. Constitution is the right to freedom of speech. Freedom of speech is closely related to freedom of press, assembly, to petition the government for a redress of grievances, and the implied rights of association and belief. Freedom of religion was, historically, closely related to freedom of speech because often the most severe speech restrictions and punishments were for religious speech. The Supreme Court interprets the extent of the protection afforded to these rights and as we will see, those protections fluctuate over time depending on how critical the court views those rights.

A. Interpreting the First Amendment from 1791 to 1920

Adopted on December 15, 1791 as one of the ten amendments that constitutes the Bill of Rights the First Amendment gave much freedom to U.S. citizens compared to those of other colonies and countries. It stated, "Congress shall make no law respecting an establishment of religion, or prohibiting the free exercise thereof; or abridging the freedom of speech, or of the press; or the right of the people peaceably to assemble, and to petition the Government for a redress of grievances." However, once in power, even the Constitution's framers were guilty of overstepping the First Amendment. In 1798, Congress passed the Alien and Sedition Act, which made it a crime for anyone to publish "any false, scandalous and malicious writing" against the government. President John Adams and the then-dominant Federalist Party used the Alien and Sedition Act to prosecute their opponents, prominent Republican newspaper editors, during the late 18th century. The Supreme Court never addressed the constitutionality of these Acts because they were repealed before they could be tested in court; however, three of the Supreme Court's justices presided over sedition trials without indicating any reservations. The leading critics of the law, Vice President Thomas Jefferson and James Madison, argued that the Act was unconstitutional based on the First Amendment and other Constitutional provisions. Jefferson succeeded Adams as president, in part due to the unpopularity of Adam's sedition prosecutions; Jefferson and his party quickly overturned the Acts and pardoned those imprisoned by them. Today, the Supreme Court would strike down the Alien and Sedition Acts as a violation of the First Amendment.

During the 19th century, criminal anarchy and criminal conspiracy laws were used to suppress the speech of abolitionists and religious minorities. During the 1830s, abolitionists began to demand the immediate end of slavery and the recognition of basic civil rights for freed slaves. In response, Southern states adopted laws criminalizing any speech that had a tendency to cause slaves to become discontent or revolt. In Virginia, anyone who "by speaking or writing maintains that owners have no right of property in slaves" was subject to a one-year prison sentence. Although mobs in the North broke up abolitionist meetings, burned their publications and destroyed their printing presses, no Northern state adopted laws criminalizing antislavery speech.

In 1856, when Benjamin Hedrick, a University of North Carolina professor, publicly endorsed Republican Presidential candidate John C. Fremont, who was antislavery, the university fired him. Upon his return to Salisbury, North Carolina, he was forced to flee the state because of threats of violence. In 1859, Daniel Worth, a Wesleyan minister in North Carolina, preached that the gospel was opposed to slavery. The American Missionary Association, which opposed slavery, supported him financially and supplied him with antislavery books and tracts. Worth was arrested and convicted of circulating antislavery materials that have a tendency to cause slaves to become discontent or revolt. On appeal, the North Carolina Supreme Court upheld his conviction, finding that the State did not have to prove that Worth's sermons and written materials reached slaves to be convicted because "its corrupting influence would eventually reach the black." As the right to free speech provisions of state constitutions were not being enforced, Republicans argued that the right to free speech belonged to all American citizens, an understanding they wrote into the 14th Amendment adopted after the Civil War.

Once the Civil War began, opponents of the war in the North were prosecuted for their anti-war speech. Clement Vallandigham, a Democratic candidate for Governor of Ohio, said that the war was "wicked, cruel and unnecessary," being fought for the freedom of blacks and the enslavement of whites. He was convicted by a military commission of interfering with the war effort. President Lincoln, instead of opposing the conviction, banished him to the Confederacy.

Congress also suppressed speech regarding sex. In 1873, Congress adopted the Comstock Act which prohibited the use of the U.S. Postal service to send obscene materials. The list of banned materials included any information about birth control.

Suppression of free speech continued in the early 20th century against suffragists, labor organizers, and pacifists using sedition and criminal conspiracy laws. In 1917, feminist Margaret Sanger was arrested for giving a lecture on birth control. Trade union meetings were banned and courts routinely granted injunctions prohibiting strikes and other labor protests. Violators were sentenced to prison. Peaceful protesters opposing U.S. entry into World War I were jailed for expressing their opinions. In the early 1920s, many states outlawed the display of red or black flags, symbols of communism and anarchy. During this era, the courts were almost universally hostile to the First Amendment rights of political minorities. Free speech issues did not even reach the Supreme Court until 1919 when, in *Schenck v. U.S.*, the Court unanimously upheld the conviction of a Socialist Party member for mailing anti-World War I leaflets to draft-age men.

The Court's meaningful exercise of judicial review under the First Amendment commenced during World War I. Its early 20th-century First Amendment jurisprudence determined that speech that could possibly harm national security could be punished. By the middle of the twentieth century, this restriction of speech was challenged, most powerfully by Justice Black and Justice William Douglas. Over time and heavily influence by the anti-Vietnam War protests, the Court recognized a spectrum ranging from no protection to varying levels of protection.

B. Literal Interpretation Never Adopted

The Supreme Court has never taken a literal approach to interpreting the First Amendment. Although the First Amendment explicitly restricts only Congress ("*Congress* shall make no law"), the court has always applied the amendment to the executive and judicial branches of the federal government. Second, while the language of the First Amendment prohibiting Congress from adopting a law abridging its freedoms is unequivocal and absolute ("Congress shall make *no* law"), Congress and the Supreme Court have always recognized numerous exceptions. Although the literalist or absolutist approach to free speech has had its supporters on the Court, notably Justice Hugo Black, the Court has never understood those words to mean that Congress could pass NO law abridging the freedom of speech. Justice Black consistently pushed for a literal reading of the First Amendment language. He argued that these clear and plain statements indicated that the Amendment's drafters performed all the balancing of expressive liberty versus the other needs of society that was necessary. He found that, by adopting the First Amendment, the founders intended "to put the freedoms protected there completely out of the area of any congressional control" (*Konigsberg v. State Bar of California*, 1961). However, Justice Black distinguished expression from expressive conduct. To him, the former was protected absolutely, whereas the government could regulate the latter. Although Justice Black may have been the most eloquent proponent of the literal interpretation of the First Amendment, his position has never garnered a majority on the Supreme Court.

Like many constitutional provisions, most of the language of the First Amendment is vague and broadly stated. The Constitution and its Amendments do not expressly define the terms, use, or boundaries of the freedoms they protect. During drafting and adoption, the First Amendment passed the House and Senate with almost no recorded debate, complicating future discussion of the Framer's intent. Thus, it is incumbent on the judiciary, especially the Supreme Court, to give meaning to these words. Where the words are clear, the Court has not interpreted them literally, and where they are not clear, the Court has had to develop its own doctrines.

The Court does not absolutely protect any category of speech. Even protected speech is subject to regulation by the government if its interest is sufficiently strong. The Court also permits the government to regulate speech if the regulation does not target the speech itself, but rather its so-called secondary effects. The court's determination of what speech is protected or unprotected (and if protected, to what extent), has changed substantially, with the arc of history showing a move toward fewer limits on speech.

C. Incorporation (Applicability to State and Local Government)

For the nation's first 134 years, the Supreme Court applied the First Amendment only to the federal government, not to the state or local government where citizens have the most contact with government and where violations of freedom of expression and freedom of religion occur more frequently. The Court interpreted the introductory words to the First Amendment, "*Congress* shall pass no law" establishing religion or abridging freedom of speech to mean that it only applied to the federal government. States were free to establish religion until the court applied the First Amendment to states through the 14th Amendment.

An early example of this dichotomy involves the establishment of religion. Several states continued official state religions after ratifying the First Amendment. Massachusetts was officially Congregationalist until the 1830s and Connecticut until 1818. Until 1877, the New Hampshire Constitution required members of the State legislature to be Protestant and until 1835 the North Carolina constitution allowed only Protestants to hold public office. From 1835–1876 it allowed only Christians (including Catholics) to hold public office. Such clauses were held by the Supreme Court to be unenforceable in the case of *Torcaso v. Watkins* (1961) when the court ruled unanimously that such clauses constituted a religious test incompatible with First and Fourteenth Amendment protections. Seven state constitutions still have religious tests for public office but they are not enforced because they are understood as unconstitutional.

When the Fourteenth Amendment was adopted in 1868, many thought that the Privileges or Immunities Clause would protect the basic rights contained in the Bill of Rights at the state and local level. This clause states: "No state shall make or enforce any law which shall abridge the privileges or immunities of citizens of the United States." Certainly, many citizens considered free speech and freedom of religion a privilege of being a U.S. citizen. However, in the *Slaughter-House Cases* decision of 1873, the Court narrowly interpreted the Privileges or Immunities Clause of the Fourteenth Amendment to disallow an application of the Bill of Rights to the states. This narrow interpretation has not yet been overruled; however the Court has provided the states with relief by allowing application through the Due Process Clause of the Fourteenth Amendment. The turning point occurred in *Twining v. New Jersey* (1908), where the Court recognized a possibility of "incorporating" the Bill of Rights to apply to local governments. Almost two decades later, the Court solidified the "incorporation" concept in *Gitlow v. New York* (1925) and held, for the first time, that freedom of speech and the press are "among the fundamental personal rights and 'liberties' protected by the Due Process Clause of the Fourteenth Amendment from impairment by the States." In its decision, the Court expressly disregarded previous decisions, such as *Prudential Ins. C. v. Cheek* (1922), which failed to protect freedom of speech at the state level. It is important to note that only certain clauses and certain amendments in the Bill of Rights have been applied (through incorporation) to the states over the nation's history. In *Everson v. Board of Education* (1947), the U.S. Supreme Court incorporated the Establishment Clause. In the majority decision, Justice Hugo Black wrote: "The 'establishment of religion' clause of the First Amendment means at least this: Neither a state nor the Federal Government can set up a church. Neither can pass laws which aid one religion, aid all religions, or prefer one religion to another . . ." In *Duncan v. State of La.* (1968), the Court reiterated that the First Amendment's clauses regarding freedom of speech, press, and religion are incorporated in the Fourteenth Amendment and therefore applicable to state and local governments.

D. First Amendment Protects Individuals from Government, not Private Interference

The Supreme Court has interpreted the First Amendment (as well as the entire Constitution and amendments other than the 13th A.) as applying to federal, state and local government actions. Private conduct generally does not have to comply with the Constitution. This means that action by private entities, be they individuals, corporations, non-profits, etc. is not protected by the First Amendment. The First Amendment protects against "state action," the word *state* meaning government. State action covers all government divisions, subdivisions, agencies and government-created companies like Amtrak and the U.S. Postal Service. If one's First Amendment rights are limited by state actors, then there is state action, but if the same limitations are taken by private actors, there will be no state action and the injured party will have no constitutional claim. Most people spend their days in contact primarily with private individuals and entities, not governmental, which means most of their speech occurs in relationships devoid of a right to free speech.

The principle idea behind limiting the application of the First Amendment to state actors is that the Constitution was designed to protect people from the power of the state. Binding private parties by the obligations of the Constitution would authorize further governmental intrusion into the lives and liberties that private parties hold. Thus constitutional law regulates public power, whereas civil law (e.g., contract or tort law) and criminal law protect people from other people. However, if governmental entities subcontract their work out to the private sector, they often can avoid constitutional rights, including the right to free speech, and thereby diminish the realm of constitutional rights.

Thus, as a general rule, only state actors can violate your constitutional rights, because it is only against the state that one has constitutional rights. For example, administrators of private law schools can restrict what law students and law professors say, where they say it, and how they say it, without infringing the First Amendment. Administrators of state law schools are much more limited in how they can restrict speech of students and professors without violating the First Amendment. Likewise, while there is no First Amendment obligation to listen to or allow someone to speak on private property whether it is a living room or a restaurant, there are substantial First Amendment protections of speech delivered on public sidewalks or a public park.

Federal and state governments can enact laws that bind private action to constitutional requirements. So, a state could adopt a law that requires private schools and universities in its state to provide the same First Amendment protections that public schools and universities receive. Of course, it would be the statute that sets these requirements and statutes can be amended and repealed.

Like all general rules in constitutional law, there are exceptions to the state action requirement; however, these exceptions are riddled with inconsistencies. One of the main reasons the Court has found exceptions is to protect individual rights. As the practice of slavery demonstrated, the abuse of private power can be just as pernicious to individual liberty as the abuse of public power. The four exceptions are: first, when private actors perform public functions; second, when public and private actor's activities are entangled; third, when the state authorizes, encourages and enforces private action; and fourth, when there is entwinement which is a hybrid of sufficient state function, entanglement, and authorization.

The first exception involves private actors performing public functions. *Marsh v. Alabama (1946)* involved a company-owned town that used general trespass law to prevent the distribution of religious literature by Jehovah's Witnesses. The use of trespass law to restrict First Amendment activities on private property is typically not problematic; People have a right to keep others off their property. However, the Court found that because this privately-owned town was the functional equivalent of a regular government-run town, the streets were public forums where the First Amendment applies, just like any other public street.

In dicta, the Court in *Marsh* also indicated that this reasoning could be extended to private parks, which serve the same function as public parks. This approach was adopted in *Evans v. Newton* (1966), where African-Americans were denied entrance to a park held in private trust for the city of Macon, Georgia. Writing for the majority, Justice William Douglas noted that the park fulfilled a municipal function, not unlike police or firemen. Therefore, the Equal Protection Clause of the Fourteenth Amendment applied. The case came back to the Court in *Evans v. Abney* (1970) after the Georgia courts decided that the trust had failed because its purpose (to keep the park for the sole use of whites) had failed due to the U.S. Supreme Court's decision. So, the argument now was that the park was entirely private and thus its owners could discriminate on the basis of race and keep African-Americans out. By this time Justice Burger had replaced Justice Warren. Justice Black, writing for the majority, declined to follow the spirit of Justice Douglas's opinion. Justice Black found that, because the park was now completely private, its owners could exclude African-Americans.

Shopping centers are perhaps the closest modern equivalent to company towns in serving the public functions that municipalities generally serve. Thus, it was not a stretch when the Court decided in *Amalgamated Food Employers Union Local 590 v. Logan Valley Plaza, Inc. (1968)* that the shopping center, like the company town, was a public forum for the purposes of allowing, under the First Amendment's guarantee of free speech, informational labor picketing that was related to a store in the mall. This ruling was narrowed in *Lloyd Corp. v. Tanner (1972)* on the grounds that the hand billing (passing out flyers, leaflets, or circulars) was unrelated to a store in the mall or the mall itself (rather, the leafleting related to the Vietnam War).

However, the Court in *Hudgens v. N.L.R.B. (1976),* another shopping mall case involving labor picketing, used this content-based distinction to overturn *Amalgamated.* The court reasoned that because the distinction between the two cases was based on the content of the message (i.e., whether the message was "shopping center related"), and because content-based regulations violate the First Amendment (discussed in section J below), then *Amalgamated* was unconstitutional. Of course, the Court could just as easily have held that it was *Lloyd* that was wrongly decided because the Court introduced content-based restrictions in that case, not in *Amalgamated.* However, these cases illustrate a trend of narrowly interpreting the public functions exception.

Hudgens has not been the end of the story. Several state supreme courts have concluded that the free speech protections of their own state constitutions protect the right of citizens to engage in expressive activities in the public areas of shopping centers. Most notable, perhaps, is the California Supreme Court's *Pruneyard* decision. The Court found constitutional protection for high school students who were soliciting signatures at a 65-store mall opposing a U. N. resolution on "Zionism." The shopping center owner took the case to the U. S. Supreme Court in 1980, arguing that the California Supreme Court's decision amounted either to a violation of *his* First Amendment rights or a taking of his private property. The U.S. Supreme Court unanimously rejected both arguments in *Pruneyard Shopping Center v. Robins (1980).*

In *Jackson v. Metropolitan Edison* (1974), the Court continued its trend of narrowly reading the public function exception. In this case, plaintiff claimed that his utilities were cut off without due process of law in violation of the Fourteenth Amendment. Based on previous cases, the court could have held that a monopoly public utility provider with exclusive power to either allow or deny one access to electricity was not only providing a public service but wielded power that was on a par with governmental power. However, the Court definitively held the modern rule that the public function exception only applies to functions that are "traditionally exclusively reserved to the state." Because public utilities have not traditionally been the exclusive prerogative of the state, the private public utility provider did not fall within this exception. Thus, even if there were a trend for states and municipalities to run public utilities, this would not be enough to satisfy this stringent test because it also requires exclusivity.

In *Flagg Bros., Inc. v. Brooks* (1978), the Court held that it was not state action when state law authorized the private sale of stored goods to enforce a warehouseman's lien. The claimant had argued that the state had delegated its traditional and exclusive power over dispute resolution to the creditor, who could now use self-help to enforce its lien. Because this was not the only way the dispute could have been resolved, the Court held that this was not an exclusive power delegated to the creditor by the state. Because dispute resolution has not always been monopolized by the state, the court held it was not a function that was "traditionally and exclusively reserved to the state."

In *Rendell-Baker v. Kohn* (1982), the Court declined to find state action where a teacher claimed that his right to freedom of expression and due process were violated when the school terminated his employment. Although the state paid 90–99% of the funding for this school, it had a private board of directors, was located on private property, and its function was not the exclusive province of the state.

The Court came to the same conclusion in *Blum v. Yaretsky* (1982). A private nursing home that received 90% of its funding from the state discharged patients without a hearing to contest the discharge. Although Justice Brennan forcefully argued in his dissent that the decisions to discharge patients were connected with state funding issues, not medical decisions, the Court reasoned that the day-to-day decisions of the nursing home were not "the kind of decisions traditionally and exclusively made by the sovereign for and on behalf of the public."

The second exception is entanglement: when state and private actors are joint actors or in a symbiotic relationship. In *Burton v. Wilmington Parking Authority* (1961), a private restaurant located in a municipal parking garage practiced racial discrimination. The plaintiff sued under the Fourteenth Amendment's Equal Protection Clause. The Court held that the city was responsible because the building was owned, rented, and maintained by the city and because of the mutual benefits that the parking authority and the restaurant received from their joint patrons. This Warren Court decision held out the possibility of a more expansive state action doctrine based on the totality of state and private actor interaction.

Although there are early cases in which the Court found that state funds given to private schools that practiced racial discrimination constituted state action, the current rule is that state funding, even if critical to the existence of a private entity, is not sufficient on its own to create state action.

Is licensing and regulation sufficient for state action? In *Moose Lodge No. 117 v. Irvis* (1972), the plaintiff sued Moose Lodge because it refused to serve him based on his race. Plaintiff asserted that since the state gave Moose Lodge its liquor license and otherwise regulated the lodge, there was state action. The Burger Court found that involvement by the state did not rise to the level of the symbiotic relationship found in *Burton*.

The third exception occurs when the state authorizes, encourages and enforces private action. In *Lugar v. Edmondson Oil Company* (1982), the Court found state action where the creditor had a sheriff help in executing a writ that the creditor obtained in an *ex parte* proceeding in violation of the plaintiff's due process rights. In *Lugar*, the Court stated at least one modern formulation of the state action rule, namely, that:

1. "The deprivation must be caused by the exercise of some right or privilege created by the state or by a person form whom the state is responsible;" and
2. "The party charged with the deprivation must be a person who may fairly be said to be a state actor." This second requirement can be fulfilled in one of three ways:
   a. If the person "is a state official;"
   b. If the person "acted together with, or has obtained significant aid from state officials;" or
   c. "Because the person's conduct is otherwise chargeable to the state."

The fourth exception is entwinement, which is a hybrid of sufficient state function, entanglement, and authorization. In *Brentwood Academy v. Tennessee Secondary School Athletic Ass'n.* (2001), the Court found that a private entity regulating high school athletics was a state actor because there was sufficient government "entwinement." The Association regulated high school athletics in Tennessee in lieu of the state Board of Education's own authority, giving the Association a state function, albeit not an exclusive and traditional state function. The entanglement came from 84 percent of the Association's membership were public schools, fees came primarily from public schools, and its staff were eligible for the state retirement program, even though their salaries were not paid by the state. The authorization element was that most of the control and management of the Association came from public high school principals and vice principals.

The Court went to great length to distinguish a similar case, *NCAA v. Tarkanian* (1989), in which the entity regulating college interscholastic sports (the NCAA), ordered the University of Nevada–Las Vegas to suspend basketball coach Jerry Tarkanian. He claimed the NCAA was a state actor because the state university had delegated its functions to the NCAA. The Court found no state action here because most of the members of the NCAA were outside the State of Nevada and the university could have retained its coach and left the NCAA. Arguably the nature of government involvement in both cases is similar and the possibility of taking one's NCAA Division I basketball team out of the NCAA is not a viable option.

E. Competing Theories of Free Speech

The broad language of the First Amendment and lack of information about the Framer's intent make the Court's interpretative job concomitantly more difficult and controversial, forcing the Court to balance competing values in its First Amendment decisions. Thus, an accurate and thorough analysis requires an understanding of the goals and underlying values of free speech. In addition to eliminating prior restraints and prosecutions of seditious libel, other goals include enhancing self-government, seeking truth, encouraging self-fulfillment, balancing stability and change, and promoting tolerance in a pluralistic society. These goals and values are not mutually exclusive, though the theory to which one adheres will influence or even determine one's views on many First Amendment issues.

1. Enhancing Self-Government

This goal argues that freedom of speech regarding governmental action and matters of public concern is foundational to democracy. For a person to make an informed political decision, he or she must be able to hear and discuss points of view from political candidates and others. This exchange permits the citizenry to develop political opinions and hold their public officials accountable for their actions.

Virtually no one would credibly dispute that freedom of political speech is a core concern of the overall freedom of expression. To do so would be to deny the historical underpinnings of the founding of our country. The Supreme Court has even described the ability to speak freely in the political context as "the central meaning of the First Amendment" (*New York Times*

Co. v. Sullivan, 1964). This concept is enshrined further in this republic's founding documents by the statement in the Declaration of Independence that governments "deriv[e] their just Powers from the Consent of the Governed." Alexander Meiklejohn said that without effective protection of political free speech, self-government cannot exist. Meiklejohn went further, including education, philosophical and scientific knowledge, literature and the arts, as well as public discussion of issues of public importance, in what must be protected to safeguard self-government.

Some have proposed that only political speech should be protected by the First Amendment. A famous proponent of this view is Judge Robert Bork, who argued that constitutional protection should only be extended to speech that is explicitly political. Adherents to this theory base their position on the lack of historical evidence that the Framers of the First Amendment intended any great protection of speech in general and because many of the founders aggressively fought to suppress speech that they thought was inimical to government. However, the Court has never taken this position. Rather, it has included a wide array of speech within the protections of the Constitution. This may be partly due to the difficulty of determining what speech is and is not political. However, the Court has also indicated a desire to include other areas of speech within the Constitution's protections because of the importance of information in making all manner of informed decisions.

2. *Seeking Truth (Marketplace of Ideas)*

This concept is founded on the idea that freedom of expression is vital for a society to effectively evaluate the rational and truth of ideas. Justice Oliver Wendell Holmes called this concept the marketplace of ideas. He wrote that testing ideas in a marketplace where free competition reigned was the best "test of truth" (*Abrams v. United States,* 1919). This theory holds that truth results most accurately and efficiently from the presentation of competing ideas in a purely competitive environment.

Holmes's theory has many adherents, including the philosopher John Stuart Mill. In 1859, Mill expressed his view of this theory in his book *On Liberty.* To him, suppressing the expression of an opinion would rob the human race, both present and future, of something of great value. He viewed the suppression of a false idea to be just as bad as the wrongful suppression of a true one because although the suppression of a true idea is wrong, humanity is deprived of enlightenment by the public refutation of the false idea.

In the marketplace of ideas, the government should suppress no ideas. Rather, every idea should be expressed regardless of its accuracy. History appears to bear this out when one looks at the travails of Isaac Newton, Galileo

Galilei, Nicolaus Copernicus, and Albert Einstein in challenging scientific ideas widely believed by their contemporaries to be absolutely and unquestionably true. In fact, most if not all significant advancement, including scientific, philosophical, theological and political, emerged from the clashing of the new ideas with the old. These clashes result in a paradigm shift that is necessary to bring about advancement and it only occurs if new ideas are expressed.

Critics claim that the marketplace of ideas fails as a theory because all ideas do not enter the marketplace and among those that do, some will win not because they are the better idea but because they are shouted the loudest, the most often, or the most effectively. Further, they argue that the best idea will not necessarily win because people are often ruled by emotion or beliefs rather than reason. Whatever idea provides the greater appeal to the greater number of people will win, regardless of the veracity or inferiority of the idea. Advocates of a marketplace of ideas acknowledge its flaws but maintain that permitting the alternative, that is, permitting the government to decide what ideas are worth expressing and what ideas are not, is worse than enduring the flaws of letting ideas compete in an open marketplace.

3. *Self-Fulfillment and Personal Autonomy*

Under this theory, freedom of expression affirms the dignity and worth of each and every member of society by allowing each person, through a journey of expressive self-discovery, to realize his or her human potential. This theory holds that free speech is essential to providing personal self-fulfillment and advancing personal autonomy. The idea is that men and women are naturally expressive beings who need the freedom to speak in order to discover who they are, what they believe, and what they want to do. Although this expression includes communicating ideas to others through a variety of mediums, sometimes the purpose of this articulation is simply to express oneself, for purposes of self-realization or self-fulfillment. Under this theory, the expression of ideas, even to oneself, can be critical to understanding oneself or to working out solutions to problems. This self-actualization is exemplified by the antiwar protester who, knowing full well that expressing her opposition to a war will not likely bring about any change in the country's policy, still participates in the protest as a method of defining herself internally and to the world.

This theory views state suppression of expression not as suppression of a person's ability to convince one person that his or her idea is the correct one. Rather, it views censorship as the state's interference with a person's individual autonomy and ability to define him or herself. Thus, whereas adherents to this view recognize the benefits of the power of expression in communicating ideas to others, they hold the power and right to define oneself both personally and publicly to be of paramount importance and immune from stifling by the government.

Critics of this theory find nothing inherently special about speech for the purpose of personal autonomy or self-realization to grant it First Amendment protection. Some critics are concerned that, if expressive conduct is included in this category, almost all conduct could be protected by the First Amendment because it arguably expresses some form of autonomy or self-fulfillment.

4. *Balancing Stability and Change*

Free speech, this theory argues, is important to promote stability and change in society. It engenders stability by allowing dissenting voices, including protesters, to turn their anger and dissent into peaceful expression. By acting as a safety valve, it allows individuals to vent in a nonviolent way. Permitting expression enables the government to channel the energy (that would otherwise be pent up and repressed) into avenues that are consistent with lawful activity. It also enables the government to understand the issues facing the people and to be able to deal with them effectively.

Governments may choose to suppress speech as a means to achieve and maintain stability or a preferred social norm. However, such suppression essentially substitutes the use of force for the application of rational debate and only drives the expression underground. This inevitably does little more than mask the underlying social problems and conflicts in a society. Although government suppression of speech may slow the pace of social change, it cannot stop it and fails as a method of ensuring loyalty among the people. Instead, it exacerbates the problems that the suppression masks because they cannot be addressed openly. When the neglected social problems eventually break through the facade, they will do so in a more violent fashion.

5. *Promoting Tolerance in a Pluralistic Society*

This theory asserts that a democratic and pluralistic society must protect freedom of speech to promote tolerance of others' viewpoints, an essential component for peaceful co-existence in an increasingly diverse society. Following closely on the heels of the enhancement of self-government argument, this approach says that instead of debating policies, a pluralistic society must respect the ideas and policies of others. To be effective, this tolerance must be extended not just to popular ideas but to distasteful and offensive ideas. Tolerance of others' ideas engenders a respect for others and a toleration of people who are different from the norm.

This theory is relatively new. Despite its recent pedigree, it has detractors. They assert that there must be a limit on the tolerance afforded to speech, particularly when the speech at issue is itself intolerant of others. When speech exhibits a lack of tolerance of others, it is likely to injure others, either emotionally or by inciting physical violence against them. Critics of absolute tolerance of speech maintain that preventing harm to others from intolerant speech outweighs the benefits of tolerating the harmful speech. The recent rise in advocacy for the punishment of "hate speech" is one particular example where some would place a limit on the tolerance of speech for the sake of enhancing tolerance of others in general.

F. Defining Speech

Before one can analyze whether a particular expression should be protected, it is necessary to define speech. Clearly, oral communication of information, ideas, or emotions from one person to another, or to a group of people is speech. Similarly, the written communication of information, ideas, or emotions also clearly constitutes speech (i.e., books, newspapers, and leaflets). However, speech is not limited to oral or written communication; conduct can be speech, as can symbolic expressions. Denying protection to these nonverbal expressions would result in the loss of some of the most effective forms of speech.

The Supreme Court has extended First Amendment protections to communicative conduct, also called symbolic speech, for more than seventy years. In the seminal case of *Stromberg v. California* (1931), the Court declared a state law unconstitutional that prohibited the display of a red flag as a "sign, symbol or emblem" representing opposition to the government. The Court also struck down a law requiring public school students to salute the flag because saluting or refusing to salute the flag is communicative conduct (*West Virginia State Board of Education v. Barnette,* 1943). The Court explained that the use of symbols is a valid method of communication that is essentially a "short cut from mind to mind." However, although some conduct communicates and thus is protected, not all conduct can be considered communicative, otherwise, no law could prohibit any conduct without violating the First Amendment's protection of expression.

Hence, the question becomes "what is communicative conduct, or when does conduct become communicative?" The Supreme Court has explained that one can find "some kernel of expression in almost every activity a person undertakes . . . but such a kernel is not sufficient" to render the activity within the protective arms of the First Amendment (*City of Dallas v. Stanglin,* 1989). The Court has identified two factors that although mildly helpful are problematic to apply. Conduct becomes communicative when:

1. The actor intended to communicate a particularized message, and
2. The circumstances were such that there was a great likelihood that the message would be understood by those who viewed the conduct (*Spence v. Washington,* 1974).

Spence involved a person who was convicted for affixing a peace sign to an American flag following the death of students at Kent State University. The students were killed while protesting the American invasion of Cambodia. After several failed attempts to disperse the protestors, the Ohio National Guard opened fire, killing four and wounding nine others. Spence argued that his conduct, taping the peace sign on the flag, was intended to communicate his opposition to the killings at Kent State and in Cambodia. The Court agreed and reversed his conviction. In a *per curiam* opinion joined by five Justices, the Court stated that Spence's action was "not an act of mindless nihilism. Rather, it was a pointed expression of anguish by appellant about the ... domestic and foreign affairs of his government." Thus, the Court found that by taping the peace sign to the flag, Spence intended to communicate a message of displeasure about the United States's activities in Cambodia and on Kent State's campus, and that the circumstances surrounding the act created a great likelihood that the message would be understood.

In *Morse v. Frederick* (2007), students unveiled a banner that conveyed the words "BONG HITS 4 JESUS" at a school-supervised event. The principal of the high school demanded that the students remove the banner, and when one student refused he was suspended for ten days. The Court recognized that the message was cryptic but stayed the suspension, holding that it was reasonable for the principal to view the banner as against the school's policy of advocating illegal drug use. In this opinion, the Court cited *Bethel School Dist. No. 403 v. Fraser* (1986), a case where a public high school student delivered a highly metaphorical speech at a student government election assembly, containing elaborate sexual allusions. The Court affirmed the school's right to protect minors by prohibiting speech that is vulgar and offensive—communication that would normally be protected by the First Amendment in a non-educational setting.

The Court has found conduct to be communicative in many other cases and situations. For example, in *City of Erie v. Pap's A.M.* (2000), the Court distinguished between being nude and nude dancing, deeming the latter expressive conduct. Some other examples include students wearing black armbands to protest the war in Vietnam, an individual's burning his selective service registration certificate on the steps of a courthouse, defacing a license plate, civil disobedience, and in some cases desecration or burning of the American flag.

In each of these cases, the Court focused on whether conduct was communicative, generally based on the presence of a particular message to be conveyed by the conduct. When there was a particular message, the conduct was deemed to be communicative and when there was no such message, the conduct was deemed non-communicative. However, the inquiry does not end there.

Once a court determines the conduct at issue was communicative, then the conduct falls within the reach of the First Amendment's protections. However, that does not mean that the symbolic speech and regulation of such conduct must comport with the regulation of so-called pure speech, non-symbolic or verbal speech. When the Court addressed the constitutionality of The Solomon Amendment, which required that law schools provide equal access to military recruiters in order to receive federal funding, it found that the language of the amendment was borderline expressive (*Rumsfeld v. Forum for Academic and Institutional Rights, Inc.*, 2006). Contrasting variances of expressive conduct, the Court compared the amendment with the flag burning involved in *Texas v. Johnson* (1989), holding it did not warrant protection under the *O'Brien* test. However, if the text of the amendment was found to be expressive conduct, it would pass the *O'Brien* test as the amendment promotes a substantial government interest.

The *O'Brien* test provides a useful four-part test for determining when the government's interest in regulating communicative conduct is sufficient to overcome First Amendment protections. In *O'Brien*, the Court stated that a government regulation of expressive conduct is permissible if:

1. It is within the constitutional power of the government;
2. The regulation furthers an important or substantial government interest;
3. The government interest is unrelated to the suppression of free expression; and
4. The restriction on First Amendment freedom "is no greater than is essential" to further the government interest (*United States v. O'Brien*, 1968).

O'Brien involved an individual who burned his selective service registration certificate on the steps of the South Boston Courthouse and was subsequently convicted for violating the Universal Military Training and Service Act of 1948. The version of the Act in force at the time, as amended through 1965, criminalized the "forg[ing], alter[ing], knowingly destroy[ing], knowingly mutilat[ing,]" or changing the selective service registration certificate in any manner.

The Court found that the Act as amended in 1965 met the four-part test it promulgated and upheld the conviction. The Act met the first part of the test because it is within Congress's power to raise and support armies and, by the Necessary and Proper Clause, to enact any legislation necessary to achieve that end. The Court determined that the second prong was satisfied because the Act furthered several government interests that were at least important, including quick determination of persons who failed to register, facilitating mobilization in emergency situations, and deterring deceptive use of the certificates. Because the Act was related to regulating all conduct concerning desecration of the certificates, not just public or contemptuous conduct, it was of general applicability and not aimed at suppression of expression, thus meeting the third prong. Fourth, the Court determined that the law imposed no greater a restriction on First Amendment freedoms than necessary to achieve the Act's purposes and thus met the last prong.

The *O'Brien* test has been applied in cases concerning laws prohibiting the desecration or burning of the American flag. In the first of these cases, the Court protected desecration and burning of the flag. However, these early cases were decided on narrow grounds and did not reach the ultimate issue of the communicative aspects of the conduct. For example, the Court reversed the conviction of a man who burned a personally owned flag in public and said, "We don't need no damn flag." The statute he was convicted under proscribed public "mutilat[ion], defac[ing], defil[ing], or defy[ing], trampl[ing] upon," or casting contempt upon the American flag by words or actions (*Street v. New York,* 1969). The Court reasoned that the statute was too vague and the man could have been convicted merely for uttering the words and not for destroying the flag.

The Court finally decided the question of symbolic speech in flag burning cases in *Texas v. Johnson* (1989). There, it invalidated a Texas statute prohibiting a person to "deface, damage, or otherwise physically mistreat" a flag in such a manner that the person knows would offend at least one person observing his actions. The five-to-four decision, written by Justice William Brennan, distinguished *O'Brien* because in *Johnson* the law specifically criminalized communicative conduct, unlike the statute in *O'Brien*. Chief Justice William Rehnquist dissented, stating that he would accord the American flag special treatment because it is such an important national symbol and that there were other methods by which a would-be flag burner could convey his or her message.

In an attempt to circumvent the Court's decision in *Johnson*, Congress adopted the Flag Protection Act of 1989. The Act criminalized the knowing mutilation, defacement, defilement, burning, or trampling of the flag, without the qualifying language in the Texas statute. However, the Court ruled that statute unconstitutional in *United States v. Eichman* (1990), with the same split in the Court that existed in *Johnson*. Justice Brennan again wrote for the majority, finding that the federal law suffered from the "same fundamental flaw" as did the Texas statute in *Johnson*. Hence, the Court clearly protects the desecration and burning of the American flag, at least as far as it is communicative. However, based on Rehnquist's dissent in *Johnson*, it is hard to find legitimate instances of flag burning that are not communicative, and thus the government is attempting to protect an important national symbol of patriotism while prohibiting specific expressions of dissent. This is clearly a distinction based on the content of the message. As will be explored later, such laws must meet strict scrutiny.

In *Holder v. Humanitarian Law Project* (2010) the Court analyzed a federal statute making it a crime to "knowingly provid[e] material support or resources to a foreign terrorist organization." Plaintiffs challenged the statute on the grounds that it was unconstitutionally vague and violated their freedom of speech rights. The Court held the statute "provides a person of ordinary intelligence fair notice of what is prohibited." Because Congress had added narrowing definitions and a knowledge requirement to the statute, Congress reduced the potential for vagueness. Applying the O'Brien test, the material-support statute did not offend free speech rights because "providing material support in any form would undermine cooperative international efforts to prevent terrorism and strain relationships with its allies." The statute was properly justified because prohibiting support in the form of service, training, advice, or personnel to foreign terrorist groups serves the Government interest of preventing terrorism. Justice Breyer dissented, saying that the Government did not meet its burden of proving that the statute, which prohibits speech and association-related activities, serves the Government's compelling interest. He also suggested that strict scrutiny analysis should have applied to this type of speech regulation. Breyer advocated that the type of political speech, such as writing and distributing publications or speaking before Congress, is the type of speech Plaintiff's engage in and is exactly the type of activity the First Amendment is supposed to protect.

In sum, expression includes what most would consider to be expression—spoken or written words communicating any idea. It also includes nonverbal artistic expressions as well as communicative conduct. In *Clark v. Community for Creative Non-Violence* (1984), a group of protesters attempted to gain a permit to sleep in a park that had not yet been approved for camping. The camping was meant to emphasize the plight of the homeless; however, this action-based form of expression was outweighed by the government's substantial interest in conserving and preventing the "wear and tear" of the park. Conduct is communicative if it is intended to communicate a particular message.

The *Spence* test also requires the Court to consider whether the attendant circumstances would indicate a great likelihood that the message would be received and understood by those who viewed the conduct. If the conduct is non-communicative, the government generally may regulate it. However, if the conduct is communicative, the analysis diverges depending on whether the statute is aimed at suppression of free speech. If so, then the law is generally unconstitutional unless it passes strict scrutiny. However, if it is not aimed at suppression of free speech, the law generally must pass scrutiny under the four-part *O'Brien* test, or else it is unconstitutional.

G. Vagueness and Overbreadth

Two powerful tools to enforce constitutionally protected freedoms, especially First Amendment free speech protections, are the doctrines of vagueness and overbreadth. As will be explained, these doctrines often overlap, but it is important to understand that they are distinct and address different statutory infirmities. There are two important commonalities of these doctrines. First, both permit a person to bring a facial challenge to the law (rather than a challenge to the application of the law to a specific situation). Second, they both operate as an exception to the standing doctrine, thus allowing a person to challenge a law without having to suffer a personal injury. In *Village of Hoffman Estates v. Flipside, Hoffman Estates, Inc.* (1982), the Court examined an ordinance that did not ban the sale of drug paraphernalia, but instead required those businesses selling "any item, effect, paraphernalia, accessory or thing which is designed or marketed for use with illegal cannabis or drugs" to get a license. Petitioner, a vender that sold literature such as "Marijuana Grower's Guide" and "A Child's Garden of Grass," challenged the statute as vague and overbroad. Justice Marshall writing for the majority, held that in a facial overbreadth challenge, a court must "determine whether the enactment reaches a substantial amount of constitutionally protected conduct." Laws that did not would not be invalidated as overbroad. In regards to vagueness, Marshall wrote that a court "should uphold the challenge only if the enactment is impermissibly vague in all of its applications. A plaintiff who engages in some conduct that is clearly proscribed cannot complain of the vagueness of the law as applied to the conduct of others." Although both doctrines could apply in some cases, it is important to understand their differences and how they apply individually to provide a complete analysis of the issues.

1. *Vagueness*

A law restricting speech is void for vagueness if a reasonable person would not know what speech is proscribed. Vagueness can void any law, not just those limiting speech. However, these issues arise frequently in the speech context so judges, out of concern for vagueness, scrutinize laws criminalizing expression. Any law that does not adequately inform a reasonable person as to what speech or conduct is prohibited and what is permitted violates due process.

The vagueness doctrine is supported by several rationales. First, it is necessary for a criminal law to place a person on notice as to what he can and cannot do. Second, a criminal law must provide adequate guidance to the government and limit the discretion of law enforcement officers to avoid arbitrary enforcement. Additionally, because the freedom of speech is a fundamental freedom that requires breathing room, governmental regulation on expression must be drawn narrowly and specifically. The regulation of free speech also raises the danger that the speech could be "chilled" by the criminal proscriptions, and that otherwise protected, and socially valuable, speech would be suppressed because the statute was not drafted with sufficient specificity. This last danger provides extra motivation to the courts in requiring that laws regulating speech receive exacting scrutiny.

A classic example of an unconstitutionally vague law (not in the context of speech) is *City of Chicago v. Morales* (1999). Chicago had adopted a statute making it a crime to loiter, defined in the law as "remain[ing] in any one place with no apparent purpose." Because the statute was aimed at preventing gang activity, the Chicago police were empowered to order a group of loiterers to disperse. Failure to do so was a misdemeanor. The Court overturned the law, with Justice John Paul Stevens writing an opinion that was a majority opinion in part. Justice Stevens found that the law was vague and unconstitutional because a person could not be certain as to what behavior would subject him or her to arrest.

Vagueness in the context of speech is illustrated in *Baggett v. Bullitt* (1964). In *Baggett*, the Court addressed the loyalty oath imposed on state employees that prevented any "subversive person" from being a state employee. The state also required its employees to swear that they are not "subversive person[s]" and that they are not part of any subversive organization. The Court found the oath and the requirement unconstitutional because of the inherent ambiguity in the word *subversive* and the ambiguous language in the statute. Those ambiguities did not give adequate guidance as to what speech or association met the proscribed category.

The Court has never formulated a bright-line test to delineate when a statute is unconstitutionally vague. It is simply impossible for the Court to do so, especially given the inherent ambiguities in language. However, case law indicates that the Supreme Court treats criminalization of expression with increased scrutiny. If a law fails to provide a reasonable person with guidance as to what speech is proscribed or if a law fails to adequately and effectively limit the power of the police in enforcing the law, then that law will probably be voided for vagueness. Thus, this doctrine is a powerful tool to challenge a law placing any restraints on freedom of speech.

2. *Overbreadth*

Closely related to vagueness, the doctrine of overbreadth is also a powerful tool when challenging any law, especially one abridging the freedom of speech. A law is overbroad if it regulates more conduct than is necessary to achieve its ends. Consider a constitutionally overbroad ordinance that provided, "It shall be unlawful and a breach of the peace for any person wantonly to curse or revile or to use obscene or opprobrious language toward or with reference to any member of the city police while in the actual performance of his duty" (*Lewis v. City of New Orleans,* 1974). The Court identified the words "obscenity" and "opprobrious" as speech falling within the confines of the Constitution and refused to group all of the statutory language into an unprotected *fighting words* category.

Under the First Amendment, a law regulating speech is unconstitutionally overbroad if it:

1. Regulates substantially more of the challenger's speech than the Constitution permits; or
2. Regulates substantially more of a third party's speech than the Constitution permits, regardless of its constitutionality as applied to the person raising the challenge.

Like the vagueness doctrine, the overbreadth doctrine permits one to raise the rights of another, a clear exception to the doctrine of standing. Standing, or *locus standi,* is the capacity of a party to bring suit in court. Federal courts only have constitutional authority to resolve actual disputes that meet the Case or Controversy requirement of the Constitution. Only parties with enough of a direct stake in an action or law have "standing" to challenge it in court.

The ability to challenge the constitutionality of a law because of its effect on a party not before the court exists because of the dangers of overbroad regulations of speech. Specifically, an overbroad law tends to chill the speech of others by preventing them from speaking in the first place. Because an overly broad law restricting speech could be seen as a prior restraint on speech, the Constitution will not tolerate such a chilling effect. The power of the overbreadth doctrine is illustrated in *Kunz v. New York* (1951). *Kunz* involved a city ordinance that proscribed religious gatherings and meetings on the streets without a permit from the city police commissioner. The defendant, a Baptist minister, had obtained a one-year permit in 1946, which was later revoked because he had "ridiculed and denounced other religious beliefs" during a meeting. He reapplied for permits in 1947 and 1948, but both applications were rejected. Following the 1948 rejection, the minister held a meeting on the street without a permit and was arrested. The Court overturned the conviction, holding that the permitting ordinance was too broad and operated as a prior restraint on speech. Writing for the majority, Chief Justice Fred Vinson explained that the ordinance vested too much power in the police commissioner because it did not provide sufficient guidance concerning the issuance and revocation of the permits. The Court invalidated the ordinance based on its effects on third parties not before the Court. Justice Robert Jackson's dissent explained that the ordinance should only be considered as applied in the case at bar.

Using the overbreadth doctrine to strike down a statute is "strong medicine," which is why the challenged law must regulate substantially more speech than the Constitution permits. For example, in *Broadrick v. Oklahoma* (1973), the Court refused to find a law facially invalid that prohibited political activities by government employees. The Court acknowledged that the law was overbroad but found it was not substantially overbroad. It further explained that any problems with the reach of the law could be addressed in "as applied" challenges on a case-by-case basis. This requirement of substantial overbreadth applies in all challenges based on the freedom of speech, even if the speech is communicative conduct and not pure speech.

Substantial overbreadth cannot be reduced to an exact definition. Notwithstanding, the Court does not find substantial overbreadth merely because one can conceive of an unconstitutional application. In *Members of the City Council of Los Angeles v. Taxpayers for Vincent* (1984), the Court explained that "there must be a realistic danger" that the law "will significantly compromise recognized First Amendment protections" of third parties. Thus, one must show a significant set of situations in which the law could prohibit constitutionally protected speech.

In *Houston v. Hill* (1987), the Court held unconstitutionally overbroad a law that prohibited citizens from interrupting police officers who were performing their duties. The defendant was convicted for shouting at police officers in an attempt to prevent them from arresting his friend. The Court explained that the law was unconstitutional because despite it being violated numerous times per day, it was enforced selectively. Because the law reached a substantial amount of constitutionally protected speech and conferred so much discretion on the police as to when to enforce it, the law was overbroad. Similarly, in *Board of Airport Commissioners v. Jews for Jesus, Inc.* (1987), the Court invalidated a resolution that banned all "First Amendment activities" from the Central Terminal Area in the Los Angeles International Airport. The lower courts had invalidated the resolution because the Central Terminal Area was a traditional public forum, but the Court invalidated the resolution because it was unconstitutionally overbroad. Writing for the Court, Justice Sandra Day O'Connor explained that the statute "reache[d] the universe of expressive activity" prohibiting all forms of protected expression. The statute did not limit its prohibitive activity to those who could interfere with airport operations or who could cause a disruption or a disturbance. It prohibited every form of expression, including simple conversations between travelers or reading. The Court found that "no conceivable governmental interest would justify such an absolute prohibition of speech."

This principle was reaffirmed in *United States v. Stevens* (2010). Congress enacted a statute to criminalize the commercial creation, sale, or possession of certain depictions of animal cruelty. The statute applied to any visual or auditory depiction "in which a living animal is intentionally maimed, mutilated, tortured, wounded, or killed." The legislation was enacted mainly to prohibit "crush videos," which feature helpless animals being tortured and killed. The statute was struck down as overbroad because a substantial number of its applications are unconstitutional. This included constitutionally protected speech, such as hunting videos or images which show an endangered species wounded or killed. The Government tried to argue the statute was limited to crush videos and depictions of animal fighting, but the Court struck down this argument saying the "language of the statute decides the constitutional question." Justice Alito dissented, saying that hunting videos or other videos involving farming used to demonstrate how the statute would be overbroad would actually fall outside the wake of the animal cruelty statute. He further concluded that the statute has a "substantial core of constitutionally permissible applications," and that Congress had only intended to limit depictions of violent criminal conduct. He also noted that this statute is closely linked with regulating criminal conduct not speech, because these violent acts of animal cruelty are committed for the sole purpose of producing videos.

In *Brown v. Entertainment Merchants Association* (2011), a California statute restricted the sale or rental of violent video games to minors. The statute covered games in which players had the option of "killing, maiming, dismembering, or sexually assaulting an image of a human being" in a manner that objectively "appeal[ed] to a deviant or morbid interest of minors." Citing *United States v. Stevens* (2010), the Court emphasized that new categories of unprotected speech may not be added to the list. Video games, like books, plays and movies, communicate ideas and social messages and thus qualify for First Amendment protection. The Court struck down California's attempt to "create a wholly new category of content-based regulation that is permissible only for speech directed at children" as both underinclusive and overinclusive. The statute was underinclusive in that it did not restrict other violent media but singled out purveyors of video games. It was overinclusive because some children may be prohibited from purchasing violent video games by the statute but not by their parents.

In contrast, if a law only proscribes a relatively small amount of constitutionally protected speech, the Court will not find it unconstitutionally overbroad. This was the case in *New York v. Ferber (1982)*, where the Court upheld a statute prohibiting child pornography. Recognizing that the law could apply to material that had serious value in the literary, scientific, or educational fields, the Court explained that such situations would amount only to a "tiny fraction of the materials within the statute's reach."

The Court in *Virginia v. Hicks* (2003) found that a policy enacted by the Richmond Redevelopment and Housing Authority (RRHA) was not overbroad even though it made it unlawful for all persons lacking a "legitimate business or social purpose" for being in a certain housing development. Hicks had been issued a written notice barring him from the area for trespassing, and was subsequently arrested after trespassing on the property again. Hicks challenged the policy under the overbreadth doctrine. The Court held the RRHA's policy was not facially invalid because the policy applied to all persons who entered the property and Hicks failed to show the policy restricted a substantial amount of speech.

Even if a law is held unconstitutionally overbroad, it can still be saved in two ways. First, if the statute could be given a construction that would limit its application, the Court may find the statute constitutional as limited by the construction. Second, the law could be saved if it contained a severability clause and the unconstitutional portion(s) could be severed from the law without undermining the reason the law was enacted in the first place. The limiting construction method of saving a law was considered in *Jews for Jesus* where the Court found that the resolution's language was not susceptible to any construction that would remove its unconstitutional aspects. The severability method was applied in *Brockett v. Spokane Arcades, Inc.* (1985). There, the state law contained a severability clause that permitted the Court to declare only a portion of it unconstitutional and sever that portion from the law.

3. Comparing and Contrasting the Vagueness and Overbreadth Doctrines

The vagueness and overbreadth doctrines both permit a person to challenge a law based on the rights of a third party not before the court when the boundaries are not clearly defined. Vagueness is aimed at providing clarity as to what conduct is proscribed and providing guidance to law enforcement, whereas overbreadth targets laws that permissibly regulate some speech but whose reach extends too far by proscribing otherwise protected speech. Understanding these similarities and differences is important to analyzing the constitutionality of laws regulating speech.

H. Content-Neutral Laws versus Content-Based Laws

The Court repeatedly has held that the First Amendment fundamentally prevents the government from regulating speech based on its content (*Forsyth County, Ga. v. Nationalist Movement*, 1992). This is a basic concept in free speech law. For example, the Court stated that, "above all else," the First Amendment prevents the government from restricting expression "because of its message, its ideas, its subject matter, or its content" (*Police Department of the City of Chicago v. Mosley,* 1972). This concept is so fundamental that the Court has based many of its decisions on the distinction between content-based and content-neutral laws. The Court has explained that such laws are "presumptively invalid" (*R.A.V. v. City of St. Paul, Minnesota,* 1992).

The Court requires that laws prohibiting speech based on its content to pass strict scrutiny, whereas a content-neutral regulation must only pass intermediate scrutiny. Note that the Court has created several categories of speech that are unprotected and less protected, many of which are necessarily content-based. Aside from these categories, content-based regulations must survive strict scrutiny and the Court requires that content-based restrictions within the unprotected and less-protected categories survive strict scrutiny.

The restrictions on content-based regulations are intended to prevent the government from targeting specific messages and viewpoints that it deems undesirable. The Court as late as 2010 acknowledged the importance of restraining the state from committing a "constitutional wrong" of disfavoring particular subjects or viewpoints, and distinguishing among speakers (*Citizens United v. Federal Election Commission*, 2010). Without such restrictions, the government could use speech regulations effectively to control thoughts by driving undesired viewpoints from the public consciousness. This is most effectively accomplished by restricting a particular viewpoint directly or by restricting the subject matter of speech.

How, then, does the Court determine whether a given regulation is content-based or content-neutral? As explained, the requirement that the government's regulation of speech remain content-neutral requires that any restrictions on expression not regulate based on

1. The viewpoint expressed, such as the ideas or the message; or
2. The subject matter or topic of the speech.

Any such content-based regulations generally must pass strict scrutiny. As an example of a content-based restriction, the Court in *Boos v. Barry* (1988) struck down an ordinance of the District of Columbia that prohibited displaying signs within 500 feet of an embassy if those signs were critical of that embassy's government. The Court found that the proscription only of signs critical of the foreign government was an impermissible viewpoint-based regulation and ran afoul of the First Amendment.

Regulation of the subject matter is similarly restricted. For example, in *Carey v. Brown* (1980), the Supreme Court invalidated a Chicago ordinance that prohibited all non-labor-related picketing in residential areas. The Court explained that, while no specific viewpoint was attacked, the ordinance restricted the subject matter of the speech. When a cable television programmer sought a declaratory judgment on the Telecommunications Act's requirement that operators scramble channels containing sexually explicit material during certain times, the Court held the regulations to be content-based and used strict scrutiny (*U.S. v. Playboy Entertainment Group, Inc.*, 2000). The government could not show that it utilized the least restrictive means necessary to achieve the purpose of protecting children from indecent conduct. By contrast, a law is content-neutral if it regulates all speech, regardless of the viewpoint or the subject matter. Thus, if a law prohibits some speech because of its viewpoint or its topic, then the law is content-based and must satisfy strict scrutiny, otherwise it is content-neutral and must only survive intermediate scrutiny.

In *United States v. Alvarez (2012)*, the Court extended First Amendment protection to false statements despite acknowledging the statements have no value in society. The Stolen Valor Act made it a crime to falsely claim receipt of military decorations or medals and provided an enhanced penalty if the Congressional Medal of Honor was involved. Alvarez was known to be a habitual liar who had broken the law when, at a local board meeting, claimed to have earned the Congressional Medal of Honor. Alvarez argued the law was an unconstitutional content-based restriction on free speech. The government argued that his false statements had no value and thus should not receive First Amendment protection. The Court held that the Stolen Valor Act was a content-based restriction of free speech that did not pass review under strict scrutiny. It reasoned that false statements about military awards did not fall into any of the categories that do not maintain First Amendment protection such as obscenity, defamation, fighting words, or fraud. The Court concluded that the government could achieve its objectives through less restrictive means and specifically, failed to demonstrate why counter-speech would not suffice.

Justices Alito, Scalia, and Thomas dissented. They argued that the majority opinion strayed far from a long line of cases recognizing that false statements that inflict harm and serve no legitimate purpose do not receive First Amendment protection. They reasoned that the Stolen Valor Act did not chill First Amendment speech because the lies have no value in society, and as Congress recognized, "the lies proscribed by the Stolen Valor Act inflict substantial harm. In many instances, the harm is tangible in nature."

Not all facially content-based laws receive strict scrutiny. A law that is facially content-based may still be deemed content-neutral if it is aimed at achieving a permissible content-neutral goal (*City of Renton v. Playtime Theaters, Inc.*, 1986). In *Renton*, the permissible content-neutral goal was the secondary effects of the speech, not the speech itself. The case involved an ordinance that prohibited locating adult movie theaters from displaying sexually explicit content within 1,000 feet of an area zoned for residences, churches, schools, or parks. The Court held that the ordinance was justified because it was not aimed at the speech but the undesirable social elements (secondary effects) associated with such theaters.

However, *Renton* and its holding have been roundly criticized both by commentators and some Supreme Court Justices. The Court sometimes has applied *Renton* and at other times has distinguished it. For example, in *City of Erie v. Pap's A.M.* (2000), the Court applied *Renton* to uphold a city ordinance prohibiting public nudity. Writing for the majority, Justice O'Connor found that, although the ordinance was aimed at shutting down a nude dancing club, the law was still content-neutral because it was aimed at the secondary effects of that type of establishment rather than at suppressing "the erotic message conveyed by nude dancing." However, the Court distinguished *Renton* in *City of Cincinnati v. Discovery Network, Inc.* (1993). Cincinnati had passed an ordinance prohibiting the distribution of commercial publications by way of news racks placed on public property. The city had been concerned about the impact of the news racks on the safety and aesthetics of the property on which they were located. Writing for the majority, Justice Stevens found that the regulation was content-based because whether a given news rack was banned from public property depended entirely on the content of the publication inside it (commercial publications were banned, whereas noncommercial ones were not). Justice Stevens distinguished *Renton* by stating that there is no set of secondary effects caused by the presence of the commercial news racks that are not also implicated by the racks the city permitted to remain on public property.

In sum, a law that facially regulates speech based on its viewpoint or its subject matter is presumed to be content-based, but the government can rebut the presumption by proving that the law has a purpose independent of the content of the speech. To do so, the government must show that the law was targeted at the secondary effects associated with the speech. If the government is successful in rebutting the presumption, then the law is deemed content-neutral. In contrast, when a regulation is facially content-neutral, the inquiry ends and the law is deemed to be content-neutral. Finally, a content-based regulation must pass strict scrutiny, else it is struck down, whereas a content-neutral regulation must only pass intermediate scrutiny to survive.

I. Prior Restraints

1. Introduction

Governments have long recognized the power of information and have sought to control the dissemination of information, often by using prior restraints on speech. A prior restraint is a restriction and, sometimes, a prohibition on expression that takes effect before the expression is even communicated (rather than after the speech has occurred). In English common law, prior restraints on speech were common and came in many forms, the most prominent of which was the old licensure provision. Because prior restraints prevent speech from occurring, the Supreme Court views them as "the most serious and least tolerable" infringements on the protections of the First Amendment.

The Court's distaste for prior restraints is well documented. Generally, the Court views them with an extremely jaundiced eye. They are burdened with a heavy presumption of invalidity (*Bantam Books, Inc. v. Sullivan*, 1963). The government, in turn, "carries a heavy burden of justification for the imposition of such a restraint" (*Organization for a Better Austin v. Keefe*, 1971). As introduced elsewhere, the Court's attitude against prior restraints partly derives from the fact that the First Amendment was largely a reaction against the licensing requirements present in England circa 1800. Although the Court's attitude toward prior restraints is clear, there is no good, clear definition as to what constitutes a prior restraint.

2. *Defining "Prior Restraint"*

In *Alexander v. United States* (1993), Justice Kennedy stated that "the term prior restraint is not self-defining." Devising a workable definition is a difficult but necessary task because of the special disfavor in which the Court holds them. Though it is true that a prior restraint prevents speech from occurring, it paints the concept with too broad a brush to say that all laws preventing speech from occurring are prior restraints. Such a definition would cause all laws regulating speech to be considered as prior restraints because they are generally aimed at discouraging certain forms of speech by the threat of post speech punishment. The clearest definition from the Court is that a prior restraint is a judicial order or an administrative scheme that prevents speech from occurring.

Sometimes the Court finds that an action that appears to have the hallmarks of a prior restraint is not in fact one. There have been several examples of laws that have appeared to be prior restraints, and yet the Court refused to hold that they were. An example is *Pittsburgh Press Co. v. Pittsburgh Commission on Human Relations* (1973). An administrative agency had ordered newspapers to cease publishing gender-based advertisements for employment opportunities, but the Court found the order not to be a prior restraint. The Court explained that the particular evil of a prior restraint is that it would stop speech before the speaker could adequately determine whether the speech was protected by the First Amendment. It found that the order was not a prior restraint because it did not stop any "arguably protected speech." The Court found that the conduct at issue was "a continuing course of repetitive conduct" which the Court did not have to speculate "as to the effect of publication." Furthermore, the Court emphasized that the order was clear and did not reach more speech than necessary to achieve its ends. Yet the Court's reasons are not clear as to why the agency's order would not amount to a prior restraint when it is very likely that a similar court order would be a prior restraint. The only distinction it provided was in a footnote, where it indicated that the administrative agency would not be able to punish a violator with a contempt citation, which a court could have done.

A more recent example that muddied the waters further is *Madsen v. Women's Health Center, Inc.* (1994). In that case, a court issued an order that restricted speech within a buffer zone of thirty-six feet around an abortion clinic. The Court refused to find the lower court's order to be a prior restraint. It based this decision on the fact that the order did not prevent protesters from speaking outside the buffer zone and that the area had been created not because of their conduct but because of their prior illicit activities. The buffer zone was created to protect the ingress and egress of staff and patients to the facility with which the protesters had previously interfered.

These cases indicate that the Court's definition of a prior restraint is opaque. The definition put forth in *Alexander* is the clearest one the Court has provided. However, it is inconsistent with some of the Court's other decisions, especially those illustrated here.

3. *The Evils of Prior Restraints*

In his famous commentaries, Blackstone forcefully stated that freedom of speech comes not from freedom from censure of criminal prosecution of speech but in countenancing "no *previous* restraint upon publication." The primary purpose and the primary evil of a prior restraint is that it prevents speech before the speech can occur. However, laws that punish speech after it occurs can have just the same effect through means of deterrence. Why are prior restraints so much worse than post speech laws having the same effect, especially when there is generally some amount of due process before the prior restraint occurs and in a licensing scheme?

The problem is that by preventing speech before it occurs, the government scrutinizes a far greater range of speech than it would if it could only react to speech. The proactive nature of prior restraints avoids the procedural protections and publicity that a post speech criminal trial provides. Additionally, government censorship of speech is antagonistic to a free society. With this power, governments are prone to suppress speech critical of the government and thereby eliminate dissenting views from political discourse. The government's argument that prior restraint can prevent a possible violent response is both conjecture as well as a failure to distinguish between speech and violent action.

Another negative aspect of prior restraints is the collateral bar rule. The collateral bar rule prevents a person from challenging a court order's legality after the person has violated the order. A court order must be followed until it is set aside, so a person who violates a court-ordered prior restraint would not be able to challenge the constitutionality of the order in his subsequent trial for criminal contempt, even if the order was illegal. In contrast, a speaker who is criminally prosecuted for violating a law proscribing speech can challenge the constitutionality of the law at trial. For example, in *Walker v. City of Birmingham* (1967), a Birmingham court ordered several civil rights protesters, including Dr. Martin Luther King Jr., to not protest on the streets unless the city issued them a permit. The protesters violated the order and were held in contempt of court. The Supreme Court upheld the contempt convictions, finding that the protesters were barred from challenging the legality of the court order because they had violated it. The Court explained that "respect for judicial process is a small price to pay for the civilizing hand of law," and that a person cannot take the law into his or her own hands and ignore the legal procedures. The only exception to the collateral bar rule that the *Walker* court permitted was an order that was "transparently invalid" or lacked even a tenuous claim to being a valid order.

However, the Court has limited the reach of the collateral bar rule by restricting its application only to court orders that follow proper procedures. For example, if the court order fails to provide due process, the Court will not require it to be obeyed. This was the situation in *Carroll v. President and Commissioners of Princess Anne* (1968), where a court order preventing demonstrations for a ten-day period resulted from an *ex parte* proceeding where the protesters received no notice of the hearing and no attempt was made to contact them. The Court explained that the procedure by which the order was issued had been fatally defective and that the First Amendment had no room for a violation of such a basic freedom (One could credibly argue that the limitation in *Carroll* was merely an example of the exception in *Walker*, because such a procedural defect would cause the order to have no viable claim to validity). Hence, the collateral bar rule requires a person to obey a court order unless it is so obviously invalid that it has no realistic claim to validity, and it prevents a person from challenging a contempt conviction for violating any other order regardless of its constitutionality. Note that the Court has sometimes enforced the collateral bar rule in systems of licensing, but only when the law requiring licensing is valid and contains due process protections. However, enforcement of the collateral bar rule in such administrative situations does not carry the same policy reasons as it does in the judicial context.

The dangers of prior restraints are clear. One who violates an unconstitutional law is free to challenge that law. And under the doctrine of standing, that may be the only situation in which a person could challenge the law. In contrast, a person is bound to obey an unconstitutional court order until it is set aside. She cannot challenge her conviction for contempt if she violates the order, unless the order is so obviously defective that it has no realistic claim to validity. It seems unduly harsh to punish a person for making constitutionally protected speech, but such is the situation with prior restraints, especially in the form of judicial orders.

4. *Forms of Prior Restraints*

Prior restraints come in different forms. Clearly, an outright ban on a particular mode of speech would be a prior restraint, such as the seizure of every copy of a periodical. However, prior restraints are most commonly found as either an administrative licensing scheme or a court-ordered injunction against speech. Laws restricting speech must be scrutinized with an eye that they arguably may be prior restraints on speech.

a. Administrative Licensing Schemes

Licensing schemes grew to prominence following the invention of the printing press. Before that time, information could be spread to a wide audience only with the expenditure of time and great effort. Because of the ease with which people could disseminate speech following the development of the printing press, the English government required publishers to submit manuscripts to the government for approval before they could be published. The license to publish the manuscript could be denied completely or granted as long as objectionable information was deleted. This is the licensing scheme against which William Blackstone railed, and it is still occasionally encountered today.

Generally, license-based prior restraints are invalid unless:

1. The government has an important reason for the licensing, and
2. There are clear criteria for the denial of a license such that the licensing authority essentially has no discretion in the matter.

The Court also requires the licensing scheme to provide procedural safeguards, such as (a) prompt action on the license application and (b) judicial review of the denial of a license application. A licensing scheme that failed to meet these requirements was held unconstitutional in *Lovell v. City of Griffin, Georgia* (1938). In this case, an ordinance prevented the distribution of all literature without first obtaining a permit from the city manager. The Court determined that the ordinance was an unconstitutional prior restraint and was facially invalid. Writing for the Court, Chief Justice Charles Hughes explained that the character of the licensing scheme strikes at the heart of the freedom of the press, and that the struggle to achieve that freedom was "primarily directed against the power of the licensor." In a second case, the Court held that a county ordinance allowing an administrator to determine assembly fees based on his suspected cost of maintaining public order from their aftermath was unconstitutional, as it was not narrowly drawn or reasonable, and lacked definite standards (*Forsyth County, Georgia v. The Nationalist Movement*, 1992).

To prevent viewpoint suppression, the Court has required that "a law subjecting the exercise of First Amendment freedoms to the prior restraint of a license" contain "narrow, objective, and definite standards to guide the licensing authority" (*Shuttlesworth v. Birmingham*, 1969). Without an important reason for the license requirement, a licensing scheme is invalid. Examples of such important reasons are content-neutral time, place, and manner restrictions designed to manage access to scarce public resources (such as a protest march in a public park or a parade). For example, in *Cox v. New Hampshire* (1941), the Court upheld a licensing scheme that required people wishing to hold a parade or protest to obtain a permit and only permitted such an application to be denied if another group was already using the venue at the same time. These restrictions are considered important because they ensure public safety, promote order, and prevent confusion by overlapping events. They also ensure that other travelers can conveniently use the streets. By contrast, the Court invalidated a North Carolina law requiring professional fundraisers to get a license before making a solicitation but placed no such restriction on volunteer fundraisers. The Court explained that just because a person receives payment for speaking does not vitiate the protections afforded that speech. North Carolina claimed that it had an important interest in regulating people who solicit money. The Court found the state's argument unpersuasive, especially when the law is not accompanied by other protections, such as prompt determination on the application. Justice O'Connor dissented, finding North Carolina's argument persuasive. She explained that the law in no way burdened charities' ability to speak—it just required them to hire licensed fundraisers, recognizing the important interest that solicitors of money be licensed by the state. For those reasons, unless there is an important reason for the licensing scheme, it will most likely be found to be invalid.

Additionally, a licensing scheme must clearly spell out the standards by which a license may be rejected and it must leave essentially no discretion in the licensing authority. This requirement of clear standards was violated in *City of Lakewood v. Plain Dealer Publishing Co.* (1988), where an ordinance regulated the placement of news racks on public property by requiring a license from the mayor. The ordinance listed several criteria that the mayor was to use in determining whether to grant a license. However, one criterion permitted the mayor to require the licensee to agree to any "other terms and conditions [he] deemed necessary and reasonable" before granting the license. The Court held the ordinance to be an unconstitutional prior restraint because it essentially gave the mayor unfettered discretion to deny a license application. Thus, a licensing scheme must provide clearly delineated standards to the licensor, leaving virtually no discretion.

Moreover, a valid licensing scheme must have at least some procedural safeguards to ensure that licenses are dealt with fairly and efficiently. Generally, valid safeguards include a prompt determination on the license application and a full and fair hearing subject to prompt judicial review before the denial of the license becomes final. The Court considered a law requiring a license before publicly exhibiting a motion picture, unanimously finding that the law was unconstitutional (*Freedman v. Maryland,* 1965). Writing for the Court, Justice Brennan explained that the Maryland law lacked sufficient procedural safeguards. Under the scheme, once a license was denied, the applicant would have to begin judicial proceedings and persuade the court that the speech was protected. Justice Brennan reversed this burden by stating that "the burden of proving that the film is unprotected expression must rest on the censor." Furthermore, after being denied, the law prohibited exhibiting the movie until a judicial determination of the denial was made, but it placed no time restrictions on the judicial action so it could conceivably drag on for some time. The Court refrained from specifying what time period was required, leaving that up to the lawmaker, but it did require the censor "within a specified brief period, either issue a license or go to court to restrain showing the film."

Thus, to be valid, a licensing scheme must meet specific criteria. There must be an important reason for the scheme, it must delineate specific criteria for the denial of a license and must provide sufficient procedural safeguards to ensure that denials are fair and applications are considered expediently. If the scheme is missing any of these criteria, it is most likely an unconstitutional prior restraint.

b. Court-Ordered Injunctions against Speech

In addition to administrative licensing schemes, the other common form of a prior restraint is a judicial order that prevents speech. Court orders restricting speech have been addressed in several areas, specifically national security, protecting fair trials and the integrity of the judicial system and preventing obscene speech. Notwithstanding, a major question is whether a judicially-imposed prior restraint is more tolerable than one issued by an administrative official.

The Court clearly answers this question in *Near v. Minnesota* (1931). There, Minnesota considered "malicious, scandalous and defamatory newspaper[s], magazine[s] or other periodical[s]" to be abatable public nuisances. The trial court issued an injunction against a newspaper, preventing it from publishing any "malicious, scandalous and defamatory" matter. The Court reversed the injunction, finding it to be an unconstitutional prior restraint. Writing for the majority, Chief Justice Hughes explained that the main purpose of the First Amendment was to prevent prior restraints on speech, and that the proper way to punish publication of restricted and unprotected speech was an after-the-fact punishment. The Court also stated that the prohibition of prior restraints was not absolute but that certain "exceptional cases" could permit their use. Among the exceptional cases, the Court included speech that is dangerous to national security, obscene publications, and incitements to violence or the forcible overthrow of the government. In his dissent, Justice Butler explained that the injunction in *Near* was not a prior restraint because it was a judicial remedy invoked after the speech had occurred. Justice Pierce Butler further explained that an injunction to prevent future speech does not "authorize administrative control [of speech] in advance," a key feature of prior restraints, but is merely an equitable remedy. Thus, *Near* established the proposition that injunctions preventing future speech are unconstitutional prior restraints on speech, even when they come after the speech initially occurred.

The first of the exceptional situations enunciated by the Court is speech that threatens national security, such as publishing troop movements and operational details, including where a military action will occur. However, the government bears a very substantial burden in showing the need for the injunction, even when national security would be jeopardized by the speech. The Court established this very heavy burden in *New York Times Co. v. United States* (1971), commonly called the Pentagon Papers case. In this consolidated action involving both the *New York Times* and the *Washington Post*, the United States sought to prevent two newspapers from publishing classified documents about the nation's involvement in the Vietnam War. The lower courts had refused to issue the injunctions against the publications, but on appeal one court reversed, issuing the injunction against the *New York Times*, and one affirmed. In a *per curiam* opinion, the Supreme Court affirmed regarding the *Washington Post* and reversed concerning the *New York Times*. The opinion did little more than explain that the government had failed to meet its burden to sustain the injunction. Each Justice in the six-to-three ruling wrote an opinion.

In their concurrences, Justices Black and Douglas took an absolutist view that prior restraints on the news were never appropriate. They explained that the language and history of the First Amendment were crystal clear and that the press "must be left free to publish news, whatever the source, without censorship, injunctions, or prior restraints." Additionally, they decried any use of injunctions to silence the press in a representative government because secrecy was inherently incompatible with open government and the government wielding any power over the press would damage the country irreparably. Justice Brennan took a slightly less absolutist position. He explained that the Court would only countenance injunctions against the press in time of war when the government must be able to act to prevent actual threats to national security, such as to prevent obstruction of its troop recruitments or the publication of the sailing dates of vessels or the strength and location of a deployment. Short of that limited scope, Justice Brennan found no support for judicial prior restraints on the media. Justices Potter Stewart and Byron White found a separation of powers issue, explaining that the courts are not competent to issue injunctions in this arena, and that that power belongs solely to the executive and legislative branches of government. Justice Thurgood Marshall noted that there was no statutory authority for an injunction, but even if there was one, if might violate the First Amendment.

The dissenters focused on the issue of time, finding that the Court had acted too quickly, and that it should not have decided the case on the record before it. Chief Justice Warren Burger explained that the Court had no appreciation for the facts of the case when it ruled, partly because of the speediness of the appeals and partly because of the delay of the *New York Times,* which had possessed the papers for some time before demanding such a quick resolution to the issue. Justice John Harlan described exactly how quickly the case had progressed. The courts of appeals had issued their opinions on June 23. By 11 A.M. on June 24, the *New York Times*'s petitions were filed with the Court and the *Washington Post* was only slightly slower, submitting its petitions in by about 7:15 P.M. on the same day. The Court held oral argument on June 26 at 11 A.M., having only received the briefs a little before 1 P.M. on June 25. The time between the decisions of the Courts of Appeals to oral argument lasted only three days. The Court issued its opinions on June 30, one week after the Courts of Appeal. Justice Harry Blackmun agreed with his fellow dissenters that the Court's handling of the case was altogether too fast and lacked the standards to evaluate the cases properly, including a properly developed record.

The rushed nature of the decision in *New York Times* prevented the Court from establishing standards by which the government might stop the press from publishing material that could damage national security. Justice Stewart found the executive and legislative branches competent to prevent such publication, not the judicial branch, but he did not provide any clear guidance on the matter. Justice White explained that some circumstances could countenance such an action by the government but also did not clearly explain the circumstances that were needed before the government could prevent such information from being published. Additionally, the Court did not provide any insight into whether the Congress could pass a law permitting such an injunction, though Justices White and Marshall indicated that such a law might permit the challenged act. Unfortunately, the Court has never been presented with these issues since *New York Times*, so it has yet to clarify the questions.

Only two other cases could have presented this issue. One was *United States v. Progressive, Inc.* (1979), but it was dismissed before reaching the Supreme Court because the challenged information was published in other outlets. The other was *Snepp v. United States* (1980). There, an ex-CIA agent published a book on the fall of Vietnam. While an agent, he had signed an agreement with the CIA that permitted it to demand that the book be submitted to them for review before publication. The former agent violated the agreement, and the Court found that the agreement was enforceable. It also explained that national security concerns would have permitted the CIA to demand such prepublication review even without an agreement or any proof that the book could damage national security.

The second major area in which the Court has addressed injunctions as prior restraints concerns orders to control pretrial publicity to preserve the integrity of the judicial process and ensure that the defendant receives a fair trial. Government regulation that has the effect of preventing communication before it occurs is permissible, as protective orders that the court issues during discovery do not amount to a prior restraint (*Seattle Times Co. v. Rhinehart*, 1984).

Nebraska Press Association v. Stuart (1976), involved a court order preventing the publication of "accounts of confessions or admission made by the accused or facts 'strongly implicative' of the accused" in a multiple murder prosecution. The district court's order was a response to the widespread coverage that the murder received in the press and represented that court's attempt to preserve the defendant's right to a fair trial. The Court created a three-part test before a court could issue a gag order preventing the press from publishing information about a criminal defendant prior to the trial. For a gag order to be valid, the court must find that:

1. The extensive pretrial publicity that would occur without the injunction would jeopardize the ability to find and select a fair and impartial jury;
2. Other, less extreme, measures would be unlikely to mitigate the effects of the pretrial publicity; and
3. The injunction would be effective in protecting against the danger of pretrial prejudice against the defendant.

On review, the Supreme Court held that the injunction was invalid because it failed to meet the three-prong test. Writing for the Court, Chief Justice Burger found that the trial court's order satisfied the first prong because it concluded that there would be "intense and pervasive pretrial publicity" that it could reasonably find might impair the defendant's right to a fair trial. The Chief Justice also found that the record did not support a finding that other, less extreme, measures would be unlikely to mitigate the effects of the publicity. He expressly stated several other alternatives that are available, such as (a) change of venue; (b) postponing the trial to let the publicity die down; (c) searching questioning of the jurors in *voir dire*; (d) "emphatic and clear instructions" to the selected jurors to consider only evidence admitted in open court; and (e) sequestration of the jury. Further, the Court determined that the injunction was not likely to be effective because of the nature of the small community of 850 people and the probability that the information would spread by word of mouth. The Court was careful to state that although it did not absolutely ban all such injunctions, it is difficult to imagine a situation in which all three prongs would be satisfied. The purpose of the Court's test in *Nebraska Press* is to keep gag orders limiting press coverage of criminal trials to a minimum, thereby maintaining the First Amendment protection of the freedom of the press. This protection is not extended to lawyers: the courts have the inherent right to regulate the legal profession because lawyers are officers of the court. It is important to note that the Court has never upheld a prior restraint to protect a defendant's right to a fair trial since *Nebraska Press*.

The Court has upheld the ability of courts to limit the access of the press and the general public to court proceedings. In *Richmond Newspapers, Inc. v. Virginia* (1980) and *Globe Newspaper Co. v. Superior Court* (1982), the Court explained that although the First Amendment protects the press's and public's right to be present at a criminal trial, the court may close the proceedings when there is a compelling state interest. However, the closure must be narrowly tailored to achieve that interest. *Globe Newspaper* involved a Massachusetts case where the court closed the trial of a defendant accused of committing sex crimes against minors. The court had acted pursuant to a state law that mandated closure in those instances. On review, the Supreme Court found the statute unconstitutional because it mandated closure even when the victim does not seek it and the victim would not be injured by the presence of the press and the public. Thus, while the Massachusetts law was supported by a compelling state interest, it was not narrowly tailored to achieve that interest.

The third major area in which the Court has addressed judicial prior restraints is obscene speech. The Court has held that an injunction preventing obscene speech is constitutionally permissible. It announced this decision in *Paris Adult Theatre I v. Slaton* (1973). However, it has limited the application of this rule only to enjoining the expression of specific material. Further, the Court does not permit the injunction to be used to shutter an establishment merely because it is used to exhibit obscene materials. This area will be more fully explored in the next section on unprotected and less protected speech, but because it involves injunctions to prevent speech before it occurs, it also qualifies as a prior restraint on speech.

Generally, the Court is suspicious of prior restraints and applies a very strict standard when determining their validity. Some Justices have even advocated an absolute prohibition on prior restraints based on the history behind the adoption of the First Amendment. Finally, it is important to remember that prior restraints, administrative or judicial, come to the court with a heavy presumption of invalidity.

J. Compelled Speech

The First Amendment protects not only the right to speak, but also the right to not speak. In *West Virginia Board of Education v. Barnette* (1943), Justice Jackson delivered the opinion of the Court, holding that it was unconstitutional to compel school children to salute the flag. He argued that "if there is any fixed star in our constitutional constellation, it is that no official, high or petty, can prescribe what shall be orthodox in politics, nationalism, religion, or other matters of opinion or force citizens to confess by word or act their faith therein."

Public-sector unions often advocate on behalf their members. However, these unions are allowed to bill both members and nonmembers for chargeable expenses. In *Knox v. Service Employees* (2012), the Supreme Court held that a California union violated First Amendment rights when it required nonmembers to pay a substantial amount of a special assessment. The temporary increase in dues was to be used as a political fund to further the union's political objectives in the 2006 special election. The Union failed to provide its members with a fresh *Hudson* notice, which would give them the opportunity to opt-out of the special assessment. By doing so, the Court stated the assessment fostered compelled speech that did not survive strict scrutiny.

The Court struck down a New Hampshire law which required all noncommercial license plates to bear the motto "Live Free or Die" in *Wooley v. Maynard* (1977). Maynard, a Jehovah's Witness, cut the words "or Die" off his license plate and was then convicted, fined and jailed. The Court held that the statute was unconstitutional, and the States could not compel its citizens to display the state motto. The State's interest of promoting its history and pride did not outweigh individual's right to free speech under the First Amendment. The Court, in *Hurley v. Irish-American Gay, Lesbian and Bisexual Group of Boston* (1995), found that compelling private citizens who organize an annual parade to include a group expressing a message that the organizers did not wish to convey violates the First Amendment.

In *Rumsfeld v. Forum for Academic and Institutional Rights, Inc.* (2006), a university challenged the Solomon Amendment, 10 U.S.C. 983(b)(1), which required universities and colleges to allow military recruiters the same access to campus as other employers in order to receive government funding. The Court found that the Solomon Amendment regulated conduct, not speech, and was therefore constitutional. Justice Roberts writing for the majority rationalized this decision in that no reasonable person would view the university allowing recruiters on campus as the university endorsing the military. In *Board of Regents of the University of Wisconsin System v. Southworth* (2000), students sued the University of Washington which charged all students an activity fee of $331.50 per year alleging that the university was using that money to fund students groups whose views they did not support. The Court found that viewpoint neutrality was the means of protecting students' First Amendment rights, and since the university allocated funds to student groups on a viewpoint neutral basis there was no First Amendment violation.

Checkpoints

- **Interpreting the First Amendment**
  - Despite the language of the First Amendment, "Congress shall make no law ... abridging the freedom of speech," the court had never adopted a literal interpretation.
  - The First Amendment was likely a reaction to the English suppression of the press and speech through licensing (prior restraints) and the crime of seditious libel.
  - Until the early twentieth century, the First Amendment was only applied to the Federal Government. This changed with *Gitlow v. New York* (1925), when the Court held that the freedom of speech and press are within First Amendment protection and "among the fundamental personal rights and 'liberties' protected by the Due Process Clause of the Fourteenth Amendment from impairment by the states."

- Free speech is vital to democracy because it allows the voters to hear and discuss a variety of viewpoints and hold public officials accountable.
- Free speech is necessary to evaluate the truth of ideas. We arrive at the truth most accurately and efficiently when we allow ideas to openly compete in the marketplace.
- Free speech is necessary to achieve personal autonomy and self-fulfillment.
- Free speech offers a safety valve for releasing pent-up frustration in a lawful activity.
- Free speech promotes tolerance of different viewpoints which engenders a respect for others, an important component to a pluralistic society.

- **Defining Speech**
  - Clearly oral and written communication of information, ideas and emotions is speech.
  - Conduct is speech when (1) the actor intended to communicate a particularized message, and (2) the circumstances are such that there is a great likelihood that the message would be understood by those who viewed the conduct.
  - Under O'Brien, government regulation of expressive conduct is permissible if:
    - The government has the power to regulate the field;
    - The regulation furthers an important or substantial government interest;
  - The government interest is unrelated to the suppression of free expression; and
  - The restriction on First Amendment freedom "is no greater than is essential" to further the government interest.
  - If the conduct at issue is speech (thus invoking the First Amendment), and the state's regulation was unrelated to suppression of free expression, then the O'Brien test applies. If the regulation is related to suppressing expression then strict scrutiny applies.
  - A federal statute that criminalizes "knowingly providing material support or resources to a foreign terrorist organization" passes the O'Brien test because it serves the governmental interest of preventing terrorism (*Holder v. Humanitarian Law Project*, 2010).
- **Vagueness and Overbreadth**
  - Vagueness and overbreadth both permit a person to facially challenge a law rather than to challenge based on a specific application, and both operate as an exception to the standing doctrine by allowing a person to challenge a law without having to suffer a personal injury.

- When determining whether a law is overbroad and vague, the Court first determines how deep the enactment interferes with constitutionally protected communication. Second, the Court examines whether the statue is facially vague, at which time the complainant must show that the law is vague in all of its applications.
- A law is void for vagueness if a reasonable person reading the law would not know what speech is illegal.
- A law regulating speech is unconstitutionally overbroad if it regulates substantially more speech than the constitution permits.
- Even if found overbroad, the Court can save the statute if (1) it can be given a limited construction; or (2) has a severability clause.

- **Content-Based Regulation and Prior Restraints**
  - Except for several categories of speech which are unprotected or less protected, government regulation of speech based on its content must pass strict scrutiny.
  - A prior restraint is a judicial order or administrative scheme which prevents speech from occurring.
  - The Court requires that "a law subjecting the exercise of First Amendment freedoms to the prior restraint of a license" contain "narrow, objective, and definite standards to guide the licensing authority."
  - Protective orders that the court issues during discovery does not amount to an unconstitutional prior restraint.
- **Compelled Speech**
  - The right not to speak is afforded the same First Amendment protection as the right to speak.
  - The government cannot force citizens to engage in speech.
  - A union requiring nonmembers to pay a substantial assessment for a political fund is compelled speech that fails strict scrutiny (*Knox v. Service Employees*, 2012).

Chapter 2

Unprotected and Less Protected Speech: Permissible Content-Based Restrictions

Roadmap

- There are several categories of speech the Court considers "unprotected" or "less protected" — advocacy of illegal action, fighting words and the hostile audience, true threats, sexually oriented speech, defamation, disclosure of private information, speech of public employees, and commercial speech.
- Quick rule is that generally, unprotected speech must only survive rational basis scrutiny, less protected speech must survive intermediate scrutiny, and protected speech must pass strict scrutiny.
- The Clear and Present Danger test used to be the test for advocacy of illegal action, but the modern test is now that the speech must be directed at producing illegal action and likely to bring about imminent lawless action.
- Words directed at a specific individual and likely to incite an immediate breach of the peace are considered fighting words.
- The hostile audience doctrine is a form of less protected speech, which must cause or be imminently about to cause a disturbance of the peace.
- Hate speech can be restricted only if it falls under one of the existing categories of less protected or unprotected speech.
- Sexually oriented speech is broken into three categories — obscenity, child pornography, and profanity. Obscenity and child pornography are not protected by the First Amendment, however language that is profane and indecent is protected.
- A public official or a public figure cannot recover for defamation under the First Amendment without a showing of actual malice.
- The government may permit a public figure to recover for intentional infliction of emotional distress or for false light invasion of privacy.
- The government can prohibit government employees from participating in political activities and speaking on matters of public concern.

- If the source of the speech is the federal government, most challenges rooted in First Amendment claims will fail.
- Commercial speech is a less protected category of speech.

I. Unprotected and Less Protected Speech: Permissible Content-Based Restrictions

The First Amendment's language contains no qualification in the mandate that "Congress shall make no law . . . abridging the freedom of speech, or of the press." However, the Court has interpreted the Free Speech Clause to protect most speech (but not all) from abridgment. To facilitate the analysis of the protected nature of speech, the Court has identified several categories of speech that it considers to be "unprotected" and "less protected." These categories are (a) advocacy of illegal action; (b) fighting words and the hostile audience; (c) true threats; (d) sexually oriented speech; (e) defamation; (f) disclosure of private information; (g) speech of public employees; and (h) commercial speech.

For speech that is not protected by the First Amendment, a law regulating or outlawing that speech need only be rationally related to the achievement of a legitimate government purpose. A regulation of less protected speech generally must be substantially related to the achievement of an important government purpose. Last, if the speech is protected by the First Amendment, any regulation of it must be narrowly tailored to achieve a compelling government purpose. The rule of thumb is that, generally, unprotected speech must only survive rational basis scrutiny; less protected speech must survive intermediate scrutiny; and protected speech must pass strict scrutiny. Thus, it is critical to know the various categories of speech because each category will determine what level of scrutiny applies.

Note, however, that a law distinguishing between speech in the same grouping must pass strict scrutiny, even if the speech is less protected or unprotected. This was the holding in *R.A.V. v. City of St. Paul, Minnesota* (1992). Before *R.A.V.*, it was widely believed that a regulation distinguishing between speech in the same grouping need only meet rational basis scrutiny. The decision in *R.A.V.* invalidated a city ordinance banning so-called hate speech based on race, color, religion, or gender if that speech was likely to anger or alarm others or cause resentment against the target group. The Court found that the speech banned by the ordinance was in the fighting words category and thus unprotected by the First Amendment. However, because the ordinance drew a content-based distinction between different forms of hate speech, the ordinance must pass strict scrutiny. Finding that the ordinance did not pass strict scrutiny, the Court struck it down. Thus, for example, a law that bans only the public exhibition of homosexual pornography but does not ban the public exhibition of heterosexual pornography must pass strict scrutiny, else it is invalid.

A. Advocacy of Illegal Action

Few would dispute that a government has the inherent right to protect itself against actions that are illegal. But when may the government prohibit speech that urges illegal violent or peaceful action? The boundaries of what expression the government can regulate were born from the forge of national security concerns in times of war, and internal foment. The early cases dealt with speech opposing war or advocating social, economic, or political change using methods that were violent and illegal. Initially, the Court read the First Amendment narrowly. This led to a constricting of the language of the Amendment such that laws punishing protesters or advocates of communism, lawlessness, or other revolutionary ideologies were upheld. However, over time, the Court's jurisprudence gradually shifted to a more expansive interpretation whereby the Amendment was seen to protect considerably more speech. Today, although advocacy of illegal action is an unprotected category of speech, the Court uses a strict definition of what speech falls in this category; much speech that would have fallen into the category in the earlier formulations will not do so today. The current test to determine whether speech is an incitement to illegality requires the speech to be:

1. directed at causing imminent illegal activity, and
2. likely to produce the illegal activity.

current interp.

1. The Development of the Clear and Present Danger Test

Initially, the Court focused on what has been called the Clear and Present Danger test: whether the speech posed a clear and present danger that would cause the very evils that Congress intended to prevent. This test was first enunciated in *Schenck v. United States* (1919). *Schenck* arose during World War I for a violation of the Espionage Act of 1917, which was passed, along with the Trading with the Enemy Act, just after the United States entered World War I in April 1917. This Act made it a crime during a time of war, to make false statements or reports with the intent to either interfere with the military success or promote the success of the enemies. Schenck had printed and distributed a pamphlet to men who had been drafted and were qualified for service in the armed forces. The pamphlet decried the draft, likening it to indentured servitude and slavery prohibited by the Thirteenth Amendment. It exhorted the draftees to stand up and resist. Schenck was charged with "causing and attempting to cause insubordination" in the ranks of the military and Navy of the United States. He asserted the First Amendment as a defense but was convicted. On review, the Supreme Court explained that the content of the speech was not solely determinative of the outcome and that the circumstances of the speech were relevant. Writing for the majority, Justice Holmes explained that, just as yelling "Fire!" in a theater is not protected, speech is unprotected when, under the circumstances, it "creates a clear and present danger" of causing illegal activity. Justice Holmes went on to state that "it is a question of proximity and degree," and that words that may not permissibly be regulated in peacetime may be regulated in a time of war. Thus, the Court found that speech advocating illegal activity may be regulated if it (1) poses a clear and present danger (2) of inciting illegal activity. This result would be reached even if no illegal activity ever occurred.

Justice Holmes further refined the Clear and Present Danger test in his dissent in *Abrams v. United States* (1919), where several self-described "anarchists," "revolutionaries," and "socialists" were convicted for violating the Espionage Act of 1917. Finding that the leaflets had the "obvious effect" of frustrating the American effort in World War I, the Court affirmed the convictions. Justice Holmes disagreed, observing that "Congress certainly cannot forbid all effort to change the mind of the country." He further explained the Clear and Present Danger test, stating that speech should not be punished as advocacy of illegal action unless it (1) "produce[d] a clear and imminent danger" of "immediate evil," or (2) the speaker intended to bring about the immediate evil. In regards to the first part, he stated that "nobody can suppose that the surreptitious publishing of a silly leaflet by an unknown man, without more, would present any immediate danger." In regards to the second test, Holmes found that the circulars were not within the reach of the statute because they were not intended to interfere with the American involvement in World War I but to help Russia and promote the Russian Revolution.

In *Abrams,* Justice Holmes employed the metaphor of a largely unregulated marketplace of ideas as the theoretical basis for the First Amendment. He wrote,

> But when men have realized that time has upset many fighting faiths, they may come to believe even more than they believe the very foundations of their own conduct that the ultimate good desired is better reached by free trade in ideas—that the best test of truth is the power of the thought to get itself accepted in the competition of the market, and that truth is the only ground upon which their wishes safely can

be carried out. That at any rate is the theory of our Constitution. It is an experiment, as all life is an experiment.

Every year if not every day we have to wager our salvation upon some prophecy based upon imperfect knowledge. While that experiment is part of our system I think that we should be eternally vigilant against attempts to check the expression of opinions that we loathe and believe to be fraught with death, unless they so imminently threaten immediate interference with the lawful and pressing purposes of the law that an immediate check is required to save the country.

2. *Revising the Clear and Present Danger Test*

In the years following *Abrams*, the states passed "criminal syndicalism" statutes that punished the advocating of communism, anarchy, or revolution. Motivated by the Red Scare (1917–1920), these statutes responded to the fear and anxiety that a Bolshevik revolution in America was imminent—a revolution that would change Church, home, marriage, civility, and the American way of Life. The Court generally held these laws to be constitutional as long as the speech had a "bad tendency." In *Gitlow v. New York* (1925), the defendant had been convicted of violating New York's criminal anarchy statute for advocating criminal anarchy. He had published a leaflet, "The Left Wing Manifesto," and a paper, "The Revolutionary Age," which advocated the violent overthrow of the government. Finding that the New York statute did not punish abstract opinions or doctrine, only the advocating of actual violent means to overthrow the government, the Court upheld the conviction. Justice Edward Sanford, writing for the Court, recognized that the First Amendment, as applied to New York through the Fourteenth Amendment, protected free speech. However, he explained that the speech outlawed by the statute posed such a substantial danger to the peace and the well-being of the government that New York was justified in punishing it. To hold otherwise would require the state to hold off until the seeds of revolution had been sown, germinated, and bore the fruit of the beginnings of violent overthrow. Thus, the Court held that a person could be punished for advocating the violent overthrow of the government, even in general terms and even if not addressed to specific individuals.

Justice Holmes dissented. He found that the Court's characterization of the publications to be an incitement was without basis, for all ideas are incitements. He explained that the manifesto and the paper simply advocated a general viewpoint and were protected by the First Amendment. However, had the publications exhorted an immediate uprising against the government rather than one at some indefinite point in the future, Justice Holmes explained that the result would likely be different.

In *Whitney v. California* (1927), the Court upheld a conviction under a California criminal syndicalism statute. The defendant had attended an organizational meeting of the Communist Labor Party, which advocated radical methods, whereas Whitney herself advocated more moderate methods. The Court upheld the conviction. Writing for the Court, Justice Sanford expressed extreme deference to the California legislature. He found that the state was within its valid police powers when it enacted the statute because of the danger to the public order posed by the advocating, teaching, or aiding and abetting of violent means to overthrow the government. He explained that the California law would only be illegal if it was an arbitrary or unreasonable exercise of the state's police power. Justice Louis Brandeis concurred. He explained that, while the First Amendment guarantees the freedoms of speech and assembly, it does not protect the acts advocated by the Communist Labor Party because they were designed to effect the violent overthrow of the government. He explained that what saved the California law was that it essentially only created a rebuttable presumption that the speech presented an immediate danger and that the defendant was free to show that the speech did not present such a danger. Because the defendant failed to show the lack of danger, and that credible evidence had been presented showing the imminent danger of illegal activity, Justice Brandeis saw no need to disturb the state's judgment.

This stage in the development of the incitement to illegality category is generally called the reasonableness phase. In these cases, the Court generally upheld the convictions because they were reasonable given the facts and circumstances. This reasonableness was buttressed by the need to protect public order and for governments to protect themselves from illegal acts intended to fell them. However, the tide eventually began to turn.

In several post-*Whitney* and post-*Gitlow* cases, the Court overturned convictions under criminal syndicalism statutes, not because of the Clear and Present Danger test but because it found that the convictions were unreasonable. For example, in *Fiske v. Kansas* (1927) and *De Jonge v. Oregon* (1937), the Court overturned the convictions under the state criminal syndicalism laws because the convictions were unreasonable. In both cases, there was no indication that the defendants or the organization actually advocated illegal acts at the meetings that led to the convictions (Although couched in terms of reasonableness, students today will recognize this as being a form of rational basis review where the Court grants deference to the legislative determination and only overturns a conviction if it was arbitrary or unreasonable).

The changes to the Clear and Present Danger standard continued into the Cold War era, slowly evolving into a more speech-protective formulation. But the evolution was gradual and generally represented an awakening to the points expressed in Holmes's and Brandeis's dissents and concurrences in *Abrams*, *Whitney*, and *Gitlow*, among other cases. The Alien Registration Act of 1940 (Smith Act) set criminal penalties for advocating the overthrow of the U.S. government and required all non-citizen adult residents to register with the government. Approximately 215 people were indicted under the Smith Act, including alleged communists, anarchists, and fascists, during the second Red Scare (1947–1957), popularly known as "McCarthyism." A key turning point occurred in 1951 when the Court reformulated the test into an analysis of the risk bordering on a formulaic approach. In *Dennis v. United States* (1951), the Court affirmed the convictions under the Smith Act of defendants who taught from books written by Karl Marx and Friedrich Engels, Vladimir Lenin, and Josef Stalin. Writing for the Court, Chief Justice Vinson explained that the question was not whether the Congress had the power to punish those who advocate the violent overthrow of the government but whether the means that Congress chose conflicted with the First Amendment. He applied the Clear and Present Danger test, finding that it did not require the government to wait until the revolution is imminent before it can act. Chief Justice Vinson adopted the formulation of Chief Judge Billings Learned Hand (Second Circuit Court of Appeals) that the "gravity of the 'evil', discounted by its improbability, justifies [the] invasion of free speech as is necessary to avoid the danger." Finding that the danger of overthrow existed and that its occurrence was likely because of the highly organized character of the Communist Party, the Court then concluded that the infringement on the freedom of speech was justified. Justice Felix Frankfurter concurred, finding that Congress was well within its power when it enacted the Smith Act, and that the Court was not empowered to overturn the law when it was not unconstitutional.

In his dissent, Justice Black explained that, by affirming the convictions, the Court had "repudiated" the Clear and Present Danger test, not merely restated it as the Court claimed. Justice Douglas also dissented, explaining that the defendants had merely taught abstract doctrine and did not advocate actual illegal acts such as sabotage, assassination, bombing, and street warfare. Instead, the defendants simply taught books that were legal to buy and read. Justice Douglas wrote that in certain situations speech loses its constitutional immunity, such as when "conditions are so critical that there will be no time to avoid the evil that the speech threatens;" however, the record in *Dennis* did not present such a situation. Thus, without such circumstances or actual advocating of illegal acts, the convictions should have been vacated.

Dennis was not the only case to reformulate the Clear and Present Danger test. However, the Court began to distinguish between the advocating of violent overthrow and mere expounding of abstract doctrine. In *Yates v. United States* (1957), the Court overturned the defendants' convictions for conspiracy to violate the Smith Act. In doing so, the Court reexamined its holding in *Dennis* and required actual "advocacy to action" for which Justices Black and Douglas had advocated in their dissents in *Dennis*. Under this new formulation, the Court upheld the conviction of a defendant in *Scales v. United States* (1961) for being a member of an organization that advocated the overthrow of the government by extralegal means. Thus, the reformulation in *Yates* of the *Dennis* test did not mark the end of prosecutions under the Smith Act, but it did require that the person or the organization actually advocate the overthrow of the government. Although not a great expansion of the protections of the First Amendment, these cases clearly afforded greater protection to the advocating of unpopular ideas, even if the ideas were inherently incompatible with the existing government, as long as the speaker did not call for illegal means of overthrowing the government.

3. The Modern Test

The Court continued to evolve the test in the late 1960s to afford greater protection to speech, even when the speech encouraged subversion of the government. Moving away from condemning the mere advocacy of illegal activity, the Court paralleled its development in the hostile audience context (explored in the next section), and moved toward a proof requirement that the speech would cause imminent harm. Today, the Court requires a three-prong test to determine if speech falls into the unprotected advocacy of illegal actions category. The next step in the evolution of the test was *Watts v. United States* (1969).

With its decision in *Watts*, the Court signaled its willingness to change standards and indicated that it would require proof that the speech would imminently cause harm. The defendant had been convicted of willfully threatening the life of the President while participating in a rally on the grounds of the Washington Monument. Specifically, he stated that he had been drafted, that he refused to report for his physical, and that "if they ever make [him] carry a rifle the first man I want to get in my sights is L.B.J." In a *per curiam* opinion, the Court reversed his conviction, though it found the statute under which the defendant was convicted to be constitutional on its face. However, because the statute criminalized pure speech, it was subject to the strictures of the First Amendment. Thus, the Court found that because the defendant's speech neither incited violence toward the President nor did it contain an actual threat of violence, it did not constitute a "true" threat as required by the language of the statute. Instead, the Court characterized the statement as mere "political hyperbole."

The Court completed its progress toward the modern test with its decision in *Brandenburg v. Ohio* (1969). *Brandenburg* involved a leader of the Ku Klux Klan who had been convicted under the Ohio criminal syndicalism law for advocating unlawful methods of terrorism to effect political or industrial reform and for meeting with others for the purpose of such advocacy. The Court explained that "abstract teaching" of the propriety or necessary of violent action against the government is not sufficient. It pointed to the prior decisions that required advocacy "directed to inciting or producing imminent lawless action" and that the advocacy must be likely to produce that action. Thus, the Court formulated the modern test: the speech must be (1) directed at producing imminent lawless action and (2) the likely to bring about the imminent lawless action. In so doing, the Court expressly overruled *Whitney* and afforded greater protection for speech critical of the government; however, the majority opinion avoided discussing the Clear and Present Danger test.

Justice Black and Justice Douglas concurred that the old Clear and Present Danger test has no place in First Amendment jurisprudence. Specifically, Justice Douglas explained that the test was inapposite in times of peace and expressed doubt that it had any utility in times of war. He further explained that the cases in which the test was applied, showed that the test left too much power in the government to undermine the protections of the First Amendment. Justice Douglas explained that the Court should have gone further by expressly overruling the Clear and Present Danger test and the line of cases derived from that flawed test. However, the Court's failure to do so is a serious ambiguity left by its decision in *Brandenburg*.

The remaining ambiguities were illustrated in *Hess v. Indiana* (1973), where the Court was divided over the imminence of the alleged harm. In *Hess*, antiwar demonstrators blocked the street and the police cleared the street without violence. However, in the process, the defendant had said either "[w]e'll take the fucking street later" or "[w]e'll take the fucking street again." The police arrested him for disorderly conduct, of which he was convicted at trial. In a *per curiam* opinion, the Court reversed his conviction. It found that the statement by the defendant was, "at worst, . . . nothing more than advocacy of illegal action at some indefinite future time." Because the statement was not directed at any identifiable person or group of people, the Court found that he could not be advocating any action. Thus, the Court found that the statement did not advocate any action, much less any imminent lawlessness, and his conviction could not stand. Justice Rehnquist dissented, joined by the Chief Justice Burger and Justice Blackmun, and explained that the Court had overstepped its permissible scope of review and conducted an independent weighing of the evidence. However, the key from *Hess* is that it strengthened the *Brandenburg* test, essentially requiring the speaker to actually advocate imminent violence or illegal action (merely advocating violence or illegality without the language being directed at causing imminent violence or illegality is not sufficient under the *Brandenburg* test as enhanced by *Hess*). The Court looks for a "working principle that the substantive evil must be extremely serious and the degree of imminence extremely high before utterances can be punished" (*Bridges v. California*, 1941). In *NAACP v. Claiborne Hardware Co.* (1982), a civil rights activist announced to a black audience that "[i]f we catch any of you going in any of them racist stores, we're gonna break your damn neck." The Court held that, because participants did not engage in violent activity and that no violent activity followed the speeches, no liability could be imposed on the speakers.

The modern test as applied by the Court in *Hess* is what the Court would use today. Remember: the importance of the test is that if the speech meets the test then it falls into the unprotected category of advocacy of illegal activity and the government's action must only pass rational basis review.

The Court has always distinguished speech for crimes like conspiracy and solicitation, and protected speech. For example, if A solicits B to rob a bank, and offers B $100,000 for successful completion of the crime, A can be convicted of solicitation. Likewise, if A & B conspire to rob the bank, they can be convicted of conspiracy to rob the bank. By contrast, if A makes a public speech calling on "every moral human being to rob a bank," the speech is protected unless the *Brandenburg* test is satisfied.

B. Fighting Words and the Hostile Audience

The next category of unprotected speech is where the listeners may use illegal force not with the speaker but against the speaker, other people or property. With this category the speaker is not advocating violence or the overthrow of the government. Instead, the speakers' words are provoking a violent response from the audience. "Fighting words" involve speech that is directed to a person and is likely to provoke a violent response against the speaker. "Hostile audience" refers to speech that provokes an audience to violence against others or property. The degree of protection afforded to speech is based on the value that the Court attributes to the speech. Because the Court considers this category to be of low value, it is largely unprotected.

1. The Fighting Words Doctrine

The fighting words doctrine encompasses speech that is so patently offensive or insulting that it would provoke a violent reaction from a reasonable person. This means that the words (1) are directed at a specific individual and (2) their mere utterance is likely to inflict emotional injury or would tend to incite an immediate breach of the peace. The Court carefully polices laws restricting this category of speech to ensure (1) that the regulation is not vague or overbroad and (2) that it is not a content based restriction.

The Court first defined fighting words as unprotected speech in *Chaplinsky v. New Hampshire* (1942). At issue in *Chaplinsky* was a New Hampshire statute that prohibited any person from "address[ing] any offensive, derisive or annoying word to any other person" in public, "nor call him by any offensive or derisive name, nor make any noise or exclamation in his presence and hearing with intent to deride, offend or annoy him," or that interferes with the conduct of his business. The defendant, a Jehovah's Witness, was distributing his church's literature on the public streets on Saturday afternoon. After a disturbance arose because of the defendant's words, the police took him to the police station. On the way, the defendant encountered the city marshal and, in response to the marshal's warning about his speech, the defendant told the marshal that he was "a God damned racketeer" and "a damned Fascist." The defendant admitted that he made those statements, except for using the word "God," after the marshal warned him. The defendant was convicted for violating the New Hampshire statute.

The Court upheld the conviction because it deemed the defendant's words to be "fighting words." The Court defined *fighting words* as words that "by their very utterance inflict injury or tend to incite an immediate breach of the peace." Writing for the majority, Justice Frank Murphy explained that such words are not protected by the First Amendment because they are not essential to the expression of any ideas and that they "are of such slight social value as a step to truth that any benefit ... from them is clearly outweighed by the social interest in order and morality." Furthermore, this use of personal verbal abuse and epithets is not essential to the communication of information or opinion, which the First Amendment was designed to protect, and punishing such speech would not be questioned under the Constitution. Justice Murphy explained that the statute was not overly broad because the New Hampshire Supreme Court put a limiting construction on the statute that expressly stated that the test is not how any given hearer would react but how men of "common intelligence" would understand words that would cause the average person to respond to them in a violent manner. It explained that the only words prohibited are those that, when delivered face to face, would tend to cause the listener to breach the peace. The Court also explained that the statute did not infringe on otherwise protected speech because the proscribed words were not intended to communicate opinions or ideas. Rather, the words falling within the reach of the statute could properly be considered epithets that would be likely to cause a violent response by the average listener.

In the 75 years since *Chaplinsky* was handed down, the Court has yet to uphold a conviction under a fighting words statute. However, in no case has the Court overturned *Chaplinsky*. In overturning convictions that may otherwise seem to fall within the reach of the fighting words doctrine, the Court has found the applicable laws to be unconstitutionally overbroad and vague, has held that the laws were impermissible content-based regulations of speech, and has narrowed the reach of the fighting words doctrine. Although this doctrine has essentially laid dormant, the Court has never overturned the decision, so it is likely still good law.

The Court narrowed the reach of the doctrine with its decision in *Street v. New York* (1969). There, the Court explained that there was only a "small class of 'fighting words'" that fits within the definition in *Chaplinsky*. In *Street*, a man was convicted of burning an American flag and exclaimed, "We don't need no damn flag.... If they let that happen to [James] Meredith we don't need an American flag." The Court explained that the speech did not qualify as fighting words unprotected by the First Amendment, despite the fact that some might have found the speech to be inherently insulting and provocative. In 1971, the Court explained the doctrine further in *Cohen v. California* (1971). There, the Court held that to qualify as fighting words they must not only be likely to inflict injury or incite the listener to a violent reaction, they must be directed at an individual person. In *Cohen*, the defendant was convicted for wearing a jacket with the words "Fuck the Draft" in a courthouse. Writing for the majority, Justice Harlan explained that the words on the jacket did not qualify as fighting words because they were not directed at any individual person. Thus, no person present who read the words would be likely to consider them a personal insult or affront.

In a series of cases the Court overturned convictions under fighting words statutes on the grounds that the law was impermissibly vague and overbroad. In *Gooding v. Wilson* (1972), the Court found that a Georgia statute banning opprobrious words and abusive language was unconstitutionally broad and vague. Writing for the majority, Justice Brennan explained that the language of the law reached more speech than was permitted under the fighting words doctrine. Relying on the definition of *Webster's Third New International Dictionary* from 1961, the Court explained that the definitions of *opprobrious* and *abusive* were broader than that of the fighting words doctrine as explained in *Chaplinsky*. Hence, the statute permitted too much speech to be regulated and gave too much latitude to juries. The Court also found that the courts of Georgia had not placed the same limiting interpretation on its statute that the highest court of New Hampshire did in *Chaplinsky*. Therefore, the Court found that the statute was unconstitutionally overbroad and vague. In dissent, Chief Justice Burger and Justice Blackmun stated that the Court's decision to find the statute facially invalid was not based on the language of the statute but on the fact that the courts of Georgia had not limited the interpretation or reach of the statute.

In *Lewis v. City of New Orleans* (1974) the Court struck down an ordinance that makes it illegal for any person to "wantonly curse or revile . . . obscene or opprobrious language toward a member of the city police while in the actual performance of his duties." The Court said that "opprobrious language" embraces words that do not fall under the fighting words definition, the word "opprobrious" embracing words "conveying or intended to convey disgrace" and found it immaterial whether the words appellant used might be punishable under a properly limited ordinance. In his concurrence, Justice Powell, remarked how unlikely it would be that a confrontation would occur between the middle-aged plaintiff and the officer, based on the fact that the woman said "you god damn m.f. police—I am going to [the Superintendent of Police] about this." Thus, a statute banning fighting words must be narrowly tailored so that it only reaches unprotected speech. Otherwise, it will be overturned for being too broad or unconstitutionally vague.

Yet another parameter on fighting words statutes is that a narrow regulation must not be too specific regarding the content of the speech, or the Court will find the statute unconstitutional for drawing an impermissible content-based restriction. In *R.A.V. v. City of St. Paul, Minnesota* (1992), a municipal ordinance banned symbols, objects, or graffiti, which included a burning cross or a Nazi swastika, from being on public or private property when one knows or reasonably should know that the banned communication would arouse "anger, alarm or resentment in others on the basis of race, color, creed, religion or gender." Writing for a unanimous court, Justice Antonin Scalia explained that the government was limited in its ability to draw content-based distinctions between speech within categories of unprotected speech. He clarified the meaning of unprotected speech by explaining that it was not that the speech was "entirely invisible to the Constitution," but that the content of the speech could be constitutionally proscribed. However, distinctions within categories of such speech must still pass strict scrutiny. Thus, the government can criminalize libel because its content is constitutionally proscribable; however, the government cannot criminalize only libel against the government unless that distinction is necessary to achieve a compelling government interest.

The Court identified two exceptions to the requirement of strict scrutiny for content-based distinctions within a category of unprotected speech. First, such a distinction is permitted if it directly promotes the rationale behind classifying the speech as unprotected in the first instance. Second, if the law is directed at the secondary effects of the speech rather than the content of the speech itself, then the distinction will not be considered to be based on the content of the speech. Justice Scalia applied the test to the ordinance at issue in *R.A.V.* and found that it was unconstitutional. Because the statute only applied to invective language likely to injure or provoke a violent response based on a few topics (specifically race, religion, creed, or gender), and not all such language, the ordinance drew a content-based distinction within the fighting words category. Additionally, the ordinance did not advance a compelling government interest, especially because other topics (such as homosexuality and political affiliation) were not covered. The Court also found that neither exception applied to these words.

Thus, to qualify as fighting words, the statute must be narrowly drawn to proscribe only those words (1) directed at an individual and (2) that simply by their utterance could injure the listener or provoke her to a violent reaction. However, the regulation must not be too narrowly drawn, else it would be invalid for drawing a content-based distinction within the unprotected category. That invalidation would not occur if the law (1) passed strict scrutiny, (2) directly advances the reason that the category of speech was unprotected, or (3) was aimed at remedying the secondary effects of the speech rather than regulating the content of the speech.

2. *The Hostile Audience*

Unlike the fighting words doctrine, which applies to unprotected speech, the hostile audience doctrine is a category of lesser protected speech that is used when speech otherwise protected by the First Amendment either provokes or has a tendency to provoke the audience to violence. Today, the Court appears to require the police to make every effort to protect the speaker before invoking this doctrine to silence him or her. The fact that a particularly impassioned demonstration would make an officer's job more difficult is not a justification to cease the demonstration or remove the speakers, as illustrated by

Edwards v. South Carolina (1963) and *Cox v. Louisiana* (1965). In the former case, the Court held that arresting a "group of Negroes" for their marching peacefully on a sidewalk to publicize their dissatisfaction with discrimination against their race, infringed on their freedom of speech rights. In *Cox*, the appellants were picketing near the court house, in violation of a federal statute. The statute was upheld, but the conduct fell short of violating the statute as the demonstrators did not present a threat to the administration of justice. This doctrine intersects with the concept of advocacy of illegal action (already discussed). The difference between the two doctrines lies in the fact that advocacy of illegal action is focused on speech that calls for the listener to act contrary to the law, whereas the hostile audience doctrine is concerned with a hostile reaction by the audience because the speech is unpopular or offensive but does not advocate illegal activity.

In the 1940s and 1950s the Court developed the hostile audience doctrine in cases that involved speech that led the audience to act out in a breach of the peace. In early cases, such as *Cantwell v. Connecticut* (1940) and *Terminiello v. Chicago* (1949), the Supreme Court applied the Clear and Present Danger test (similar to the one applied in the advocacy of illegality). In *Cantwell*, the defendant had been convicted for playing a record attacking the Roman Catholic faith on the corner of a public street. The Court overturned the conviction because although a clear and present danger of "riot, disorder, interference with traffic on the public streets, or other immediate threat to public safety, peace, or order" would clearly permit the government to intervene, such a danger was not present based on the speech at issue. Thus, the government cannot use the guise of such authority to punish speech that is otherwise protected simply because the speech is unpopular. There must be an actual likelihood of imminent threat to public peace and order based on the speech itself. The Court reached a similar conclusion in *Terminiello*, where the defendant had been convicted for calling his opponents "slimy scum," "snakes," and "bedbugs." Several disturbances resulted despite a substantial police presence. The Court overturned his conviction for disturbing the peace because the speech did not pose a clear and present danger of imminent lawless action. The Court explained that speech sometimes best serves its purpose when it "creates dissatisfaction," "stirs people to action," and "induces a condition of unrest." The Court clarified that to be regulated, the speech must pose a clear and present danger of causing "a serious substantive evil that rises far above public inconvenience, annoyance, or unrest."

The Court applied the same standard in *Feiner v. New York* (1951) to uphold a conviction. There, the defendant was addressing a gathering crowd of blacks and whites via a loudspeaker. He was trying to get people to attend a meeting he was holding that evening, but in the process he made derogatory remarks about various public officials, including President Harry Truman, the American Legion, and the mayor of Syracuse. The police made no attempt to interfere with the speech, but the crowd began to grow restless when he appeared to be exhorting the blacks in the audience to rise up and fight for equal rights. Some in the crowd threatened the police with violence if they did not control the crowd, and the police asked the defendant to stop speaking. After he refused several times, the police arrested him. He was convicted of disorderly conduct for "ignoring and refusing to heed and obey reasonable police orders." The disorderly conduct statute proscribed, *inter alia*, gathering with others on a public street and refusing to move when ordered by the police. Relying on its reasoning in *Cantwell*, the Court upheld the conviction. Writing for the majority, Justice Vinson explained that although the hostile audience doctrine could not be used if the crowd was merely murmuring and objecting to the speech, it is an entirely different situation when the speech is going beyond "the bounds of argument or persuasion and undertakes incitement to riot." Because the defendant refused to stop speaking at the request of the police, which was made after the crowd began to threaten violence, the Court held that the statute was not unconstitutional as applied.

Justice Black, writing in dissent, argued that the facts of the case did not show an imminent threat of a riot or other uncontrollable disorder. The scene as found in *Feiner* was not far from any similar scene where the crowd disagrees, sometimes violently, with a speaker. Justice Black argued that before silencing the speaker's constitutional right to speak in the name of preserving order, the police must make all reasonable efforts to control the crowd. Only after all such efforts have failed and violence is imminent, can the police silence the speaker. He went on to describe that the Court's holding amounted to permitting the government to silence unpopular speakers.

A difficult question in the hostile audience doctrine is whether the speaker ought to be punished for the reactions of his or her audience. To do so essentially permits a mob to silence an unpopular speaker through its actions. Additionally, because the police themselves may be more likely to agree with the crowd, if only because it is easier to control an individual than a crowd, their own attitudes may shade the perception of the threat of disorder, causing them to act prematurely. In more recent rulings, the Court appears to have followed Justice Black's *Feiner* dissent. In *Edwards v. South Carolina* (1963), the Court explained that police protection at the scene was sufficient to prevent any foreseeable disorder. The Court emphasized the ability of the police to control the crowd in overturning a conviction in *Cox v. Louisiana* (1965), where the speaker protested racial segregation at lunch counters and urged a sit-in (some in the audience found the speech inflammatory). The Court reached a similar result in *Gregory v. City of Chicago* (1969), even where the crowd became angry with the speaker and began throwing rocks.

Thus, the hostile audience doctrine still exists as a form of less protected speech. To qualify, the speech must cause an imminent threat of a substantial disturbance of the peace. However, it also appears that the police must make all reasonable efforts to control the crowd before they can invoke the doctrine and silence the speaker.

C. Hate Speech

Laws that prohibit the expression of hate, against individuals or groups based on national or ethnic origin, sex, race, sexual orientation, or religion are common outside the U.S. Justifications for these laws include protecting the dignity of the individual, avoiding discrimination, and lowering societal tensions that lead to violence. In the U.S., free speech interests prevail so there is no judicially or legislatively created category of unprotected or less protected speech called hate speech. Hate speech in the U.S. is only proscribed to the extent that it falls under one of the existing categories of less or unprotected speech such as advocacy of illegal action, fighting words, hostile audience or the true threats doctrine. Although legally classifying speech as "hate speech" is of relatively recent vintage, it goes without saying that hate speech has been around from time immemorial and was legally prosecuted in the U.S. until the modern era.

The questions of what constitutes hate speech and how such speech should be handled is still a developing area of the law. The most active attempts to curb such speech involve hate speech codes passed on college campuses. This revival of hate speech codes began in the 1980s and continues today. However, every time these codes are challenged in court, they are struck down as an infringement of the First Amendment.

1. *Group Libel*

The Court has examined different theories that seek to justify hate speech restrictions. In 1952, the Court addressed a challenge to an Illinois law proscribing the portrayal of "depravity, criminality, unchastity, or lack of virtue of a class of citizens" based on race, creed, color, or religion if the portrayal would expose such citizens to contempt, derision, or which would cause a breach of the peace or riots. In that case, *Beauharnais v. Illinois* (1952), the Court upheld the convictions of several people. Specifically, the individuals had called for whites in Chicago to unite and for the city to "protect" white neighborhoods from blacks, whom they saw as invading, harassing, and encroaching on their neighborhoods. The Court held that the government can forbid defamatory language directed at a defined group of individuals. The Court based its decision on the government's power to make defamation against an individual illegal. The Court considered the speech by the defendants against an identified group as essentially the same as libelous defamation directed at an individual. Justice Frankfurter's majority opinion also explained that the Court did not need to apply the Clear and Present Danger test because the speech was essentially defamatory and as such was already within the government's power to control.

The Court's decision in *Beauharnais* established the rule that one can libel an identified group (called group libel). This decision has never been overruled. However, intervening decisions have called its holding into question. It is doubtful that the Court would uphold *Beauharnais* today. One reason is that courts have repeatedly refused to follow the Court's holding. A classic example is the case of *National Socialist Party of America v. Village of Skokie* (1977). There, the Court upheld the right of Nazis to march in Skokie, Illinois, a town populated mostly by Jews, including many survivors of the Nazi concentration camps. After the case was remanded, the Seventh Circuit found attempts by the town to prohibit publication and distribution of material that promoted and incited hatred of others based on their religion or race and to ban the display of the swastika to be unconstitutional. In its decision, the Seventh Circuit expressly stated that it no longer regarded *Beauharnais* as good law.

Another reason that *Beauharnais* may no longer be good law is that its underpinnings have since been eroded. When deciding the case in 1952, the Court expressly based its decision on the government's unlimited ability to proscribe defamation. However, in *New York Times Co. v. Sullivan* (1964), the Court rejected this unlimited power and placed rather strong limits on the ability of the government to curb defamatory speech.

Another challenge to *Beauharnais* is the doctrine of void for vagueness and overbreadth and the doctrine of content-based discrimination. It is likely that statutes similar to that in *Beauharnais* would be deemed overbroad, vague or content based. Therefore, today hate speech probably cannot be successfully proscribed under the group libel theory.

2. Fighting Words and True Threats

Hate speech regulation could be justified under the fighting words doctrine. However as previously stated, the Court has not upheld a statute banning fighting words since *Chaplinsky* and such a statute would need to survive a challenge of void for vagueness or overbreadth, and of *R.A.V.*'s application of strict scrutiny to content-based distinctions within a category of unprotected speech.

Another tool to combat hate speech is the true threats doctrine. Although the Court has never defined what constitutes a true threat, numerous federal statutes have, the broadest of which makes it a crime to transmit in commerce any communication containing any threat to injure another person. As interpreted by the lower courts, the speaker need only intend the threatening communication. He or she need not actually intend to carry the threat out (or even have the ability to carry it out). Though this doctrine is often linked to hate speech, it is not limited to hate-based threats. In fact, it was initially developed to address threats made against the President or Vice President of the United States. In *Watts v. United States* (1969), the Court explained that the Constitution did not protect speech that was intended as a threat to the life of the President and upheld a federal statute banning such speech. However, the Court also explained that the threat must be an actual threat of illegal, violent harm, and not merely a "very crude offensive method of stating a political opposition to the President." In making its determination, the Court looked at the totality of the circumstances. In *Watts*, the defendant, protesting the draft and police brutality, stated that he had received his draft classification as 1-A and that he had to report for his physical on Monday. He then said, "I am not going. If they ever make me carry a rifle the first man I want to get in my sights is L.B.J." In a *per curiam* opinion, the Court explained that, when taken in context, the speech only indicated the speaker's disagreement with the President and that it did not actually threaten him with illegal violent harm.

The seminal case addressing true threats in the context of hate speech is *Virginia v. Black* (2003), in which the Court addressed a Virginia statute banning cross burning with the intent to intimidate a person or a group of persons. The statute went further and found that the mere fact of cross burning raised a presumption that the burning was with the intent to intimidate, requiring the defendant to rebut that presumption. The Court struck down the Virginia statute because of the presumption it permitted based on the defendant's conduct. Justice O'Connor's opinion, a majority opinion in part and a plurality opinion in part, explained that, without the presumption that burning a cross was prima facie evidence of intent to intimidate, the statute would have been constitutional. Justice O'Connor also explained that the statute need not ban all intimidating speech to be constitutional. Rather, she explained that cross burning is especially intimidating given its history with the Ku Klux Klan and that because of its especial virulence, the government could ban only that speech if it chose. Specifically, Justice O'Connor expressed that such intimidating hate speech is intended to be a threat of illegal violent harm to the hearer, and burning a cross has traditionally been used to communicate that threat. Thus, under the logic of *Black*, hate speech may be proscribed without offending the First Amendment because it is intended to threaten and instill fear in the hearer, rather than communicate ideas.

Another possible avenue under exploration by legislatures around the country is tacking on additional penalties to crimes involving hate as a motivation. Commonly known as hate crimes laws, the Court has lent at least a measure of legitimacy to these enhancements. For example, in *Wisconsin v. Mitchell* (1993), the Court upheld a statute that provided for greater criminal punishments when the victim was chosen on grounds of race. Chief Justice Rehnquist, writing for a unanimous Court, explained that the nature of crimes committed based on hatred for another due to race involves a greater harm to society in general and also inflicts "distinct emotional harms on their victims." Rehnquist also stated that they have a greater likelihood of provoking a breach of public order or riots. Note that hate crimes laws are not aimed directly at preventing hate speech. However, the trend is to use hate speech as an indication of the animus behind the crime and as evidence of the hateful motivation. Thus, although not directly targeting hate speech itself, hate crimes legislation may have the side effect of deterring hate speech to avoid the penalty enhancements created by the legislation.

Another approach to proscribing hate speech involves the doctrines of incitement to imminent illegality and the hostile audience. These two doctrines were already discussed, but they are also applicable in the context of hate speech. First, under the *Brandenberg* test, the government enjoys the ability to protect itself from change caused by "violence, revolution, and terrorism." The ability to protect the citizenry from violence and to preserve the peace are also valid exercises of the police power of the state. However, under the *Brandenberg* test, the bar is set very high: The speech must present a threat of imminent violence. To be proscribed under these doctrines, the hate speech must be intended to cause imminent violence or it must be provoking a crowd against the speaker to the point that, absent silencing the speaker, will lead to imminent lawlessness. Recall that the Court tends to follow Justice Black's dissent in *Feiner v. New York* (1951), which requires the police to take all reasonable steps to control the crowd first and only permit silencing the speaker if the police are unable to do so.

Due to the many Court created doctrines protecting free speech, most hate speech is protected under the First Amendment. The Court's method of banning it by group libel theory in *Beauharnais* would probably not hold up today, and treating hate speech as fighting words will be difficult due to *R.A.V.* and the tests of vagueness and overbreadth. That said, speech that incites to imminent violence or clearly threatens or intimidates may be proscribed, and hate crimes legislation can succeed in combating hate speech. Nonetheless, this is still an active and developing area of free speech law.

D. Sexually Oriented Speech

The regulation of sexually oriented speech is always a controversial topic in First Amendment law. The court has long recognized that the government can regulate such speech, but it has struggled with what constitutes "obscenity." In 1948, Doubleday was convicted of violating the N.Y. obscenity statute for selling *Memoirs of Hecate County*, written by literary critic Edmund Wilson, because it contained two scenes describing sexual intercourse. An evenly split Supreme Court (Justice Felix Frankfurter disqualified himself because he had talked to the author about the book) left a New York Court of Appeals decision to uphold the obscenity conviction in place (*Doubleday & Co., Inc. v. New York*, 1948). The following year, a Pennsylvania court acquitted book publishers and sellers charged with violating the state obscenity statute for publishing and selling works by authors such as Erskine Caldwell, James T. Farrell, William Faulkner and Calder Willingham (*Commonwealth v. Gordon*, 1949).

In finding that the Court had endorsed punishment of obscenity *qua* obscenity, the judge relied on several statements by the Supreme Court. In *Chaplinsky v. New Hampshire* (1942), the Court stated that there were "certain well-defined and narrowly limited classes of speech" that were not protected by the First Amendment and included "lewd and obscene" material in such a class. The Court's endorsement of prosecuting obscenity continued after the acquittal in *Gordon*. For example, Justice Murphy included the "lewd and obscene" among the speech that has no value to society in *Beauharnais*. The Court has since refined its position on sexually oriented speech by dividing it into three groups: obscenity, child pornography, and language that is profane and indecent. The Court finds that the first two categories, obscenity and child pornography, are not protected by the First Amendment; the third category is generally protected, but there are exceptions.

1. *Obscenity*

Although the Court has permitted the legislature to ban obscene speech, the Court has found it extremely difficult to define obscenity . In fact, its attempt to define obscenity led to the famous quote from Justice Potter Stewart's concurrence in *Jacobellis v. Ohio* (1964), "Perhaps I could never succeed in intelligibly . . . [defining hard-core pornography]. But I know it when I see it." Although the Court has progressed from this and provided substantial guidance as to what constitutes obscenity, sometimes it appears that the Court just "know[s] it when [it] see[s] it."

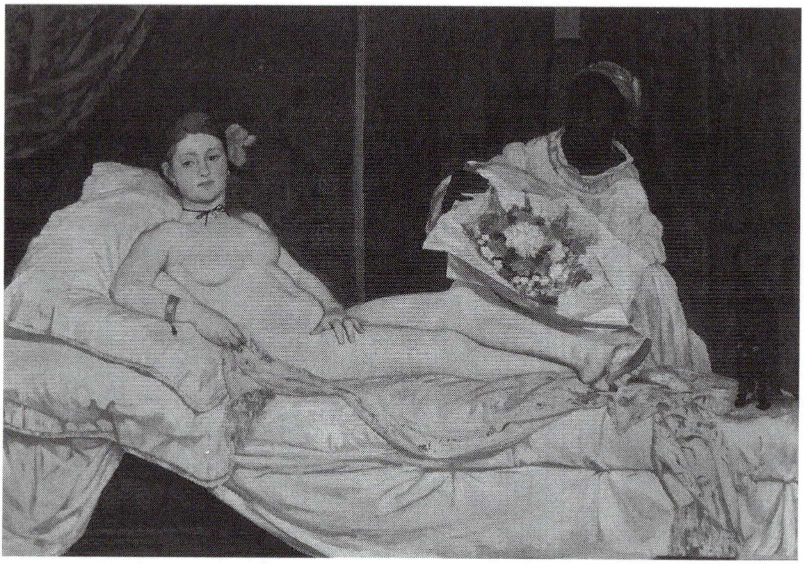

Manet's *Olympia* was considered obscene in 1865, but today is considered a masterpiece. As tastes in the arts change, the legal definitions of obscenity and free expression change as well.

The Court first addressed obscenity directly in *Roth v. United States* (1957), a case that still forms the core of the Court's obscenity jurisprudence today. In *Roth*, the Court expressly held that obscenity was not protected by the First Amendment. In so holding, the Court relied on past dicta in *Chaplinsky* and *Beauharnais*. In his majority opinion, Justice Brennan noted that the Court had always assumed that obscene speech fell outside the protections of the First Amendment. He grounded this understanding of history in the fact that the Court had long held that ideas with at least some redeeming value, no matter how slight or how unpopular, were protected by the Constitution unless the speech infringed on "more important interests."

After finding that obscenity was not protected, Justice Brennan divorced much sexual expression from obscenity. He explained that to be obscene, the material must "deal with sex in a manner appealing to prurient interest," and that displays of nudity or sex in art, literature, science, and similar forums were not obscenity. Justice Brennan then qualified the "prurient interest" language, explaining that the theme of the work must be judged as a whole by applying contemporary community standards from the viewpoint of the average person in the community. He then stated that generally, there would be no violation of due process if a statute banning obscenity were found to be less precise than desirable, as long as the statute provided "adequate warning" as to what conduct was proscribed. Thus, under *Roth*, the Court articulated a three-part test for obscenity. To qualify as obscene, the material must (1) appeal to a prurient interest in sex; (2) have no redeeming artistic, scientific, literary, or other similar value; and (3) on the whole, be offensive to the average person applying contemporary community standards.

The Court has continually held that obscene speech is not protected by the Constitution; however in the years after *Roth*, the Court struggled with how to define obscenity and how to justify its finding that obscenity was not protected speech. In *A Book Named "John Cleland's Memoirs of a Woman of Pleasure" v. Attorney General* (1966), the Court overturned a conviction based on a finding that the book had at least some "social value" and thus was not obscene. The Court was badly fractured, however, and could not muster a majority opinion in the case. Justice Brennan's opinion stated that the three elements of the *Roth* test were independent of each other, and material was not obscene if it passed any of the three elements. The confusion continued with *Ginzburg v. United States* (1966). There, the Court found commercial publications devoted to sex to be obscene because they were commercial ventures that exploited erotica solely for their prurient appeal. With his decision in *Ginzburg*, Justice Brennan ran directly counter in his opinion in *Memoirs* because he never considered any potential social value of the publications. Thus, the Court seemed to indicate that if the material is intended to appeal solely to prurient interests, that intent outweighed any social value that the material may have had.

The Court eventually came through the fog with its decision in *Miller v. California* (1973). Again, the Court reaffirmed that obscene material was not protected by the First Amendment. It also created the test for obscenity that is still used today. First, it abandoned the post-*Roth* approaches of treating the *Roth* elements independently and that material intended to appeal solely to prurient sexual interests would override any vestige of redeeming social value. The *Miller* test was based on the *Roth* elements but expanded on them. Under *Miller*, material is obscene if (1) the average person applying contemporary community standards would find that, viewed as a whole, the work appealed to the prurient interests; (2) the work describes or depicts sexual conduct defined by the applicable law in a patently offensive way; and (3) as a whole, the work lacks serious literary, political, scientific, or artistic value. As examples, the Court explained that patently offensive depictions or descriptions of ultimate sex acts would fall within the *Miller* test, as would patently offensive descriptions or depictions of masturbation, excretion, and lewd exhibition of genitalia. The dissents decried the new test as one that endorsed censorship by permitting suppression simply based on individual predilections.

In *Paris Adult Theatre I v. Slaton* (1973) the Court found that states can make "the morally neutral judgment" that obscene materials "injure the community," "endanger the public safety," and threaten a "decent society." The Georgia Supreme Court described the films being displayed at the theater as "hard core pornography" which left "little to the imagination." The defendant argued that the films were protected speech because they were shown for adult consumption only. However, the Court rejected that argument, recognizing the longstanding and legitimate interest of states to regulate obscene material in local commerce and "in all places of public accommodation." However, the Court went further and explained that, because depictions of obscenity could have a "corrupting and debasing impact" that may lead to antisocial behavior, states could ban such depictions under legitimate police powers. The fact that the speech was only made to adults did not lend it talismanic immunity under the First Amendment. The Court emphasized the governmental interest in avoiding the negative effects on a community by such establishments congregating in a single community.

In other decisions, the Court addressed the issues of possessing obscene material and distinguished it from commerce involving obscenity. In *Stanley v. Georgia* (1969), before *Miller*, the Court upheld the right to possess obscene materials because the states only have a legitimate interest in regulating obscenity in commerce and public discourse. It found that the First and Fourteenth Amendments protected private possession of obscene materials. However, in *United States v. Reidel* (1971), the Court explained that although a person cannot be prosecuted for possessing obscene materials under *Stanley*, there is no constitutionally protected right to sell or deliver those materials to that person.

Historically, the Court has focused on the defendant's conduct, which includes material that the defendant markets and displays. Such is illustrated in *Ginsburg v. U.S.* (1966), where the Court held that while the material by itself was not obscene, the sordid way the venders pandered the material was in violation of the statute that prohibited mailing of certain materials. Defining pandering as "the business of purveying textual or graphic matter openly advertised to appeal to the erotic interest of their customers" and considering the trial court's finding that only four of the fifteen articles appealed to the prurient interest, the way that the vendors emphasized the provocative aspects of the literature rendered it obscene. In this decision, the Court cited an objective to avoid material that is sold to produce sexual arousal from being exempt from regulation, just because it has been disguised as speech.

Thus, the Court has upheld an individual's right to possess obscenity. But no one has a right to buy or sell such materials. Further, the government is not prohibited from banning obscenity as long as the law passes the three-prong *Miller* test. However, the *Miller* test is not limited only to material that potentially could be viewed by children. Under *Paris Adult Theatre I*, the fact that minors are not permitted in to view material in a publicly accessible place does not shield the speech from being regulated, especially given the effects that such places have on the community. Thus, the government generally has the right to regulate the dissemination of obscene speech but not the possession of such materials.

Today, the multibillion-dollar adult film industry and its enormous presence on the internet may have changed "community standards" so as to make prosecutions difficult to impossible. This may explain why obscenity prosecutions for adult pornography have dropped precipitously in the past decade. However, community standards can continue or reverse direction and the *Miller* test allows for this change.

Feminist legal scholars are represented on both sides of the pornography debate. Catherine Mackinnon and Andrea Dworkin argue that pornography that portrays women as "sexual objects for domination, conquest, violation, exploitation ... or positions of servility or submission," is a form of sex discrimination. They argue that this type of pornography should be suppressed because it causes (and is itself a form of) violence against women. However, sexually explicit material that did not fit this description, would be protected. On the other side, Nadine Strossen is a civil libertarian and free speech advocate. She argues that adult obscenity laws are "hopelessly vague," enforced unevenly by traditionalist governments against disfavored groups such as feminists, gays, and lesbians, perpetuate the stereotype of women as victims requiring protection from the patriarchy, and distract us from concrete discriminatory conduct.

In *American Booksellers Assn. v. Hudnut (1985)*, the U.S. Court of Appeals for the Seventh Circuit struck down an Indianapolis, Indiana obscenity statute that had adopted MacKinnon's approach to obscenity. The Court found the statute impermissibly discriminated based on content and viewpoint. This discrimination occurred because sexually explicit speech that treated women in the approved way was legal, while sexually explicit speech treating women in the disapproved way was illegal, without regard to literary, artistic or political qualities as a whole. The Court held that the state cannot restrict speech based on a preferred viewpoint.

2. Child Pornography

Child pornography is a category of unprotected speech, but because it is a content-based restriction of obscenity, it must pass strict scrutiny. As a category of unprotected speech recognized by the Supreme Court, it is of relatively recent vintage. It developed as one branch of the outgrowth of the Court's creation and application of the strict scrutiny test to content-based restrictions on speech. The doctrines of vagueness and overbreadth had developed sufficiently by the 1980s such that any new test would have to survive scrutiny under their requirements. When the Court recognized the category of child pornography as unprotected speech in 1982, it not only considered the state interest involved and the fit of the law to the interest but also ensured that the law not be unconstitutionally vague or overbroad.

The seminal case where the Court recognized this category was *New York v. Ferber* (1982), where it held that the government could prohibit the advertising, selling, display, and distribution of pornographic materials involving children. Specifically, the Court upheld a New York law that prohibited the promotion of "a sexual performance by a child." It defined such a sexual performance as one "which includes sexual conduct by a child less than sixteen years of age" and sexual conduct as "actual or simulated sexual intercourse, deviate sexual intercourse, sexual bestiality, masturbation, sado-masochistic abuse, or lewd exhibition of the genitals" (The defendant was the owner of a bookstore specializing in sexually oriented materials which sold two films depicting young boys masturbating). The Supreme Court unanimously upheld the conviction.

The Court based its finding in *Ferber* on the compelling need to protect children, listing five supporting premises. First, it recognized the state's compelling interest in protecting the physical and psychological well-being of children, stating that preventing sexual abuse and exploitation is a "government objective of surpassing importance." It further observed that the use of children as subjects of pornographic productions harms the children physiologically, emotionally, and mentally, and that virtually all states have statutes prohibiting child pornography. Second, distribution of child pornography is directly related to the state's compelling interest because (a) the materials are a permanent record of the child's participation in the activity with the distribution exacerbating the harm to the child and (b) the distribution network encourages the distribution and thus the exploitation and abuse of children. Third, the advertising and sales of this material provides an economic incentive which, in turn, feeds the growth of the industry and the exploitation of the children. Fourth, the value of such materials, if any, is "exceedingly modest, if not *de minimis*" and, if there were any artistic, literary, scientific, or educational value, it could be met by activity by a person of legal age who appears to be younger. Fifth, recognizing child pornography as a category of unprotected speech is not contrary to existing case law precedent.

Additionally, the Court held that the test for validity of child pornography laws is different than the obscenity test as articulated by the *Miller* court. Specifically, the validity of laws proscribing child pornography need not appeal to the prurient interest of the average person or be portrayed in a patently offensive manner under community standards. In addition, the work need not be considered as a whole. However, the Court noted one specific exception. It retained First Amendment protection of distributing descriptions or other non-obscene depictions of sexual conduct that do not involve live performances, photographic, or other visual reproductions of live performances. The Court emphasized that criminal responsibility cannot be imposed without having to prove some element of scienter against the defendant.

The Court's decision in *Ferber* is important for three main reasons. First, it delineated the standard by which the constitutionality of anti-child pornography laws would be judged. Second, the Court did not actually define child pornography. Rather, it merely passed on the constitutionality of the definition provided in the New York statute. Third, it provided that the doctrines of vagueness and overbreadth could be applied to such laws but found that they were not applicable to the New York law. Justice O'Connor's concurring opinion stressed that, although New York's law was not facially unconstitutional, it may be found unconstitutional as applied in certain situations because it may proscribe acts that do not threaten the harms against which the state may legitimately protect. Specifically, she found that the statute may criminalize clinical depictions of adolescents like those that may have a place in medical textbooks, and that there may be other applications that do not implicate the "kiddie porn" market that New York was attempting to control. The Court extended *Ferber* to mere possession of child pornography in *Osborne v. Ohio* (1990).

Congress sought to expand the amount of speech that would be categorically outside the protection of the First Amendment by criminalizing the use of simulations of adolescents in sexual positions. In *Ashcroft v. Free Speech Coalition* (2002), the Court struck down two overbroad provisions of the Child Pornography Prevention Act of 1996 (CPPA). These provisions proscribed "virtual pornography" by outlawing sexually explicit images that purported to depict minors. The content at issue used adults who looked like minors or computer-generated images. Analyzing the statute under *Ferber*'s protection of children, the Court found that when no actual minors were used in the creation of what appeared to be child pornography, the state's interest in preventing child abuse was not implicated because no children were harmed. The Court later described this as the rejection of the "can't-make-an-omelet-without-breaking-eggs" approach to the First Amendment, meaning that it is impermissible to prohibit protected speech based on the possibility that it could be unprotected. The Court recognized that experts sometimes find it difficult to decipher the difference between computer-generated images using real children versus computer graphics; however, it remains unacceptable to put a blanket provision on all images. To do so would "turn the First Amendment upside down." The Government argued that without the CPPA, child molesters might use virtual child pornography to seduce children. The Court responded that "there are many things innocent in themselves, however, such as toys, movies, games, video games, candy, money etc. that might be used for immoral purposes, yet we would not expect those to be prohibited because they can be misused."

The problem with the provisions of the CPPA at issue in this case was that they included categories of speech other than obscenity and child pornography, and thus were overbroad. A provision at issue prohibited "any visual depiction, including any photograph, film, video, picture, or computer or computer-generated image or picture" that "is, or appears to be, of a minor engaging in sexually explicit conduct." The Court concluded that the "CPPA prohibits speech despite its serious literary, artistic, political, or scientific value." In particular, it prohibits the visual depiction of teenagers engaged in sexual activity which is, a "fact of modern society and has been a theme in art and literature throughout the ages." The Court mentioned such as Romeo and Juliet, Traffic and American Beauty as examples. The Court found that "if these films, or hundreds of others of lesser note that explore those subjects, contain a single graphic depiction of sexual activity within the statutory definition, the possessor of the film would be subject to severe punishment without inquiry into the work's redeeming value. This is inconsistent with an essential First Amendment rule: The artistic merit of a work does not depend on the presence of a single explicit scene."

Thus, the CPPA prohibited speech for a different reason than anti-child pornography laws. Laws prohibiting the distribution and possession of child pornography ban speech because of the manner in which it is produced, regardless of its serious literary or artistic value. But speech prohibited by the CPPA "records no crime and creates no victims by its production." Child pornography is not necessarily without value, but it is illegal because of the harm that making and distributing it necessarily inflicts upon children.

Following *Ashcroft*, Congress re-wrote the CPPA and called it The Prosecutorial Remedies and Other Tools to end the Exploitation of Children Today

Act (The PROTECT Act of 2003). In *U.S. v. Williams* (2008) the Act faced a constitutional challenge. The Act prohibited the "pandering" of child pornography: any person who "knowingly . . . advertises, promotes, presents, distributes, or solicits through the mails . . . including by computer . . . material [that] contains "an obscene visual depiction of a minor . . . or a visual depiction of an actual minor." Williams was discovered posting sexually suggestive pictures of children on the Internet, including photographs of his four-year-old daughter being molested, and was subsequently arrested for pandering and possession of child pornography. His correspondence with an undercover agent, who solicited the pornography, ultimately lead to his arrest. Focusing on these transactions, the Court disagreed with the Eleventh Circuit's interpretation that offers to provide child pornography must be commercial, and that small-scale personal transactions are included under the language of the statute. The Court focused on the fact that Williams simply offered something that is unlawful to possess and is unprotected by the First Amendment.

The government may regulate and proscribe child pornography without meeting the requirements of *Miller*, but only when actual minors are used in the production of the challenged material. When the material uses youthful-looking adults, computer-generated images, or other simulated minors, the Court applies the *Miller* test.

3. *Profanity and Indecency: Protected but Low-Value Speech*

Speech that does not meet the definition of either obscenity under the *Miller* test or qualify as child pornography under *Ferber* but is otherwise profane or indecent is generally protected by the First Amendment. The Court finds that such speech, even if it is of only low value to society, is protected. It bases this on the difficulty of separating the speech from the ideas that it is intended to express. To hold otherwise would essentially open the door to censorship because the speech was unpopular or generally offensive.

Justice Stevens clearly illustrates the principle that material containing sexual content could not be the basis for regulation in *Young v. American Mini Theatres, Inc.* (1976) when the Court held, "[s]elective exclusions from a public forum may not be based on content alone, and may not be justified by reference to content alone."

The classic case is *Cohen v. California* (1971), in which the Court concluded that the government may not punish expression simply because those to whom the speech is expressed find it offensive. In *Cohen*, the defendant had been arrested for wearing a jacket bearing the words "Fuck the Draft" inside the Los Angeles Courthouse. In overturning the conviction, Justice Harlan wrote that one cannot forbid speaking certain words without inherently suppressing the ideas that the words were intended to convey. He was concerned that once the state has the ability to proscribe specific words because others may find them offensive, there would be no rational boundary between those words and other words that may be offensive. Harlan also refused to categorize the speech as a "fighting word" under *Chaplinsky v. New Hampshire*, because no "individual actually or likely to be present could reasonably have regarded the words on appellant's jacket as a direct personal insult."

A similar rational prevents the general proscription of speech that has sexual content but is not obscene. The Court addressed this issue in *Erznoznik v. City of Jacksonville* (1975). *Erznoznik* involved a challenge to a Jacksonville, Florida, ordinance proscribing drive-in theaters from exhibiting motion pictures depicting nudity if the images are visible from any public street or public place. The Court found that the statute was underinclusive because it did not protect people from all movies that might offend them. Further, Justice Lewis Powell, writing for the Court, explained that the ordinance was overinclusive because it would ban motion pictures that would not be considered obscene, such as educational movies, including those about peoples for whom public nudity is common, war documentaries showing nude victims of the war, and a film that shows a baby's unclothed bottom. The Court also stated that such an ordinance could be saved if the state courts had given it a narrowing construction. However, the state courts of Florida had not done so, and the plain language of the ordinance was not amenable to such a construction. Thus, because the material banned was not obscene, the Court found that it was within the protection of the First Amendment, and the Jacksonville ordinance was invalid.

The Court has found two exceptions to this protection. First, speech in schools that may offend others may be proscribed if it is inconsistent with the educational mission of the school. In *Bethel School District No. 403 v. Fraser* (1986), a student had been punished for giving a nominating speech at a school assembly that, while it did not contain profane language, was replete with sexual innuendo. The Court upheld the student's punishment because the speech was "wholly inconsistent with the 'fundamental value' of public school education."

Second, the Court has recognized the government's ability to prohibit profanity and indecency broadcast over the airwaves. In *FCC v. Pacifica Foundation* (1978), the Court upheld the ability of the Federal Communications Commission to punish indecent speech broadcast over radio or television. The Court explained that although the government could not ban all indecent speech, it could do so over the radio, especially where the speech was patently offensive, because the speech accosts the individual at his or her home, where a person has a right to be left alone. The Court found that the expectation of privacy, insofar as being left alone, overrode the First Amendment rights of the intruder. It explained further that placing warnings bookending the different segments of the speech would not be sufficient because that would not protect a person who happened to tune in between the warnings.

The Court has refused to extend these exceptions to other forms of media, including telephones, cable television, and the Internet. First, in *Sable Communications v. FCC*, (1989), the Court addressed a federal statute that was targeted at banning the "dial-a-porn" industry by banning indecent or obscene speech over the telephone. The Court explained that the speech could not be banned merely because it was indecent or obscene. Further, the speech was not made to a captive audience because, except for wrong numbers, the caller generally intended to encounter the speech.

The Court ruled along similar lines in *Denver Area Educational Telecommunications Consortium, Inc. v. FCC* (1996), where it addressed the Cable Television and Consumer Protection and Competition Act of 1992 (CTCPCA). Several provisions of the CTCPCA were challenged. One proscribed material on cable television that was considered patently offensive and sexually oriented. Another required that cable systems permitting such material segregate it on a single channel and require the subscriber request access to the channel in writing. The last provision allowed cable systems to prohibit material on public, educational, or governmental channels that was sexually explicit. Though it could not muster a majority opinion, the Court upheld the first provision and invalidated the last two. The Court recently restated the right of the F.C.C. to regulate content it deems indecent on non-cable television stations (*F.C.C. v. Fox Television Stations, Inc.*, 2009). The controversy arose from two different occasions. The first was during the 2002 Billboard Music Awards, when the singer Cher said, "I've also had critics for the last 40 years saying that I was on my way out every year. Right. So fuck 'em." The second involved the 2003 Billboard Music Awards, when Paris Hilton and Nicole Richie, actors from the television show "The Simple Life," were presenting an award. Hilton publicly reminded Richie to "watch the bad language," in which Richie responded, to the audience, "Why do they even call it 'The Simple Life'? Have you ever tried to get cow shit out of a Prada purse? It's not so fucking simple." The FCC found both broadcasts to be patently offensive under community standards for the medium and the language to be "vulgar and shocking." The Court reversed the Second Circuit to hold that it is reasonable for the F.C.C. to regulate television programs to provide "conscientious parents a relatively safe haven for their children." Thus, its decision to fine the networks was neither arbitrary nor capricious.

Finally, the Court has refused to apply *Pacifica* to the Internet. In *Reno v. ACLU* (1997), the Court, by a vote of seven to two, invalidated several portions of the Communications Decency Act of 1996. Writing for the majority, Justice Stevens recognized the importance of protecting minors from access to this material but found that the government could not restrict access by adults to achieve that end. The Court refused to modify its jurisprudence on regulating material in *Ashcroft v. ACLU 1* (2002). A facial challenge was brought against the Child Online Protection Act (COPA) because it utilized the Miller test to ban offensive material on the Internet. Justice Thomas announced the opinion of the majority that the use of the "community standards" prong of the Miller Test to identify what is harmful to children did not cause COPA to be substantially overbroad. The Court addressed the issue again in *Ashcroft v. ACLU 2* (2004), where it further considered COPA. Justice Kennedy, writing for the majority, explained that this second attempt to "make the Internet safe for minors," failed the strict scrutiny test. The Court recognized the state's interest in protecting minors from exposure to profanity and indecency on the Internet. However, it found that preventing access to such material by adults or making it difficult using methods like filtering software were not narrowly tailored to protecting children. Justice Kennedy explained that the Congress could pass a law encouraging the use of filtering software, not mandating it, which would give parents the ability to protect their children without criminalizing protected speech.

The Court has addressed the question of whether Congress could condition federal assistance for Internet access to public libraries on the installation of software that blocked obscene or pornographic images, or other material which could be dangerous for minor children. In *United States v. American Library Association* (2003) the Court ruled that Congress has the authority to require public schools and libraries receiving E-Rate discounts to install web filtering software as a condition of receiving federal funding. In a plurality opinion, the Supreme Court ruled that: 1.) public libraries' use of Internet filtering software does not violate their patrons' First Amendment free speech rights; and 2.) The Children's Internet Protection Act is not unconstitutional. The Court stated that Internet access in public libraries "is neither a 'traditional' nor a 'designated' public forum." A public forum is created when the government makes an affirmative choice to open up an area for use as a public forum. Libraries, however, do not acquire Internet terminals in order to "create a public forum for Web publishers to express themselves, any more than it collects books in order to provide a public forum for the authors of books to speak." The Court explained that the Internet is simply "another method for making information available in a school or library ... [and is] no more than a technological extension of the book stack."

The court heard a free speech challenge to the "disparagement clause" of the Lanham Act in *Matal v. Tam* (2017). This case concerned a rock band's application for federal trademark registration of the band's name, "The Slants." "Slants" is a derogatory term for persons of Asian descent and members of the band are Asian-American. They thought that by taking that slur as the name of their band, they could "reclaim" the term and drain its denigrating force. The Patent and Trademark Office (PTO) denied the application based on the "disparagement clause" of the Lanham Act which prohibits the registration of trademarks that may "disparage or bring into contempt or disrepute" any "persons, living or dead." The court held that the disparagement clause violates the Free Speech clause because it offends a bedrock principle of the First Amendment: Speech may not be banned on the ground that it expresses ideas that offend. The court also dispensed with the government's arguments that trademarks are government speech (if they are, "the Federal Government is babbling prodigiously and incoherently" and "saying many unseemly things" besides "endorsing a vast array of commercial products and services") and that trademarks are a form of government subsidy (subsidy cases involve cash subsidies or their equivalent from the government whereas here the applicant for trademark registration must pay fees to the government).

Thus, the Court has found that speech that may be offensive or indecent because of its near-obscenity or its profane content is generally protected by the First Amendment. However, the Court recognizes exceptions to the general rule for speech in schools that are contrary to the mission of the school and such speech broadcast over the radio or television waves. However, the Court has refused to extend that proscription beyond those two exceptions. Thus, obscene and indecent speech over telephone lines, cable television, and the Internet are protected under the First Amendment.

The court has recently looked at attempts to keep sex offenders off the internet. In *Packingham v. North Carolina* (2017), the court reviewed a North Carolina law that made it a felony for a registered sex offender "to access a commercial social networking Web site where the sex offender knows that the site permits minor children to become members or to create or maintain personal Web pages." North Carolina had prosecuted over 1,000 people for violating this law, including petitioner, who was indicted after posting a statement on his personal Facebook profile about a positive experience in traffic court. The Court unanimously held that the statute impermissibly restricts lawful speech in violation of the First Amendment. Writing for the court, Justice Kennedy noted that even if the Court assumed that the statute was content neutral and thus subject to intermediate scrutiny, it could not survive because it was not "narrowly tailored to serve a significant governmental interest." He observed that a fundamental First Amendment principle is that all persons have access to places where they can speak and listen, and then, after reflection, speak and listen once more. He recognized that today, one of the most important places to exchange views is cyberspace, particularly social media, which offers "relatively unlimited, low-cost capacity for communication of all kinds."

Kennedy wrote that the Court assumed that the First Amendment permits a State to enact specific, narrowly-tailored laws that prohibit a sex offender from engaging in conduct that often presages a sexual crime, like contacting a minor or using a website to gather information about a minor. However, the statute here, as Justice Alito wrote in his concurrence, "sweeps far too broadly to satisfy the demands of the Free Speech Clause." The Court noted that social media allows users to gain access to information and communicate with one another on any subject that might come to mind but with one broad stroke, North Carolina barred access to what for many are the principal sources for knowing current events, checking ads for employment, speaking and listening in the modern public square, and otherwise exploring the vast realms of human thought and knowledge. Foreclosing access to social media altogether thus prevented users from engaging in the legitimate exercise of First Amendment rights. Kennedy wrote that even convicted criminals—and in some instances especially convicted criminals—might receive legitimate benefits from these means for access to the world of ideas, particularly if they seek to reform and to pursue lawful and rewarding lives.

E. Defamation

Defamation is the issuance of a false statement about another person, which injures the reputation of that person. Defamation is divided into spoken defamation (slander) and written defamation (libel). Traditionally, states had the ability to define and punish defamatory speech through tort law without implicating the First Amendment because the Court had long recognized such speech to be outside the protection of the First Amendment. For example, as recently as the 1950s, in *Beauharnais v. Illinois* (1952), the Court explained that libelous speech is not protected by the First Amendment because it is of "such slight social value as a step to truth" that the social interest in social order and morality outweighed any benefit provided by such speech. However, today, defamatory speech has been found to fall within the protections of the First Amendment, especially when the speech concerns a public official or a public figure. As we will see, the tendrils of the First Amendment do reach speech concerning private persons. The ongoing tension in this area is the protection of the right of free speech with a person's right not to have his or her dignity besmirched by the exercise of another's right to free speech.

The Court began to constitutionalize defamation with its decision in *New York Times Co. v. Sullivan* (1964). Before *New York Times*, states were free to define and punish the tort of defamation as they saw fit. In *New York Times*, the Court held that the ability to recover against a tortfeasor for defamatory speech was circumscribed by the First Amendment. In doing so, the Court supplemented the all states' tests for defamation when the speech was about a public official with the requirement that the speech be made with "actual malice." The Court defined actual malice as publication of the speech "with knowledge that it was false or with reckless disregard of whether it was false or not."

New York Times involved a defamation suit by a city commissioner of Montgomery, Alabama. The defendant, the petitioner in the Court, had published an advertisement containing an allegation that after black students had protested at the Alabama state Capitol by singing "My Country, 'Tis of Thee" the Alabama state college expelled their students and "truckloads of police armed with shotguns and tear-gas ringed" the campus. Further, the advertisement alleged that the police sought to "starve [the students] into submission" by locking them in the dining hall after the entire student body refused to reregister. The plaintiff was responsible for supervising the police and fire departments of the city, and he claimed that this reference to the police defamed him. At trial, he won and was awarded $500,000 in damages, which the Supreme Court of Alabama affirmed. The Supreme Court granted *certiorari* and reversed.

Writing for the Court, Justice Brennan began with Alabama law providing that once a plaintiff established that the speech was libelous *per se*, the defendant's only defense is to prove that the speech was "true in all [its] particulars." If he cannot prove that the speech was true, then damages were presumed and the plaintiff could be awarded damages without proof that his reputation was actually damaged. Justice Brennan examined this law against the policies underlying the First Amendment, that public debate should be "uninhibited, robust, and wide-open," and that that debate will sometimes involve unpleasant attacks on public officials. The Court then focused on the fact that in free and vigorous public debate, erroneous statements are inevitable and that they must be protected to ensure that free speech has the "breathing space" that the First Amendment intended it to have. As such, putting the onus of proving truth on the speaker in the face of libel *per se* does not comport with the protections of the First Amendment when the speech involves a public official. Hence, the defamatory content of speech nor factual error suffice to "remove the constitutional shield" from criticizing official conduct of public officials.

Justice Brennan then explained that states cannot use the civil law of libel to accomplish what it cannot do with criminal law. Furthermore, the Alabama law permitted damages *per se* that was 1,000 times greater than a criminal fine and 100 times greater than that under the Alien and Sedition Acts. Under this scheme, the threat of successive civil judgments against a publisher would have a substantial chilling effect on free speech and would risk silencing public debate over crucial issues. Finding that the *New York Times* published the advertisement without checking its own files and that a reasonable examination of the files would have turned up the false nature of the allegations are not sufficient to show that it knew that the publication was false. Furthermore, the paper was not reckless as to the falsity of the advertisement because it did not have a substantial reason to suspect the false nature of the claims because they had come from sources with a strong reputation for accuracy. The Court found that at most, the paper's actions constituted negligence that failed to meet the standard required to show actual malice.

New York Times dealt with a public official plaintiff against a private party, but it did not address situations involving defamation of private persons who have achieved fame and notoriety. It also did not distinguish between speech relating to purely private concerns and speech on matters of public issues. In *Rosenblatt v. Baer* (1966), the Court explained that all public employees are not public officials. Rather, it applies, at a minimum, to public employees who have or are perceived to have "substantial responsibility for or control over the conduct of governmental affairs." The Court's constitutionalization of defamation continued over the next three decades as it clarified the test and its application to situations, including those above.

Three years after it crafted and applied the actual malice standard to public officials, the Court extended it to public figure plaintiffs in *Curtis Publishing Co. v. Butts* (1967), but it could not muster a majority opinion. *Curtis* was a consolidated case involving the former head football coach at the University of Georgia, the incumbent athletic director at the school at the time of the suit, and a former general in the U.S. Army. Articles were published claiming that the athletic director had fixed a football game while he was the head coach and that the former general had commanded a crowd in a racial protest, orchestrating an assault on federal marshals. Writing for the plurality, Justice Harlan explained that the actual malice standard applied to public figures because, like public officials, they command "sufficient continuing public interest" and they have sufficient access to channels of communication to combat the statements in the media. Further, he differentiated public figures into two forms: (1) the person who is a public figure merely because of his position, and (2) the person who injects himself into the " 'vortex' of an important public controversy."

The Court solidified its actual malice standard in *Gertz v. Robert Welch, Inc.* (1974). Writing for the majority, Justice Powell explained that the actual malice standard developed in *New York Times* was applicable only to public officials and public figures and not private plaintiffs. Furthermore, he used the distinction, introduced in *Curtis*, between people who are public figures for all purposes and those who are public figures solely because of their intentional involvement in a controversy of public importance. The first form of a public figure was called a public figure for all purposes, and the second form was called a public figure for the limited issues into which she injected herself. The Court explained that the lessened protection of public officials and public figures was balanced by their access to the channels of communication to use self-help to combat the defamatory statements. Because private persons do not generally command the same access, they need additional protection. To that end, the Court held that the states are free to define defamation as it applies to publishers or broadcasters of defamatory material that harms a private individual. Further, it placed two important limits on the states' ability to permit recovery for defamation. They cannot provide liability without fault, and they cannot permit recovery of presumed or punitive damages without meeting the actual malice standard as defined in *New York Times*. Additionally, the Court refused to adopt the content-based distinction suggested by the plurality in *Rosenbloom v. Metromedia, Inc.* (1971), where a private individual would have to meet the actual malice standard if the issue was one of public interest even if she did not inject herself into the controversy.

The *New York Times* actual malice standard, which allowed the public to criticize a public official for his conduct, was extended in the 1970s to include anything related to fitness for office, *Ocala Star-Banner Co. v. Damron* (1971). In *Damron*, a small newspaper published that a city mayor had been charged with perjury, which turned out to be false due to an editor's inadvertent mix-up. The newspaper printed two retractions before the election period, however, the city official sued for libel believing his reputation was permanently damaged. The trial judge incorrectly did not instruct the jury to apply the actual malice standard, and on appeal the Court took the opportunity to reiterate that a criminal charge against a public official, no matter how remote in time or place, is always "relevant to his fitness for office," in application to the *New York Times* rule of reckless disregard of the truth, as it held in *Monitor Patriot Co. v. Roy* (1971).

Thus, today there is a substantial distinction between the protections that states can provide to victims of defamation that is based solely on their status in the public eye. A public official or a public figure is accorded less protection because of access to the media to refute the defamatory statements. Consequentially, one must show that the publication or broadcast was made with actual malice that is, knowing that the statement was false or acting in reckless disregard of the falsity of the statement. A person may become a public figure by either (1) holding a position that by its nature generates public interest in that person, or (2) injecting him or herself into the forefront of a public controversy. However, a person who is not a public official and who is not a public figure enjoys the greatest protection. The state is free to permit her to recover under the traditional common law tort of defamation as long as it does not (1) permit strict liability, or (2) permit recovery for presumed or punitive damages without meeting the actual malice standard. Such is illustrated in *Time, Inc. v. Firestone* (1976), where a newspaper published false statements about dissolution of marriage litigation between a wealthy and well-known couple. The Court held that the wife of the industrial scion was not a public figure and that the act of filing for divorce or holding a press conference was not enough to make the issue one of public controversy.

F. Disclosure of Confidential Information and Other Speech-Related Torts

The Court has addressed the application of the First Amendment to the government's ability to provide relief for other speech-related torts aside from defamation. The Court holds that the *New York Times* standard limits the ability of the government to permit recovery by public officials or public figures for intentional infliction of emotional distress and for false light invasion of privacy. Regarding public disclosure of private facts, the Court holds that the First Amendment prohibits recovery for information that is not of legitimate public concern if (1) it was obtained from public records, (2) it was not obtained unlawfully, and (3) it was reported truthfully.

1. *Intentional Infliction of Emotional Distress*

The Court definitively applied its First Amendment jurisprudence regarding intentional infliction of emotional distress in *Hustler Magazine v. Falwell* (1988). The plaintiff, a nationally known Christian minister and active commentator on politics and public affairs, was the subject of an advertisement in the defendant's magazine. The ad was a parody of another ad that featured a transcript of a fictional interview with the plaintiff that portrayed him as a drunk and immoral and suggested that he only preached when he was intoxicated. The Court held that public officials and public figures may only recover for intentional infliction of emotional distress when the publication was made with actual malice as defined in *New York Times*. Writing for the majority,

Chief Justice Rehnquist explained that such parodies are protected by the First Amendment for the same reasons that defamatory speech is protected. He traced the long and storied history of parodic publications in American political and public debate, finding that the quality of American political dialogue "would have been considerably poorer without them."

In *Snyder v. Phelps* (2010), the Court reaffirmed the applicability of the actual malice standard to IIED cases and the proposition from *Connick v. Myers* (1983) that "speech on public issues occupies the highest rung of First Amendment values" even when the form of such speech is unsettling to the general public. Fred Phelps, the founder and leader of the Westboro Baptist Church (Westboro) of Topeka, Kansas, and his followers believe that God hates America for tolerating homosexuality and is punishing the country by killing United States military members who are serving abroad. Seeking media coverage for their message, Westboro attends military funerals to protest, holding signs declaring "God Hates Fags," "Thank God for IEDs," "Thank God for Dead Soldiers," and other things. Westboro held such a demonstration near the funeral site for Marine Lance Corporal Mathew Snyder and subsequently his father, Albert Snyder, filed suit for Intentional Infliction of Emotion Distress and other tort claims.

Writing for an 8–1 Majority, Chief Justice Roberts found that the speech of Westboro was on a matter of public concern and despite the proximity to Snyder's funeral, was protected by the First Amendment. Justice Roberts observed that "While these messages may fall short of refined social or political commentary, the issues they highlight—the political and moral conduct of the United States and its citizens, the fate of our Nation, homosexuality in the military, and scandals involving the Catholic clergy—are matters of public import." He also noted that "The signs certainly convey Westboro's position on those issues, in a manner designed, unlike the private speech in *Dun & Bradstreet*, to reach as broad a public audience as possible. And even if a few of the signs—such as "You're Going to Hell" and "God Hates You"—were viewed as containing messages related to Matthew Snyder or the Snyders specifically, that would not change the fact that the overall thrust and dominant theme of Westboro's demonstration spoke to broader public issues."

The Court held that merely finding that speech is "outrageous" for the purposes of applying state tort law does not overcome the "special protection" afforded to speech on matter of public concern. Westboro did not disrupt the funeral and picketed peacefully on public land 1,000 feet from the church hosting the funeral. The Court reaffirmed that even hurtful speech, which pertains to public issues, can be important to public debate and so Mr. Snyder could not recover for his tort claims.

Justice Alito dissented arguing that "it is well established that [IIED] can be satisfied by speech" and where a defendant is not disputing that the rigorous standards if IIED are satisfied and that their speech "go[es] beyond all possible bounds of decency" the speaker cannot argue that the First Amendment "gave them a license to engage in such conduct." Alito believes that the content of the Westboro church goes "far beyond commentary on matters of public concern" and were purposefully attacking the deceased in an attempt to garner attention for their message. Moreover, Alito emphasizes that unlike in *Hustler* the plaintiff here is not a public figure and so the purposeful targeting of such a person should diminish First Amendment protections targeting such a person. Justice Alito would have reversed the lower court and remanded in support of Mr. Snyder's tort claim.

2. *False Light Invasion of Privacy*

The tort of false light invasion of privacy involves the (1) publication, (2) of private information, (3) that is reasonably believed to be factual, and (4) places the person in a false light. The Court addressed this tort in the context of public officials and public figures in *Time, Inc. v. Hill* (1967). *Hill* involved the publication of an article about a play that closely mirrored the plaintiff's experience in which his family was held prisoner by three escaped convicts. The article expressly drew the comparison between the play and the plaintiff's ordeal, which had been widely reported in the media when it happened. Foreshadowing its later decision in *Rosenbloom v. Metromedia, Inc.* (1971), the Court held that because the article involved events of public concern, the tougher *New York Times* standard applied and required the plaintiff to meet the actual malice standard. However, the modern standard for false light invasion of privacy mirrors the standard from *Gertz*. Private persons may recover actual damages as long as the state does not permit strict liability, but they may only recover presumed and punitive damages if they meet the *New York Times* actual malice standard; public figures must meet the *New York Times* actual malice standard to recover actual damages.

3. *Publication of Private Facts*

The tort of publication of private facts involves the (1) publication, (2) of private facts, (3) that are not of legitimate public concern, and (4) would be offensive to a reasonable person. The Court holds that the First Amendment prevents recovery when the facts are obtained from public records, were lawfully obtained, and reported truthfully. The leading case is *Cox Broadcasting Corp. v. Cohn* (1975). *Cox Broadcasting* involved the publication of the name of a rape victim. The information was true, and it was publicly available because it was contained in court documents that were a matter of public record. The Court found that the First Amendment prevented recovery in this situation. Justice White, writing for the majority, explained that once information had been disclosed to the public by its inclusion in court documents, the press could not be punished for reporting it. To hold otherwise "would invite timidity and self-censorship" that would likely lead to suppression of information that should be available to the public.

In *Bartnicki v. Vopper* (2001), the Court addressed a similar issue. *Vopper* involved a situation in which published information was obtained by lawful means, was truthful, and involved matters of public concern. However, the information was obtained by an intermediary third party who received the information unlawfully. The information at issue dealt with negotiations between the Pennsylvania State Education Association, a teachers' union, and the local school board. The negotiations which had been contentious, received wide coverage in the media. During one conversation between the president of the teacher's union and the union's chief negotiator, the union president said that if the board did not move, the union would go to the homes of the board members and "blow off their front porches" because they had "to do some work on some of those guys." The Court held that, because the information was a matter of such public concern, the defect in the chain between the source and the publisher was not sufficiently tainted to remove the First Amendment's protection of that speech.

In sum, the Court has applied the First Amendment to speech-related torts other than defamation. The First Amendment requires the *New York Times* actual malice standard to limit recovery for the torts of intentional infliction of emotional distress and false light invasion of privacy, holding public officials and public figures to a higher standard of proof than private plaintiffs. The ability of states to permit recovery for the tort of public disclosure of private facts has also been circumscribed by the First Amendment such that once otherwise private information has been disclosed in public documents, the information may be published with impunity as long as the information was lawfully acquired.

G. Attempts to Add New Categories of Unprotected Speech

The Court has permitted content-based restrictions on speech only for a few historic categories of speech, including incitement, obscenity, defamation, speech integral to criminal conduct, so-called "fighting words," child pornography, fraud, true threats, and speech presenting some grave and imminent threat the Government has the power to prevent.

Periodically the Court is asked to create new categories of speech not protected by the First Amendment. Typically, the Court refuses. This chapter has already addressed two such attempts, hate speech (unrelated to true threats, incitement to imminent violence or fighting words) and computer simulations of adolescents in sexual positions. The following three cases are notable for the large majorities the Court commanded in each case, showing that current First Amendment doctrine is widely accepted on the Court.

In *United States v. Stevens* (2010) the Court ruled (8–1) that a federal law banning depictions of animal cruelty violated the First Amendment. The law had been enacted primarily to prevent the production of so-called "crush" videos, in which a small animal is stomped or crushed to death, often by a woman wearing high heels. Congress enacted 18 U. S. C. §48 to criminalize the commercial creation, sale, or possession of these depictions of animal cruelty. The statute did not address underlying acts harmful to animals, but only portrayals of such conduct. The acts depicted in crush videos are prohibited by the animal cruelty laws enacted by all 50 States and the District of Columbia.

The Court held that depictions of animal cruelty should not be added to the list of constitutionally unprotected categories of speech, because "depictions of animal cruelty" are not well defined, and there is no history of excluding such depictions from First Amendment protection. The Court rejected the government's proposal that a claim of categorical exclusion from the First Amendment should be based on a simple balancing of relative social costs and benefits. The Court stated, "the First Amendment itself reflects a judgment by the American people that the benefits of its restrictions on the Government outweigh the costs." The Court tried to distinguish its relatively recent creation of child pornography as a category outside First Amendment protection. The Court argued that "*Ferber* presented a special case: The market for child pornography was "intrinsically related" to the underlying abuse, and was therefore "an integral part of the production of such materials, an activity illegal throughout the Nation."

The Court found the statute overbroad. For example, the statute does not require that the depicted conduct be cruel; "wounded … or killed" is sufficient so the depiction of the humane slaughter of a stolen cow is illegal. The Court found that the exemptions clause did not save the statute ("any depiction that has serious religious, political, scientific, educational, journalistic, historical, or artistic value"). Most hunting videos would fall outside the exception because they are primarily entertainment, not educational.

In *Brown v. Entertainment Merchants Association (2011)* the Court examined whether a California law imposing restrictions on violent video games comported with the First Amendment. The law prohibited the sale or rental of "violent video games" to minors, and required their packaging to be labeled "18." In a 7–2 decision the Court struck down the law, ruling that video games were protected speech like other forms of media. Writing for the majority, Justice Scalia said, "Like the protected books, plays, and movies that preceded them, video games communicate ideas—and even social messages—through many familiar literary devices (such as characters, dialogue, plot, and music) and through features distinctive to the medium (such as the player's interaction with the virtual world). That suffices to confer First Amendment protection."

Finally, in a 6–3 decision, the Court in *United States v. Alvarez (2012)* struck down *The Stolen Valor Act*. This federal law had made it a crime to falsely claim receipt of military decorations or medals and provided an enhanced penalty if the Congressional Medal of Honor was involved. The government argued that false statements have no value and hence no First Amendment protection, pointing to defamation and fraud as examples. However a plurality of the Court applied strict scrutiny and concluded that falsity alone was not sufficient to exclude speech from First Amendment protection. The Court noted that in addition to falslity, defamation required a knowing and reckless falsehood. Fraud typically requires justifiable reliance by the alleged victim on the false statement, and injury to the alleged victim as a result. Another two justices applied intermediate scrutiny and concluded that while false statements were entitled to some protection, the Stolen Valor Act was invalid because it could have achieved its objectives in less restrictive ways. Writing for the plurality, Justice Kennedy said, "Permitting the government to decree this speech to be a criminal offense, whether shouted from the rooftops or made in a barely audible whisper, would endorse government authority to compile a list of subjects about which false statements are punishable. That governmental power has no clear limiting principal. Our constitutional tradition stands against the idea that we need Oceania's Ministry of Truth" (invoking George Orwell's novel *1984*).

H. Speech of Public Employees

Thus far, we have considered freedom of speech in the context of private persons. However, does the First Amendment extend the same protection to the speech of government officials and public employees? The Court has addressed this question in two distinct areas. First, the Court has held that the government can prohibit participation in political activities by government employees. Second, the government may prohibit its employees from speaking on matters of public concern if its interest in efficient operations outweighs the employee's interest in such speech.

1. Prohibition of Participation in Political Activities

The Court upheld the government's power to prohibit its employees from participating in partisan political activities in *Union Public Workers of America (C.I.O.) v. Mitchell* (1947). The plaintiffs sought to enjoin the enforcement of Section 9(a) of the Hatch Act based on the First Amendment's protection of free speech. Section 9(a) of the Hatch Act read, "[n]o officer or employee in the executive branch of the Federal Government [shall] take any active part in political management or in political campaigns." Writing for the majority, Justice Stanley Reed explained that the government has the ability to regulate the political conduct of its employees, including political contributions of money. He then compared the provisions of the Hatch Act to statutes regulating political contributions of money by public employees, finding that the Hatch Act was a regulation of the political contributions of time and energy. The Court held that the government can "regulate the political conduct of government employees" so long as the regulations fall "within reasonable limits." Thus, the government has the power to prohibit its employees from participating in partisan political activities as long as the regulations are reasonable.

Justice Black wrote in dissent that there was no rational distinction between First Amendment protections of private citizens and those of government employees. Further, he argued that while a few high-ranking government employees may abuse their positions to coerce citizens, "muzzl[ing] millions of citizens" was not an appropriate response.

2. Speech by Government Employees in the Workplace

The Court has addressed the government's ability to punish its employees for their speech in the workplace. In *Connick v. Myers* (1983), the plaintiff, an assistant district attorney, was terminated because she created and distributed a survey among her co-workers about the office's transfer policy, its morale, and the need for a committee to address employee grievances. The plaintiff distributed the survey because she had been informed that she would be transferred to a different section. Shortly after she distributed the questionnaire, she was terminated for insubordination (and because she refused to accept the transfer). The Court held that the government's interest in efficient operation outweighed the First Amendment interest implicated by the termination.

Writing for the majority, Justice White expanded on the Court's decision in *Pickering v. Board of Education* (1968). He explained that the Court must weigh the government's interest in efficient operation against the speaker's interest because the questionnaire contained a question involving a matter of public interest. However, because it only contained one question, it only touched on matters of public concern in a very limited context. Justice White characterized it as an employee's grievance regarding an internal policy of the district attorney's office. Balancing against the plaintiff's slight interest in the speech was the fact that the speech occurred at the office, it involved the application of the policy at issue to the speaker, and the plaintiff had to disrupt her own work to distribute the questionnaire. Thus, the Court found that the government's interest in efficient operations and avoidance of disruptive activities outweighed the plaintiff's relatively slim interest in speaking. Justice Brennan's dissent, joined by Justices Marshall, Blackmun, and Stevens, wrote that the Court's decision would deter public employees from making statements critical about the operation of government agencies.

The Court addressed the same issue in *Rankin v. McPherson* (1987) and applied *Connick* in reaching its decision. The plaintiff, a low-level probationary employee who could be fired at any time and for any reason, had been fired because of a racially charged remark she made about her own race. The remark concerned the attempted assassination of President Ronald Reagan and was made in the presence of another employer whom the plaintiff did not know was present. The Court found that the plaintiff's interest in making the statement outweighed the government's interest in efficient operations and held that her discharge was improper.

Writing for the Court, Justice Marshall found that the statement addressed a matter of public concern and that the test outlined in *Pickering* and expanded in *Connick* applied. Weighing in favor of the government was the fact that the plaintiff made the statement at work in the government office. However, the plaintiff's statement did not disrupt the office's operation, and it had not disturbed or interrupted other employees. She did not bring disrepute onto the office because she spoke in the office and not in public, and nobody else heard the statement. Furthermore, Justice Marshall pointed out that the plaintiff had been fired because of the content of the speech and that her position in the office was not sufficiently high to subject the content of her speech to such scrutiny. He also explained that to uphold the plaintiff's discharge would unnecessarily burden other similarly situated employees by causing them to censor themselves because their boss could overhear them and deem them unworthy to serve in the office. Therefore, the Court found that the plaintiff's interest in speaking outweighed the government's interest in maintaining an efficiently operating agency. Justice Scalia, in a dissent joined by the Chief Justice, Justice White, and Justice O'Connor, wrote that the statement by the plaintiff was so close to words that receive no protection from the First Amendment that it should not enjoy protection in this context.

In *Garcetti v. Ceballos* (2006), the Court analyzed whether a public employee should be afforded First Amendment protection when that expression was made pursuant to their duties in the workplace. Ceballos was a deputy district attorney in Los Angeles who wrote a memo to his superiors after becoming concerned that an affidavit contained serious misrepresentations. The memo recommended the case against the defendant be dropped and raised a considerable amount of debate with Ceballos' superiors. In the aftermath of the events, Ceballos claimed he was subjected to retaliatory employment actions, including the denial of a promotion. The Court held that First Amendment protections did not extend to Ceballos' expressions because they were in furtherance of his duties as a deputy attorney. Unlike in *Pickering*, the expressions made here were not of public concern which would render greater First Amendment protection.

In their dissent, Justices Souter, Stevens, and Ginsburg reasoned that First Amendment protection should not be classified by where and how it occurs but rather by the content of the expression: "Private and public interests in addressing official wrongdoing and threats to health and safety can outweigh the government's stake in the efficient implementation of policy, and when they do public employees who speak on these matters in the course of their duties should be eligible to claim First Amendment protection."

Justice Breyer also wrote a dissenting opinion because he believed the court should apply the *Pickering* standard, "even though the government employee speaks upon matters of public concern in the course of his ordinary duties . . ." He reasoned that by nature, government functions deal with matters of public concern. Here, the fact that Ceballos was speaking in furtherance of his professional duties does not negate the fact that he was speaking on an issue that concerns the general welfare of the public.

The Court also addressed the rights of public employees to associate in *Elrod v. Burns* (1976). In 1970 a newly elected Democratic Sheriff proceeded to fire several employees who were members of the Republican Party. Historically, the practice of the new Sheriff was to replace all non-civil-service employees with members of his own party. This practice is referred to as patronage. Because they were non-civil-service employees, they were not protected from arbitrary discharge by any statute or ordinance. The Court held that the practice was unconstitutional and relied on earlier rulings holding the government could not condition public employment on political faith.

In *Heffernan v. City of Paterson, New Jersey* (2016) Heffernan was demoted from his position as a detective in the office of the chief of police after fellow officers saw him holding a yard sign and speaking with campaign workers for the challenger in the Paterson, N.J., mayoral race. Although the challenger was a good friend of his, Heffernan was not involved in the campaign (and, as a non-resident of Paterson, was not even eligible to vote in the election); he was picking up a sign for his bedridden mother, whose sign had been stolen from her yard. Nevertheless, he was demoted the following day because of his "overt involvement" in the challenger's campaign, although his supervisors were mistaken about that involvement. The Court held that "when an employer demotes an employee out of a desire to prevent the employee from engaging in political activity that the First Amendment protects, the employee is entitled to challenge that unlawful action under the First Amendment . . . even if, as here, the employer makes a factual mistake about the employee's behavior." The Court found that whether the employer's act was based on a factual mistake or not did not matter because it can still "cause the same kind, and degree, of constitutional harm."

Hence, speech by public employees is substantially less protected than speech by private persons. The First Amendment does not protect such speech unless it is about a matter of public concern. Once the speech is found to be a matter of public concern, then the Court balances the employee's interest in speaking against the government's interest in efficient government operations. If the government's interest outweighs the employee's interest, the speech may be regulated.

I. Government Speech

Another category of speech outside First Amendment protection or challenge is government speech. The government may promote its own speech and message without requiring viewpoint neutrality. The government is not infringing the free speech rights of individuals when the government declines to use content and viewpoint neutrality in its own speech. When the government expresses a message based on policy choices, it necessarily is involved in content and viewpoint based discrimination. For the government to communicate policy choices, it must be free to do so without fear of a First Amendment challenge.

In *Rust v. Sullivan* (1991), physicians filed suit challenging the facial validity of a Congressional Act. Title X of the Public Health Service Act was a program that provided government funding for family planning services. The program prohibited doctors from providing any type of counseling on the use of abortion as a method of family planning. Women were still able to receive referrals for abortions and general counseling so long as it was not part of the government funded program. The physicians claimed the limitations violated both the First and Fifth amendments. The Supreme Court held the "Government can, without violating the Constitution, selectively fund a program to encourage certain activities it believes to be in the public interest, without at the same time funding an alternative program which seeks to deal with the problem another way." The Court reasoned that the government could choose what speech and viewpoint it funds, which naturally excludes other messages, and this would not be considered viewpoint discrimination for First Amendment purposes.

In *Rust*, the Court addressed a regulation on government funding of a public message. This is distinguishable from the issue in *Legal Services Corporation v. Velazquez* (2001), which dealt with government funding of private speech. In 1974 Congress enacted the Legal Services Corporation Act. The Act established the Legal Services Corporation (LSC) as a nonprofit organization in the District of Columbia. The purpose of the LSC was to distribute funds to local grantee organizations "for the purpose of providing financial support for legal assistance in noncriminal proceedings or matters to persons financially able to afford legal assistance." The issue arose out of one of the restrictions placed on LSC grantees and their clients. The condition at issue prohibited "legal representation funded by recipients of LSC moneys if the representation involves an effort to amend or otherwise challenge existing welfare law." This restriction was interpreted to prevent an attorney "from arguing to a court that a state statute conflicts with a federal statute or that either a state or federal statute by its terms or in its application is violative of the United States Constitution."

The Court held this restriction on speech unconstitutional. The Court reasoned that the purpose of the government funds was to provide indigent clients access to attorneys who would advocate on their behalf. The attorney speaks for the indigent client, not the government. The Court was particularly concerned with how the limitation would impair the function of the judicial system. The Court stated the restriction "sifts out cases presenting constitutional challenges in order to insulate the Government's laws from judicial inquiry." Further, problems would arise in situations where attorneys were forced to withdraw from a case once a challenge to a statute arose. In those cases, the clients would likely not be able to procure representation through any other source. Unlike in *Rust*, where women had alternative access to abortion counseling, indigent clients would not have an alternative source to receive "vital information respecting constitutional and statutory rights bearing upon claimed benefits."

In *Johanns v. Livestock Marketing Association* (2005), the Court confirmed the constitutionality of a government-compelled subsidy for the purpose of funding the government's own speech. Several beef farmers objected to provisions within the Beef Promotion and Research Act of 1985. The Act established a government policy of "promoting the marketing and consumption of 'beef and beef products,' using funds raised by an assessment on cattle sales and importation." The program included various domestic television and print campaigns, market and food science research, and overseas marketing. The farmers filed suit claiming the forced subsidy violated the First Amendment by compelling speech they did not agree with. Prior to this case, the Court had only addressed compelled speech where the individual was forced to personally express a message they disapproved of, and cases where the government forced an individual to subsidize a message from a private party. Here, the challenge was to a forced subsidy that funded the government's own message. The Court held the case involved a First Amendment challenge to government speech. And therefore, regardless of the details surrounding the speech, the government was immune to a constitutional challenge on First Amendment grounds.

The Court dealt with the issue of whether a religious group could force the Government to allow the group to erect a monument in a public park in *Pleasant Grove City, Utah v. Summum* (2009). The public park contained 15 permanent monuments, including a wishing well, historic granary, the City's first fire station, a September 11 monument and a Ten Commandments monuments. 11 of these 15 displays had been donated by private groups of individuals. Summum, a religious organization, wrote the City on two separate occasions requesting permission to erect a monument which would contain "the Seven Aphorisms of SUMMUM." The City denied these requests, and the religious group filed suit alleging the City violated their free speech rights. Justice Alito, delivering the unanimous opinion of the Court, upheld the City's refusal of the Summum monument because the City's decision to accept certain privately donated monuments while rejecting others is a form of government speech not subject to First Amendment scrutiny.

The court affirmed that the Free Speech Clause only restricts government regulation of private speech, it does not regulate government speech. The Court recognized that public parks are traditionally public forums, however monuments in public parks are closely associated with the viewpoints of the government and convey the government's message. The key issue is whether the government is creating a forum for private speech, which is governed by the First Amendment, or whether the government is the speaker, in which case the First Amendment does not apply.

In *Agency for International Development v. Alliance for Open Society International, Inc.* (2013) the Court held that the requirement that nongovernmental organizations wishing to receive funding from the federal government for HIV and AIDS programs overseas, adopt a policy explicitly opposing prostitution violates the First Amendment. Chief Justice John Roberts, writing for the majority, said that the government cannot force a private organization to publicly profess a viewpoint that mirrors the government's view but is not held by the organization itself. Such a requirement would be considered a form of "leveraging" and in violation of the First Amendment protection of free speech.

The Court addressed the issue of whether specialty license plates were government speech in *Walker v. Texas Division, Sons of Confederate Veterans, Inc.* (2015). In a 5–4 split, the Court held that Texas's specialty license plate designs constituted government speech and therefore Texas was entitled to reject a proposal for plates featuring a Confederate battle flag. The Court's rational was threefold. First, history shows that States, including Texas, have long used license plates to convey government speech, e.g., slogans urging action, promoting tourism, and touting local industries. Second, Texas license plate designs "are often closely identified in the public mind with the [State]." Each plate is a government article serving the governmental purposes of vehicle registration and identification. The governmental nature of the plates is clear from their faces: the State places the name "TEXAS" in large letters across the top of every plate. Texas also requires Texas vehicle owners to display license plates, issues every Texas plate, and owns all of the designs on its plates. The plates are, essentially, government IDs, and ID issuers "typically do not permit" their IDs to contain "message[s] with which they do not wish to be associated." Third, Texas maintains direct control over the messages conveyed on its specialty plates, by giving the Board final approval over each design. Like the city government in Summum, Texas "has effectively controlled the messages [conveyed] by exercising final approval authority over their selection." These considerations, taken together, show that Texas's specialty plates are similar enough to the monuments in Summum to call for the same result.

Justice Alito authored the dissent and argued that these license plates were private speech because although they unquestionably contain some government speech, with over 350 specialty plates in Texas, they were little mobile billboards. The messages on the plates honor numerous colleges and universities, high schools, fraternities or sororities, the Masons, the Knights of Columbus, the Daughters of the American Revolution, a realty company, and even a favorite soft drink. To deny the Sons of Confederate Veterans their requested plate is viewpoint discrimination. "Texas, in effect, sells that space to those who wish to use it to express a personal message — provided only that the message does not express a viewpoint that the State finds unacceptable. That is not government speech; it is the regulation of private speech."

J. Commercial Speech

Commercial speech, over time, has moved from being unprotected speech to partially or less protected. Traditionally, commercial speech was a completely unprotected category of speech so the government could regulate commercial speech without regard to the First Amendment. However, in the mid-1970s, the Court began to extend the protections of the First Amendment to commercial speech. The level of protection afforded to commercial speech is less than that of the fully protected categories, thus commercial speech is a less protected category of speech. The current analysis of protection of commercial speech first requires the court to determine whether the speech is commercial speech. Once the speech is found to fall in that category, the court must determine whether the speech is protected. For commercial speech to be regulated, the Court uses a four element test: (1) the speech must be about lawful activities and it must not be misleading, (2) the government interest must be substantial, (3) the law must advance the interest directly, and (4) the regulation must only be as extensive as necessary to achieve the interest.

1. *What Is Commercial Speech?*

The Court has developed a definition that, although appearing to be specific, fails to provide sufficient clarity to be a bright-line test. Its definitions are focused on speech that advertises. However, it has yet to fully consider what speech, other than advertisements, would qualify as commercial speech. Not all advertisements constitute commercial speech, and paid editorial advertisements fall within the protection of the First Amendment in order to promote the interchange of ideas. The current test consists of three elements: (1) the speech must be an advertisement, (2) the speech must refer to a specific product, and (3) there is an economic motive behind the speech.

When the Court indicated that the First Amendment protected commercial speech in *Virginia State Board of Pharmacy v. Virginia Citizens Consumer Council, Inc.* (1976), the Court defined commercial speech as speech that only proposes a commercial transaction. Unfortunately, this definition proved difficult to apply in practice because it was understood to mean advertisements, but there were advertisements, such as political campaign ads, that were clearly not commercial. The Court altered the definition of commercial speech in *Central Hudson Gas & Electric Corp. v. Public Service Commission of New York* (1980). In *Central Hudson*, the Court expanded commercial speech to include expression that solely concerns the economic interests of the speaker and its audience. However, this definition was more extensive than necessary because it could reach the content of publications or broadcastings, which, although being solely concerned with the economic interests of the speaker and the audience, would fall within the protections of the First Amendment.

The expansion of commercial speech dealing with the campaigns continued in *McIntyre v. Ohio Elections Commission* (1995). A woman was arrested for distributing leaflets expressing her opposition to a proposed school tax levy. The distribution of campaign literature without the name and address of the author was a violation of the Ohio Elections Commission Code. The Court found this Ohio Code provision was a violation of the First Amendment because the freedom to publish anonymously is protected. Justice Stevens explained, "the interest of having anonymous works enter the marketplace of ideas unquestionably outweighs any public interest in requiring disclosure as a condition of entry." The Court further held that bans of this kind were regulations of core political speech.

The Court expressed the modern test for whether speech is commercial speech in *Bolger v. Youngs Drug Products Corp.* (1983). *Bolger* involved a condom manufacturing company that also published informational pamphlets about sexual topics. Some of the brochures dealt with condoms in general, and others addressed the specific products made by the company. The Court examined the pamphlets and determined that they constituted commercial speech. The Court explained that its previous tests were not sufficient, and it formulated the modern test. It said that just because the pamphlets were advertisements was not sufficient to find that the speech was commercial, thus it rejected *Virginia State Board of Pharmacy*. Further, the Court rejected *Central Hudson* and stated that because the pamphlets were produced under an economic motive would not suffice on its own. The Court concluded that the proper test was the combination of all of these characteristics. Thus, commercial speech is (1) advertisement, (2) referring to a specific product, (3) motivated by economics.

2. *The Test for Regulation of Commercial Speech*

As stated in the previous section, the Court began to lend some protection to commercial speech in its decision in *Virginia State Board of Pharmacy v. Virginia Citizens Consumer Council* (1976). A few years later, the Court announced the test that has survived until today. In *Central Hudson Gas & Electric Corp. v. Public Service Commission of New York* (1980), the Court's four-part test for regulating commercial speech requires: (1) the speech must not be misleading and must concern lawful activity, (2) the government must have a substantial interest in regulating the speech, (3) the regulation must directly advance the government interest, and (4) the regulation must be no more extensive than necessary to serve the government interest. Stated another way, the Court applies intermediate scrutiny to regulations of commercial speech regarding lawful activities that are not misleading. Although this test has generally survived, there is still some debate over the degree of deference to be accorded the government in determining its compliance with the last two elements of the test.

The debate has centered on whether the Court requires that the regulation be the least restrictive alternative in achieving the government interest. In addressing this question, the Court has not provided clear and consistent direction. However, as of today, it appears that although the Court does not require that the regulation be the least restrictive means of advancing the government interest, it must still be narrowly tailored to achieve that interest.

Board of Trustees of the State University of New York v. Fox (1989) involved a challenge to the state's regulation of commercial solicitations on college campuses. The majority rejected requiring the regulation be the least restrictive alternative. The Court interpreted the restrictions of the last two prongs of the test to require only that the regulation be narrowly tailored to achieve the government interest. Writing for the majority, Justice Scalia expressly drew a distinction between commercial speech and noncommercial speech. He stated that the former enjoys "'a [more] limited measure of protection'" than noncommercial speech because it held a "'subordinate position in the scale of First Amendment values.'"

The Court appeared to take a less deferential view of the extent to which regulation advances the government interest and the breadth of the regulation in *Rubin v. Coors Brewing Co.* (1995). In *Rubin*, the Court required the regulation to directly and materially advance the asserted government interest. Writing for the Court, Justice Clarence Thomas further required the government to prove that the dangers that it asserts are posed by the commercial speech to be regulated are real and that the regulation "'will in fact alleviate them to a material degree.'" This language is clearly inconsistent with the language in *Fox*. The Court continued to struggle with the formulation of the last two elements of the *Central Hudson* test over several years, producing two plurality opinions with diametrically opposed viewpoints on the question.

However, the Court appeared mostly to settle the issue in its recent decision in *Lorillard Tobacco Co. v. Reilly* (2001). *Lorillard Tobacco* involved a Massachusetts regulation on the advertising and sale of cigarettes, smokeless tobacco, and cigars. The regulations placed various restrictions on advertising and promotional materials placed outdoors and at the point of sale, product samples, cigar labels, and retail and mail order transactions for tobacco products. The Court expressly rejected the petitioners' request to jettison the *Central Hudson* test and replace it with a strict scrutiny test. Instead, it reaffirmed *Central Hudson* and explained that the First Amendment only requires that the regulation be narrowly tailored to achieve the government's objective. While the Court mustered a majority behind the *Central Hudson* test, four Justices dissented in part. This reveals that there is still some indecision in the application of the last two elements of the *Central Hudson* test. For now, the Court holds that the last two elements only require the regulation to be narrowly tailored to achieving the substantial government interest.

3. *Application to Specific Situations*

a. *Commercial Speech about Illegal Activities & Commercial Speech That Is Misleading or False*

The Court has held that commercial speech about illegal activities, or that is misleading or false, is not protected by the First Amendment. The Court has only addressed the advertisement of illegal activity in *Pittsburgh Press Co. v. Pittsburgh Commission on Human Relations* (1973). There, the Court explained that commercial speech advertising illegal activity could be regulated without offending the Constitution. Note that this case was decided before the Court extended any protection to commercial speech and before the Court announced the *Central Hudson* test. However, because the *Central Hudson* test expressly excludes illegal speech from its reach, the Court's later decision clearly excluded this speech from the reach of First Amendment protection.

The same analysis holds for commercial speech that is deceptive or misleading because such speech does not contribute to the public dialogue in any meaningful manner. Though the First Amendment protects false, deceptive, and misleading speech in the noncommercial context (as discussed in the section on defamation and other speech-related torts) it does not protect such speech in the commercial context.

b. *Solicitation of Clients by Attorneys and Accountants*

The Court initially established that putting a complete ban on legal service advertisements in newspapers was unconstitutional (*Bates v. State Bar of Arizona*, 1977). Though the Court initially held that attorney advertising could not be regulated, it has since held that attorneys may engage in truthful advertisement of their services so long as the advertisement is not deceptive, subject to regulation. It is permissible to regulate the in-person solicitation of potential clients by attorneys if motivated by profit. Yet lawyers may solicit potential clients where they will represent the client for free and may not be punished for doing so. In *Ohralik v. Ohio State Bar Association* (1978), the Court found that Ohio's punishment of an attorney for in-person solicitation of the victim of a car accident was permissible when the solicitation was in person and in the hospital. The Court reasoned that personal solicitation of legal services for profit inherently risked fraud, undue influence, or misrepresentation. On the same day that it decided *Ohralik*, the Court decided *In re Primus* (1978), where it found that the punishment of an attorney for in-person solicitation of a potential client violated the First Amendment because the lawyer offered to represent the person free of charge. Thus, in-person solicitations by attorneys are not protected when they are motivated by profit, but are protected when the representation will be for free.

The Court stopped this permissible regulation of attorney solicitation at the personal level. Any solicitation by targeted, direct mail is protected, whether the representation would be for free or was motivated by profit. In *Shapero v. Kentucky Bar Association* (1988), the Court invalidated a Kentucky law that prohibited such solicitation because the parties are at less of a risk of deceptive or unfair practices by the attorney because the solicitation was in writing and there would be a paper trail for a court to follow. Although it may not be prohibited, it may still be regulated. In *Florida Bar v. Went For It, Inc.* (1995), the Court upheld a Florida law prohibiting direct mail solicitations of potential personal injury or wrongful death clients within thirty days of the accident leading to the cause of action. The Court found that such direct solicitation was invasive and intended to preserve the public's confidence in the profession. The dissent disagreed, finding that such solicitation was not invasive and could harm the victims by delaying their ability to get representation. Therefore, attorneys may make direct mail solicitations of clients, but this may be regulated to some degree.

In contrast to the regulation of in-person solicitation of clients by attorneys where the solicitation is motivated by profit, the Court prevents such regulation of solicitation by accountants. In *Edenfield v. Fane* (1993), the Court held invalid a state law prohibiting certified public accountants from soliciting business in person. The Court distinguished *Ohralik*, finding that such solicitations by accountants did not pose the same dangers as in-person lawyer solicitations for profit. Thus, states may not regulate in-person solicitation of accountants like it can for lawyers.

c. Regulating the Trade Names of Businesses

The Court has found that the use of trade names by a business was not protected by the First Amendment. It considered the speech to be commercial speech "and nothing more." The Court found that a state law constitutional that prohibited optometrists from advertising or offering their services under a trade name in *Friedman v. Rogers* (1979). The Court justified this because it found that the use of trade names inherently risked deception. A bad optometrist could simply change the trade name under which he practiced, hiding his true identity. This would permit him to assume the identity of a reputable optometrist who retired or went out of business and then fool the public into thinking he was the good optometrist. Because the Court couched its decision in the inherent deceptiveness of trade names, it seems likely that other speech that is inherently deceptive can be regulated. One could even analogize this with the Court's decision to allow regulation of in-person attorney solicitations for money, just discussed, because the overreaching it feared would be a form of deception. Thus, governments have the ability to regulate trade names for businesses and, arguably, any other speech that inherently risks deceiving the public.

d. Regulation of Commercial Speech as a Means to Combat Other Problems

The Court generally prohibits states from limiting commercial speech where the justification is that people will be better off without the information. The First Amendment value is that people are better off when they have more information. The Court has upheld some restrictions on commercial speech that is truthful, nondeceptive advertising of legal activities when the restrictions are aimed at addressing other problems, such as traffic safety.

The Court has upheld such restrictions on speech where the speech would negatively impact traffic safety. But this is an unsettled field. An example of a case upholding this type of regulation was *Railway Express Agency v. New York* (1949). There, the Court upheld a city ordinance that banned advertisements on trucks where the advertisement was not related to the usual business of the truck owner. The Court applied what was later called rational basis scrutiny and found that the city may have determined that those who advertise their own business on their own trucks do not pose the same traffic problems as those whose trucks contain the advertisements of others.

More than thirty years later, the Court upheld a city ordinance banning all outdoor billboards in *Metromedia, Inc. v. City of San Diego* (1981), to the extent that the ordinance only applied to commercial advertisements. Noncommercial advertisements, such as by candidates for political office, could not be banned. The Court explained that the restriction on commercial speech was permissible because it was a less protected category of speech and billboards are traffic hazards and unattractive.

The soundness of *Metromedia, Inc.* is in doubt due to the Court's decision in *City of Cincinnati v. Discovery Network, Inc.* (1993). In *City of Cincinnati* the Court invalidated a city ordinance prohibiting the distribution of commercial newspapers on news racks but permitting the sale of noncommercial papers on the same racks. The Court explained that because the law was a content-based distinction that was unrelated to the asserted "other purpose," it was unconstitutional.

The Court has also generally limited the ability of the government to regulate certain activities or products with the goal of reducing participation in the activities or consumption of the products. The Court addressed this question regarding alcohol at the federal level in *Rubin v. Coors Brewing Co.* (1995) and at the state level in *44 Liquormart, Inc. v. Rhode Island* (1996). In both cases, the law ran afoul of the *Central Hudson* requirement that the regulation be narrowly tailored. Similarly, the Court struck down a state regulation of tobacco advertising in *Lorillard Tobacco Co. v. Reilly* (2001) because it also failed the narrow tailoring requirement of the *Central Hudson* test.

However, the Court has permitted states to regulate gambling advertisements to reduce gambling. In *Posadas de Puerto Rico Associates v. Tourism Company of Puerto Rico* (1986), the Court upheld a law prohibiting casino advertisements. The Court explained that the regulation was a valid exercise of the state's police power to protect the health, safety, and welfare of its citizens and that the law was narrowly tailored to achieve those ends. The Court extended these findings to advertisements for lotteries in *United States v. Edge Broadcasting Co.* (1993). In this case, a federal law prohibited the advertisement of one state's lottery by a station located in another state that did not have a lottery. The Court followed *Posadas* and upheld the law because of the government's interest in discouraging gambling. In *Greater New Orleans Broadcasting Association, Inc. v. United States* (1999), the Court struck down a federal law banning advertising by casinos because it was not narrowly tailored to achieve the goal of reducing gambling (the many exceptions permitted advertisements by casinos located on Native American reservations).

The Court has also clearly held that the government may not restrict the advertising of abortion services or of contraceptives. The Court has held that such advertising is strictly within the protection of the First Amendment, and that prohibiting such advertisements because they may offend or embarrass others, as claimed in *Carey v. Population Services International* (1977), is not permitted.

Similarly, the Court has long held that truthful and non-deceptive advertisements by professionals are protected by the First Amendment. State regulation of lawyer advertising has generated many cases. For example, in *Zauderer v. Office of Disciplinary Counsel of the Supreme Court of Ohio* (1985), the Court held that lawyer advertisements are protected by the First Amendment as long as they are not deceptive. The attorney had been disciplined because his advertisement contained information about a specific legal problem, included an illustration, and was deceptive. The Court struck down the first two bases for the discipline but upheld the third.

Similarly, the Court has held that signs advertising property for sale may not be proscribed by the government. In *Linmark Associates, Inc. v. Township of Willingboro* (1971), the Court addressed an ordinance banning the display of "for sale" or "sold" signs to deter white flight from a racially integrated neighborhood. The Court accepted as valid the ordinance's goal of preventing white flight but held that the government could not achieve that goal by "restricting the free flow of truthful information." The Court unanimously held that such restrictions based on the theory that people are better off with less information were invalid and violated the First Amendment.

Checkpoints

- **Unprotected and Less Protected Speech**
    - Advocacy of Illegal Action—Modern Test
        - The speech must be (1) directed at producing imminent lawless action and (2) the likely to bring about the imminent lawless action.
    - Fighting Words and the Hostile Audience
        - Speech that is so patently offensive or insulting that it would provoke a violent reaction from even a reasonable person constitute fighting words.
        - Under the hostile audience doctrine speech must cause or be imminently about to cause a disturbance of the peace.
    - True threats of illegal, violent harm are not protected by the 1st A. (Watts v. U.S., 1969).
    - Hate Speech can only be restricted if it falls under an existing category of restricted speech.
    - Sexually Oriented Speech
        - The Court has created three categories of sexually oriented speech: (1) obscenity; (2) child pornography; and (3) profanity and indecency.
        - Obscenity and child pornography are unprotected speech and laws prohibiting them need only pass the rational basis test.
            - Under *Miller*, material is obscene if:
            1. The average person would find that the work appeals to the prurient interests when viewing the work as a whole and applying contemporary community standards;

2. The work describes or depicts sexual conduct defined by the applicable law in a patently offensive way; and
3. As a whole, the work lacks serious literary, political, scientific, or artistic value.

- Under *Stanley*, one has a constitutionally protected right to possess obscene materials.
- However, under *Reidel*, no one has a constitutionally protected right to produce, distribute, or sell obscene materials.
- Under *Ferber*, the government may regulate or proscribe child pornography without applying the *Miller* test when the material depicts minors in sexual acts and actual minors were used.
- However, under *Ashcroft v. Free Speech Coalition*, where the material purports to depict children engaging in sexual acts, but no actual children were used, the *Miller* standard applies.

- Profane and indecent speech are protected by the First Amendment, thus laws punishing this speech must pass strict scrutiny.
- However, the Court has identified limited exceptions to this protection for such speech in schools and on the broadcast media.
- But the Court has refused to extend those exceptions to First Amendment protections to telephones, cable television, and the Internet, thus they are protected under the First Amendment.
- Public libraries and schools are neither traditional nor designated public forums so Congress can condition federal assistance for Internet access to them on the installation of software that blocks obscene or pornographic images.

- Defamation
  - The First Amendment requires that a public official or a public figure cannot recover for defamation without proving that the publication was made with actual malice, defined as knowing that the publication was false or acting with reckless disregard of its falsity.
  - A public official is a public employee who controls, or is perceived to control, the conduct of governmental affairs.
  - Under *Damron*, a criminal charge against a public official, no matter how remote in time or place, is always "relevant to his fitness for office."
  - There are two kinds of public figures:
    - A person who, by virtue of her position, generates public interest in her, is a public figure for all purposes and in all contexts; and

        - A person who injects himself in the forefront of a public controversy becomes a public figure for the limited purposes of that controversy and related issues.
    - A private person still enjoys protection from defamation under the traditional definition, except that states cannot permit a private person to recover on a strict liability theory.
    - Further, a private person may not recover presumed or punitive damages without meeting the amplified actual malice standard.
- Speech-Related Torts Other Than Defamation
    - The *New York Times* standard applies to the ability of public figures and public officials to recover for intentional infliction of emotional distress and for false light invasion of privacy.
    - The First Amendment prevents recovery for publication of true information that is private, once that information is released to the public, such as through publication in court documents, and is obtained lawfully.
- Speech by Public Employees
    - The government can prohibit participation in political activities by government employees.
    - The government may prohibit its employees from speaking on matters of public concern if its interest in efficient operations outweighs the employee's interest in such speech.
    - This prohibition is lawful when the speech contains matters of public concern yet is made in furtherance of the employee's job.
- Government Speech
    - Speech on behalf of the federal government is generally immune to constitutional challenges.
    - The government may promote one idea or activity at the exclusion of another without being viewpoint discriminatory.
    - The government is prohibited from enacting restrictions or conditions on funding that interferes with private speech or the judicial function.
    - The government cannot force a private organization to publicly profess a viewpoint that mirrors the government's view but is not held by the organization itself
    - Government may compel the payment of subsidies to be used in funding government speech.

  - Specialty license plate designs constitute government speech and therefore states are entitled to reject a proposal for plates based on its message.
- Commercial Speech
  - Commercial speech is (1) an advertisement; (2) that refers to a specific product; and (3) is motivated by economic motives.
  - The First Amendment protects commercial speech, but it protects it less than noncommercial speech. Not all advertisements constitute commercial speech, and paid editorial advertisements fall within the protection of the First Amendment.
  - The Court applies a four-part test to determine the validity of regulations of commercial speech. This test requires: (1) a substantial interest in regulating the speech; (2) the regulation must directly advance the interest; (3) the regulation must be no more extensive than necessary to serve the interest; and (4) the speech must not be misleading and must concern lawful activity.
  - The last two prongs of the test are understood only to require that the regulation be narrowly tailored, not the least restrictive means, to achieve the government interest.
  - The First Amendment does not protect commercial speech that is misleading, deceptive, or false or concerns illegal activities. Thus, a regulation of such speech need only pass rational basis scrutiny.
  - It is unconstitutional to put a complete ban on legal service advertisements.
    - Attorneys may engage in truthful advertisement of their services as long as the advertisement is not deceptive, subject to regulation.
    - Any solicitation by targeted, direct mail is protected, but may be regulated to some degree.
    - In-person solicitations by attorneys are not protected when they are motivated by profit, but are protected when the representation will be for free.
  - The use of trade names by a business is not protected by the First Amendment.
  - States generally cannot limit commercial speech where the laws were enacted under the theory that people will be better off without the information.
    - However, the Court has upheld some restrictions on commercial speech that is truthful advertising of legal activities when the restrictions are aimed at addressing other problems, like traffic safety.

- The Court has struck down regulations of certain activities or products with the goal of reducing participation in the activities or consumption of the products.
- But the Court has permitted states to regulate gambling advertisements to reduce gambling in the state.

Chapter 3

Level of Free Speech Protection Differs Based on Location of Speaker

---

Roadmap

- **Impact of Location on Freedom of Speech**
  - The First Amendment protects not only free speech, but where and when speech may occur.
  - There are three categories of public spaces—public forums, limited public forums, and nonpublic forums.
    - A public forum is a public place that has been traditionally been open to the public for speech.
    - A limited public forum in a public space opened by the government specifically to be used for speech.
    - A nonpublic forum is government property that is neither a public forum nor a limited public forum.
  - There is no right to free speech on private property.
  - The government may regulate the speech of its employees, and may choose to fund speech that could be attributed to promoting a government message.
  - The Court grants deference to speech occurring in schools, prisons and militaries because of the unique characteristics of these environments.

I. Level of Free Speech Protection Differs Based on Location of Speaker

The many forms of expression that constitute "speech" occur in a multitude of locations. Historically, the vast majority of people lacked access to the mass media (i.e., radio, TV, newspapers, magazines, etc.) so their opportunities for expression were to go door to door, hand out tracts or demonstrate on street sidewalks, or organize meetings in public parks or meeting halls. The internet changed this lack of access to the larger community. The internet is the dominant and pervasive technology of the Information Age and much of the entire world is now connected. Thus an individual can potentially reach millions of people with a message. Of course, the First Amendment began before the advent of electricity so free speech cases began with simple or no technology and have progressed up to today's internet age.

All speech occurs in a place and through a medium. First Amendment jurisprudence delineates the levels of speech protection based on when and where speech occurs as well as its medium. Typically, these issues arise when people try to use public property for their speech, however, they also arise when people try to speak on private property they do not own, such as shopping centers. Today there is no right to use private property for speech purposes because the constitution only applies to the government, not individuals or private entities.

This section examines the Court's decisions regarding the places where speech occurs. It covers speech on public property, private property, and finally, speech restricted environments, which are certain domains the Court finds to be substantially less protected by the First Amendment, such as schools, prisons or the military.

A. Government Properties

Initially, the Court rejected that the public had any right to speak on public property. It refused to recognize that there was any difference between speech on public property and speech on private property. In the early cases involving speech on public property, the Court held that the government can control speech on public property just as strictly as a private person may control speech on his or her property. In *Davis v. Massachusetts* (1897), the Court upheld the conviction of a minister for preaching in Boston Common without a license. In so holding, the Court expressly stated that the government has the power to control the manner in which the public may utilize public property and analogized the government's power to that of the owner of a private residence. To the *Davis* court, this power was inherent in the government's role as the representative of the public, and it could not logically be limited unless it interfered with proprietary rights.

This attitude persevered until 1939 when the Court began to recognize that the public had the right to speak on at least some public property that had been traditionally opened for and used by the public for the exchange of ideas. This revolution in thought began with *Hague v. Committee for Industrial Organization* (1939), when the Court found a Jersey City, New Jersey, ordinance facially invalid. The ordinance prohibited all public meetings in the streets and other public places unless a prior permit had been obtained. In his plurality opinion, Justice Owen Roberts wrote that regardless of the ownership of streets and public parks, they have, since time immemorial, "been held in trust for the use of the public and, time out of mind, have been used for purposes of assembly, communicating thoughts between citizens, and discussing public questions."

The revolution in the Court's jurisprudence continued in *Schneider v. New Jersey* (1939). In that consolidated case, a majority of the Court invalidated city ordinances from different states that prohibited the distribution of pamphlets by individuals on public property. The cities attempted to validate their ordinances as valid exercises of the police power because they were motivated by prevention of littering in the streets and that permitting such distribution of pamphlets would encourage littering. Justice Roberts, writing for the majority, rejected this argument. He explained that the government may regulate the use of the streets to protect the health, safety, and welfare of the public as long as it does not infringe with the right of free speech or other fundamental liberty interests. He contrasted the ordinance with other methods of controlling the public's use of the streets such as blocking traffic on the streets or prohibiting the act of littering by explaining that such regulations would not necessarily have any relationship to the freedom to write, speak, or distribute information. To hold otherwise would be to permit the police to determine which ideas may be expressed and which ideas may not be expressed. However, Justice Roberts was very careful to state that the holding in *Schneider* did not extend to commercial solicitations or canvassing, which could be regulated by the state as necessary, even under the ordinances at issue in the case.

The Court's decision in *Hague* began the legal recognition of the concept of a public forum. A public forum is a public place that has either traditionally been open to the public to use for speech or a place that is specifically designated by the government as being open to the public for speech.

The Court expressly articulated the concept of a public forum and provided three categories of public spaces—public forums, limited public forums, and nonpublic forums—in *Perry Education Association v. Perry Local Educators' Association* (1983). There, the Court described the streets and parks as "quintessential public forums" because they have "by long tradition or by government fiat . . . been devoted to assembly and debate." These public spaces enjoy the greatest free speech protection. The Court then explained that places that the government has "voluntarily opened" for the public to use for communication also receive substantial protection, but they are more limited because the government may close down these limited public forums. Finally, the Court described those places that are not traditionally considered public forums and forums the government does not open for purposes of communication. In these nonpublic forums, the government is free to reserve the space for its intended use and may more readily restrict the speech that occurs there. The constitutionality of a speech regulation on public property depends on the characterization of the public space. Thus, whether a public place is a public forum, a limited public forum, or a nonpublic forum is the threshold question in analyzing restrictions of speech in public spaces, and that determination may be determinative of the regulation's constitutionality.

1. *Public Forums*

Under *Perry Education Association*, the Court recognized that the public's interest in speaking in public forums is very strong. Public forums are those public places that have been traditionally devoted to speech and assembly or have been so designated by government fiat. Sidewalks and parks are the archetypical public forums. In public forums, the government's ability to regulate speech is sharply curtailed by the First Amendment.

The *Perry Education Association* court expressly stated that the government cannot prohibit all expressive activity in public forums. To determine the constitutionality of a regulation of speech in a public forum, the law must be either a reasonable content-neutral time, place, and manner restriction, or it must pass strict scrutiny. If the restriction is a content-neutral time, place, and manner restriction, it must also serve an important government interest and leave adequate alternative venues for the speech. Finally, the restriction must be narrowly tailored to achieve the government interest, but it need not be the least restrictive alternative.

a. Content-Neutral Speech

To be content-neutral, the regulation must not restrict either the viewpoint or subject matter of the speech. As an example, *Boos v. Barry* (1988), discussed elsewhere, the Court invalidated a city ordinance prohibiting signs critical of a foreign government to be displayed within 500 feet of that government's embassy. The Court held that the regulation targeted political speech on sidewalks, traditionally recognized as public forums. However, the Court upheld another aspect of the ordinance that permitted the police to disperse crowds within 500 feet of the embassy of a foreign government if the crowd threatened the peace or public safety. This latter aspect of the ordinance was sustained because it was a valid exercise of the police power that applied regardless of the subject matter or the viewpoint expressed in the speech.

Regulations of demonstrations provide difficult questions and can lead to different results on apparently similar facts. Contrast *Carey v. Brown* (1980) with *Hill v. Colorado* (2000) and *McCullen v. Coakley* (2014). In *Carey*, the Court invalidated a state statute prohibiting people from picketing or demonstrating around an individual's residence unless the residence was used either as a place of business or as a place of employment and was involved in a labor dispute. The Court found that the statute was not content-neutral because it treated certain views on a certain subject differently than others. However, the Court took a different view of demonstrations and protests outside an abortion clinic. In *Hill*, the Court sustained the regulation of protests within 100 feet of any health care facility, finding that the regulation was content-neutral. The regulation prohibited any person from knowingly coming within eight feet of another person, without that person's consent, for the purpose of passing literature, showing a sign, or orally protesting, educating, or counseling the other person. The Court explained that the law was content-neutral because it applied regardless of the subject matter or viewpoint expressed in the speech. The dissent argued that the law was clearly content-based because it had the purpose of curtailing a specific message.

In *McCullen v. Coakley* (2014), a unanimous Court found that a Massachusetts law that criminalized standing on a public road or sidewalk within thirty-five feet of a reproductive health care facility violated the First Amendment. The majority concluded that the law, although targeting abortion clinic protests, is content and view-point neutral and therefore not subject to strict scrutiny under the First Amendment (The Court in *Hill* reached the same conclusion about the buffer zones in Colorado). The Chief Justice in *McCullen* then applied lesser (but still substantial) scrutiny reserved for neutral laws restricting the time, place, and manner of speech, as did the Court in *Hill*. But while Justice Stevens and his majority found that the buffer zone in *Hill* was narrowly tailored, the Chief Justice's majority in *McCullen* found that the Massachusetts's law was not. One could argue that, even though *McCullen* did not explicitly overrule *Hill*, its rationale effectively renders buffer zones like Colorado's unconstitutional. Perhaps the determining factor was the difference between the laws in the two cases: *Hill* involved an eight-foot floating buffer zone around individuals within a hundred feet of abortion clinics, while *McCullen* involved a thirty-five-foot fixed buffer zone.

One could reconcile *Carey*, *Hill* and *McCullen* by noting that the Court appears to focus on whether a law is justified on some content-neutral grounds, regardless of its intent and effect.

b. Time, Place, and Manner Restrictions

The Court has long held that the government can regulate the time, place, and manner in which individuals may use a public forum to speak. Time, place and manner restrictions are a crucial aspect to the police power because they help the government ensure that the public's use of space for nonspeech purposes, such as transportation in the case of the streets, is not hampered by the speech that occurs there. Furthermore, they help the government regulate the use and availability of scarce public resources. However, a time, place and manner regulation must be content-neutral and reasonable. If the regulation is content-based or unreasonable, the regulation must pass strict scrutiny.

In *Cox v. New Hampshire* (1941), the Court addressed a state statute that forbade unlicensed parades, processions, and other public performances on a public street. The statute set out the requirements for licensure in the margin of the statutory text. 68 people were arrested for violating the statute. They, along with twenty others, had met and divided into groups before marching on the sidewalk. Each marcher carried a staff with a religious message written on it. The marchers also passed out religious leaflets. On review, the Court found that the statute was a content-neutral and reasonable time, place, and manner restriction. The Court explained that the licensing provision was not a prior restraint on speech because of the limiting guidelines the statute provided. Requiring the permit provided the authorities with sufficient prior notice of the event so that they could "prevent confusion by overlapping parades or processions . . . secure convenient use of the streets by other travelers, and minimize the risk of disorder." Because the statute was not discriminatory (and was not applied as such), it was a reasonable restriction.

In *Reed v. Town of Gilbert* (2015), the Court examined a municipal ordinance that regulated the manner in which signs could be displayed in public areas. The ordinance imposed stricter limitations on signs advertising religious services than signs that displayed "political" or "ideological" messages. When the town's Sign Code compliance manager cited a local church for violating the ordinance, the church filed a First Amendment challenge based on freedom of speech. Writing for a unanimous Court, Justice Clarence Thomas held that the town's sign ordinance was "content based on its face" in light of the fact that the "restrictions in the Sign Code that apply to any given sign [depend] entirely on the communicative content of the sign." Because the church's signs were "treated differently from signs conveying other types of ideas," strict scrutiny applied. Justice Thomas rejected the Ninth Circuit's conclusion that the ordinance was content-neutral because the regulations were not based on "disagree[ment] with the message conveyed" and the reasons for regulating the various categories of signs were "unrelated to the content of the sign[s]." Rather, he emphasized that "[a] law that is content based on its face is subject to strict scrutiny regardless of the government's benign motive, content-neutral justification, or lack of 'animus toward the ideas contained' in the regulated speech." Justice Thomas explained that "innocent motives" do not eliminate the danger of censorship, because governments may one day use content-based laws to regulate "disfavored speech."

In *Heffron v. International Society for Krishna Consciousness, Inc.* (1981), the Court upheld a state regulation restricting to designated areas any group distributing literature, selling materials, and soliciting donations at a state fair. This rule applied to all groups—nonprofits, charitable organizations, and commercial vendors—equally. Although the representatives of a group could walk around the fairgrounds and communicate orally with the patrons, distribution and sales could only occur at a booth leased from the fair. The booths were leased on a first-come, first-served basis and in a nondiscriminatory fashion. The state fair in question was located on a 125-acre tract of public property. In the preceding five years, the twelve-day fair had attracted an average of 115,000 people on weekdays and 160,000 people on weekends. The Court found the regulation to be a valid time, place, and manner restriction. Justice White explained that the regulation did not discriminate based on the content of the speech. Furthermore, it did not prohibit speech—only where and how it could occur at a certain time. Finally, the regulation was directed at an important government interest: protecting public safety and ensuring orderly conduct at the fair. Justice White emphasized that the restriction need not be the most reasonable restriction to achieve the interest, it must merely be a reasonable restriction.

In contrast, consider *Police Department of Chicago v. Mosley* (1972). There, the Court addressed the constitutionality of a Chicago ordinance prohibiting disorderly conduct. The statute expressly defined disorderly conduct to include "picket[ing] or demonstrat[ing] on a public way within 150 feet of any ... school" during school hours. However, the statute expressly excluded "peaceful picketing of any school involved in a labor dispute." The respondent, a frequent picketer of a Chicago high school because it practiced racial discrimination, challenged the ordinance as violating his right to picket the school. The Court found the statute unconstitutional because it provided for different treatment of speech based on the content of that speech (picketing in a labor dispute with the school was permissible, but no other picketing or demonstrating was). The Court explained that this content discrimination violated the Equal Protection Clause of the Fourteenth Amendment as well as the First Amendment. Justice Marshall explained that the ordinance designated certain speech as impermissible by its content, not by how, when, or where the speech occurred, which "is never permitted." The ordinance did not permit all peaceful picketing, only peaceful picketing on a certain subject. Therefore, the Court found the ordinance unconstitutional.

The time, place, and manner restriction must also serve an important government interest. Such interests include maintaining good public order, preventing public disturbances, and maintaining order and discipline in schools. In *Heffron*, the Court upheld the prohibition on distributing literature or soliciting money at a state fair, except in a booth, to control foot traffic and ensure public safety. Similarly, the use of loudspeakers on trucks or other devices to amplify sound could be controlled to prevent disturbing the public. The Court has also permitted the regulation of speech outside a school during school hours to protect against disruption of the school's "peace or good order." All of these restrictions were valid time, place, and manner restrictions because they did not ban all such speech, did not permit some speech but forbid other speech based on content, and were intended to achieve an important government interest.

In *Pleasant Grove City, Utah v. Summum* (2009), a private group fought to have its permanent monument of the Ten Commandments erected in a park, based on the fact that the government had erected other donated monuments. The Court recognized that parks are public forums but distinguished speech in parks from the display of a permanent monument. The latter circumstance is not subject to forum analysis as it is a form of government speech not subject to strict scrutiny (otherwise, if the government were regulating the speech, only reasonable time, place, and manner restrictions would be allowed and the Court would use strict scrutiny).

In *McCullen v. Coakley* (2014), the Court heard a challenge to Massachusetts's Reproductive Health Care Facilities Act, which made it a crime to knowingly stand on a "public way or sidewalk" within 35 feet of an entrance or driveway to any "reproductive health care facility," defined as "a place, other than within or upon the grounds of a hospital, where abortions are offered or performed." The Court observed that the Act was neither content nor viewpoint based, so strict scrutiny did not apply. The Court stated that buffer zones serve the state's legitimate interests in maintaining public safety on streets and sidewalks and in preserving access to adjacent reproductive healthcare facilities. Writing for a unanimous court, Chief Justice Roberts held that 35-foot fixed abortion buffer zone violated the First Amendment because it limited free speech too broadly. The Court observed that the buffer zones "impose serious burdens on petitioners' speech, depriving them of their two primary methods of communicating with arriving patients: close, personal conversations and distribution of literature. Those forms of expression have historically been closely associated with the transmission of ideas." The Court found that the State had not sought a less intrusive approach and stated: "to meet the narrow tailoring requirement, however, the government must demonstrate that alternative measures that burden substantially less speech would fail to achieve the government's interests, not simply that the chosen route is easier."

Thus, the test for a valid time, place, and manner restriction is fourfold. First, it must be content-neutral, both on the subject matter and the viewpoint. Second, the regulation must reasonably restrict the time that speech can occur, where it can occur, and how the speech can be made. This kind of restriction can also protect licensing schemes, as was the case in *Cox*. Third, the restriction must serve an important government purpose. Fourth, it must be narrowly tailored in order not to limit free speech too broadly.

2. *Limited Public Forums*

The Court has also determined that speech on public property that is not a traditional public forum is protected by the First Amendment. According to the Court in *Perry Education Association v. Perry Local Educators' Association* (1983), a limited public forum is a place that the government has opened to the public to use for expressive activities. The distinguishing factor between a limited public forum and a traditional public forum is that, because the government opened the limited public forum to the public to use for speech, it can revoke that access at any time. However, that factor is relevant only to the fact that a limited public forum can be closed to public speech, whereas a traditional public forum cannot. During the time the limited public forum is open for the public to use for speech, the Court has held that that speech enjoys the same protection as that made in traditional public forums. In *Good News Club v. Milford Central School* (2001), Justice Thomas explained that although the government may limit the speech that can be made in a limited public forum, it cannot discriminate based on the viewpoint of the speech. The restriction must also be reasonable when considering the purpose for which the forum is used. Thus, the crucial inquiry is whether the public property is a limited public forum.

Unlike traditional public forums, limited public forums must be opened by the government to the public for purposes of speech. As such, they can and do take many different forms. Public schools and universities who open their property for use by students have been held to be limited public forums. More difficult questions are government spaces that are open to the public, even if not expressly for speech, such as an airport.

In *International Society for Krishna Consciousness, Inc. v. Lee* (1992), the Court addressed just this situation. The case involved a regulation adopted by the Port Authority of New York and New Jersey that prohibited the "repetitive solicitation of money" as well as the distribution of literature. The regulation only governed speech inside the airport terminals and was inapplicable to the sidewalks outside the terminal buildings themselves. The parties did not dispute that the solicitation at issue in the case was speech protected by the First Amendment. The question was the character of the airport terminals: Are they public forums or not? The Court held that they were not. Writing for the majority, Chief Justice Rehnquist began his analysis by recognizing that public streets and parks are traditional public forums because they have been made available for speech since time immemorial. He clarified that statement by describing the traditional public forum as one that has the free exchange of ideas as a principal purpose of the space.

Rehnquist then explored the limited public forum concept. The government must affirmatively act to create a limited public forum. Government inaction by failing to proscribe or restrain speech cannot cause a nonpublic forum to become a public one. Similarly, permitting people to visit or use freely a place owned or operated by the government is not sufficient to promote it to the status of a public forum. Rather, the government must "intentionally open a nontraditional forum for public discourse." He also found that the location of property is relevant to the public forum inquiry. Property separated from "acknowledged public areas" may indicate that the separated property is "a special enclave" and speech there enjoys less protection.

The Court concluded that airport terminals are not traditional public forums or limited public forums. Airport terminals are not traditional public forums because they have only recently become places where great numbers of people come; thus, even if they have been held out for speech, they have not been so held out for a sufficiently long time. Further, it is only within the recent history of airports that they have been used by religious and other nonprofit groups to distribute literature, solicit funds, recruit members, and similar activities. Similarly, airports are not limited public forums. The government has not opened them to public access to use for speech purposes (rather, they are opened for use as transport hubs). The fact that the government has not objected to the use of these airport terminals by religious and other nonprofit groups for speech purposes does not create a limited public forum. Accordingly, the Court upheld the ban on solicitation activity in airport terminals. However, the Court overturned the ban on distribution of literature, finding that the ban was not a reasonable restriction on speech in the nonpublic forum.

The Court recognized schools as a limited public forum in *Christian Legal Society Chapter of the University of California, Hastings College of the Law v. Martinez* (2010). Here, the Court examined a public law school's anti-discrimination policy with which all registered student organizations (RSO) must comply. Christian Legal Society (CLS) required members to sign a "Statement of Faith" and conduct their lives in accordance with prescribed principles, one of those being renouncing homosexuality. CLS was denied RSO status by Hastings "on the ground that the group's bylaws did not comply with Hastings's open-access policy because they excluded students based on religion and sexual orientation." The Court held that the limited public forum precedent was the proper framework for assessing both CLS's First Amendment challenges because the government has the ability to impose reasonable restrictions on speech on property within its control. Justice Ginsburg delivered the opinion of the majority, holding that the anti-discrimination is a reasonable, viewpoint-neutral condition to gain access to the RSO forum. The policy was found to be reasonable because: 1) the Court grants schools much deference when making decisions for their students; 2) the anti-discrimination policy encourages that all students are able to participate in all RSOs; 3) the policy encourages students with different backgrounds to come together instead of allowing groups to exclude members because of their backgrounds; and 4) the policy promotes state-law proscriptions against discrimination. The policy was viewpoint-neutral because it did not favor or disfavor one group over another (the requirements to become a RSO applied to all student groups evenhandedly).

3. *Nonpublic Forums*

The third category of forum is the nonpublic forum. Under the test in *International Society for Krishna Consciousness v. Lee* (1992), a nonpublic forum is a space that is not:

1. traditionally available to the public to use for speech, or
2. opened by the government for the public to use for communication.

Unlike public and limited public forums, the nonpublic forum receives substantially less protection. The Court, in *Perry Education Association v. Perry Local Educators' Association* 1983), stated that with a nonpublic forum, "the state may reserve the forum for its intended purpose, communicative or otherwise, as long as the regulation on speech is reasonable and not an effort to suppress expression merely because public officials oppose the speakers' views."

When the Court held in *International Society for Krishna Consciousness v. Lee* (1992) that airport terminals were nonpublic forums, the Court permitted the airport to prohibit solicitation of airport patrons as a reasonable restriction on speech. However, the Court refused to permit the airport to prohibit distribution of literature by the same group. The Court based its holding on several precedents finding several other places to be nonpublic forums, including advertisement space on buses and military bases.

In *Lehman v. City of Shaker Heights* (1974), the court found a "car card space" on a public transportation bus to be a nonpublic forum because it was not an area traditionally held out to the public for communication. The Court distinguished the car card space from traditional public forums such as "open spaces ... meeting hall[s], park[s], [and] street corner[s]." The Court analogized advertisement in the car card space to advertisements in newspapers, explaining that such an advertisement was not the primary purpose of either venture (and thus, both ventures could exercise discretion in what advertisements they selected). Therefore, the car card space on the public transportation bus was not a public forum.

The Court determined that military bases are not public forums in *Greer v. Spock* (1976). At the time, Fort Dix permitted the public access to nonrestricted areas of the military installation but prohibited them from certain forms of expression, including demonstrations, political speech, and protest marches. The Court recognized that the primary purpose of a military installation is to provide for the training of soldiers, not to provide a public forum for communicative purposes. The Court explained that a commanding officer of a military installation has had the "historically unquestioned power ... summarily to exclude civilians from the area of his command."

The Court upheld the ability of a state to restrict the use of its property and prohibit its use for communication by the public in *Adderley v. Florida* (1966). There, civil rights demonstrators had been convicted for holding a rally outside a jail and for failing to disperse at the order of the police. The divided Court found that as long as the state did not act in a discriminatory manner, the state could exclude the public from using its property to communicate. The dissenting justices reasoned that a jail is a seat of government like an "executive mansion, a legislative chamber, [or] a courthouse," and when the public feels that a prisoner is being unjustly held, the public should be permitted to demonstrate to that effect outside the jail.

4. *Restricted Environments*

The relevance of where the speaker speaks or wishes to speak extends to other contexts. Some places that the government controls, such as schools, prisons, and the military, the Court has granted great deference in regulating speech. Although each of these environments is different, they share some similarities that have led the Court to treat them similarly. Because these environments are places (1) where people are often involuntarily present and (2) that are generally authoritarian out of necessity, the Court tends to accord great deference to regulation of speech and expressive activities in them. However, the restrictions still must be appropriate and the deference not too extreme.

a. Government Workplace — Government as Employer

The Court upheld Congress' ability to regulate government employees' participation in political activities in *United Public Workers of America (C.I.O.) v. Mitchell* (1947). Congress had enacted the Hatch Act in 1940, which made it unlawful for federal employees to engage in certain political activities. A man named Poole, who worked at the polling station and was a ward committeeman, challenged the Act. Justice Reed, writing for the majority, held that Congress may regulate the political activities of government employees "within reasonable limits." The Court emphasized that government employees were still able to voice their opinions at the ballot box. Justice Black dissented, asserting that § 9 of the Hatch Act was overbroad, and had the potential to limit millions of citizens from engaging in political activities, such as federally funded farms and business subsidiaries.

The government also has the ability to punish employees for speech in the workplace. In *Garcetti v. Ceballos* (2006), a deputy district attorney, Ceballos, asserted he was subjected to retaliatory employment action after writing a memo to his supervising attorney regarding possible misrepresentation in an affidavit and advising his supervisor with how to proceed with the case. The Court held that when government employees are speaking as private citizens and not in their official capacity, then their speech in protected. However, when speaking in their official capacity, speech restrictions are justified because "employers have a heightened interest in making sure employees' official communications are accurate, demonstrate sound judgment, and promote the employer's mission." Applying this rule, the Court found that because Ceballos was communicating as part of his official duties, his speech was not protected and could be punished. This was a 5–4 decision and the dissent was concerned about protecting whistleblowers from reprisals.

The Court again found the government could regulate employee's speech in *Connick v. Myers* (1983). When Myers was informed that she would be transferred to a different section of the criminal court, she strongly opposed. Myers prepared a questionnaire concerning several intra-office policies, including the transfer policy. Myers's employment was terminated that afternoon for refusing to accept the transfer. She brought suit, alleging her free speech rights had been violated. The Court relied on *Pickering v. Board of Education* (1968), which established the test that, when determining whether a public employer has properly discharged an employee for engaging in speech, the Court must balance interests. The interest of the employee, as a citizen, in commenting on matters of public concern, must be balanced against the interest of the State, as an employer, in promoting the efficiency of the public services it performs through its employees. Myers speech was held to not be a matter of public concern, only speech which reflected "one employee's dissatisfaction with a transfer and an attempt to turn that displeasure into a cause célèbre."

In *Rankin v. McPherson* (1987), the Court found that an employee's First Amendment rights outweighed her employer's interest in discharging her for speech relating to a matter of public concern. McPherson was a clerical employee, who after learning of the attempt to assassinate President Reagan made the remark to a co-worker "If they go for him again, I hope they get him." The Court again relied on the balancing test of *Pickering.* The Court found that McPherson's comment about the assassination attempt was a matter of public concern, and the comment did not disrupt the work of the office, and so the statement was protected.

In *Lane v. Franks* (2014), the Court held that the *Pickering* test protected an employee who provided truthful testimony in response to a subpoena regarding things that he had discovered in the course of his employment. According to the Court, the question was whether the government had "an adequate justification for treating the employee differently from any other member of the public" based on the government's needs as an employer. In particular, the Court cited the employer's legitimate "interests in the effective and efficient fulfillment of their responsibilities to the public," including "promoting efficiency and integrity in the discharge of official duties," and "maintaining proper discipline in public service." The Court noted that the employer's side of the *Pickering* scale was "entirely empty" because it did not "assert, and cannot demonstrate, any government interest that tips the balance in their favor. There is no evidence that Lane's testimony at Schmitz' trials was false or erroneous or that Lane unnecessarily disclosed any sensitive, confidential, or privileged information while testifying."

Government employees do retain the right to freedom of association. A plurality opinion in *Elrod v. Burns* (1976) found that employees dismissed because of their political beliefs and association violated the First Amendment. Employees at the Cook County's Sheriff's Office, all Republicans, were dismissed or threatened with dismissal after a new Democrat Sheriff was appointed. The employees challenged, alleging their patronage dismissals violated the First Amendment, Fourteenth Amendment, and various statutes. The Court agreed and found that patronage dismissals severely restrict political belief and association, which are at the core of the First Amendment. It found that the government may not force an employee to relinquish his beliefs or association for a public job without severely inhibiting that employee's rights. Justice Powell dissented, arguing that employees who accept patronage jobs, such as at the Sheriff's Office, benefitted because of their patronage, and therefore have not been penalized because of their affiliation.

Public schools can regulate student speech when that speech might be attributable to the school. In *Hazelwood School District v. Kuhlmeier* (1988) the Court found that student speech could be restricted. Students, who were staff members of the school newspaper, were unable to publish stories relating to pregnancy, sexual activity, divorce and birth control. The students challenged the school's ability to censor the content of the newspaper. The principal deleted the stories and published the remainder of the paper. The students attempted to rely on *Tinker v. Des Moines Independent School District* (1969), and argued their rights to freedom of speech "did not end at the schoolhouse gate." The Court disagreed, holding that school's do not offend the First Amendment by exercising control over student speech in student-sponsored expressive activities so long as their actions are reasonably related to legitimate teaching concerns.

b. Government as Funder

The government can regulate funding to certain programs and organizations that essentially promote a government-sponsored message. In *Rust v. Sullivan* (1991), a facial challenge was brought against a statute enacted by Congress that limited Title X funding for family-planning services. The statute restricted any funding from being dispersed to programs where abortions were performed. Those challenging the regulations asserted that restricting funding to programs where abortion was an option resulted in viewpoint discrimination (and thus violated the First Amendment). The Court upheld the statute, recognizing that Congress may "selectively fund a program to encourage certain activities it believes to be in the public interest, without at the same time funding an alternative program which seeks to deal with the problem in another way." The statute was found to not encroach on a doctor's ability to provide or a women's right to receive information concerning abortion-related services outside of the Title X project. Justice Blackmun dissented and was joined by Justices Marshall, Stevens and O'Connor in finding that the statute's limitation of Title X funding to only non-abortion programs clearly targeted a viewpoint. Blackmun further stated that physicians and counselors should provide patients with the full range of information and options, which includes information related to abortions.

In *National Endowment for the Arts v. Finley* (1998), a group of performance artists challenged the National Endowment of the Arts (NEA) grant-making procedures. Congress had enacted an amendment to the NEA criteria that no funds could be used "to promote, disseminate, or produce materials which in the judgment of the NEA may be considered obscene ... when taken as a whole, do not have serious literary, artistic, political, or scientific value." The artists had been recommended for grants by the NEA before the "decency and respect" amendment enacted by Congress, but their applications were subsequently rejected. The Court held that the Government has wide latitude to set spending priorities it believes to serve the public purpose. The "decency and respect" criterion was held not to silence speakers by "expressly threatening censorship of ideas." It merely chose not to fund certain speech and was therefore constitutional.

However, in *Legal Services Corp. v. Velasquez* (2001), the Court held the funding provision of the Omnibus Consolidated Rescissions and Appropriations Act of 1996 (OCRAA), which limited funding distribution of the Legal Services Corporation (LSC), to be unconstitutional. OCRAA prohibited the LSC from funding any organization that represented clients who challenged welfare laws. LSC attorneys challenged the restriction as being unconstitutional, and the Court agreed. In a 5–4 decision delivered by Justice Kennedy, the Court held the funding provision impermissibly limited the arguments attorneys were allowed to make for their clients and therefore violated the First Amendment.

In *Agency for International Development v. Alliance for Open Society International, Inc.* (2013) the court struck down a requirement that to receive federal funding for HIV and AIDS programs overseas, organizations had to adopt an anti-prostitution policy. The Court held that the government cannot force private groups to publicly express certain views as a condition to receiving funding. The Court characterized this coercion as a form of "leveraging" money to compel unwanted speech and a violation of the First Amendment.

The Court did find that the government can prohibit organizations receiving government funding from using the federal funds to cover the costs of speaking out in contradiction to the government's views. Such a restriction, the Chief Justice indicated, assures that funds do not underwrite contrary views. But when the government seeks to control the recipient's views on policy issues, the government pushes beyond the program's limits and violates the First Amendment. The dividing line, the Court held, is between conditions that "define the limits of the Government spending program" by limiting what speech the money can be spent on (which is permissible) and conditions that seek to leverage funding to regulate speech outside the program (which is impermissable).

c. Speech in Public Schools

Arguably, speech restrictions in public school are antithetical to the school's purpose of education, namely to hear and debate a spectrum of views. Two primary issues arise under the First Amendment in the context of restricting speech in public schools. First is the question of the freedom of students to express their ideas. Second is the school's ability to control student access to "objectionable" materials.

Concerning student speech, the Court has recognized that there is some need for order and discipline in the educational settings. As a result, the Court generally defers to the school's determination of what speech is permissible and what would tend to disrupt the order and discipline necessary to further educational objectives.

Early Court decisions were strongly protective of the right of students to speak while in school. In *West Virginia State Board of Education v. Barnette* (1943), students refused to salute the flag at the beginning of the school day. Though it rested its argument primarily on the Religion Clauses of the First Amendment, the Court found that saluting the flag was a form of speech, and schools could not force students to speak. Furthermore, in *Tinker v. Des Moines Independent Community School District* (1969), the Court upheld the right of students to protest the Vietnam War by wearing black armbands. Writing for the Court, Justice Abe Fortas made the famous statement that "neither students [n]or teachers shed their constitutional rights to freedom of speech or expression at the schoolhouse gate." To hold otherwise would be to turn public schools into "enclaves of totalitarianism" (because the wearing of the armbands was a silent protest, it did not disrupt the school's educational efforts). Thus, the Court held that speech was protected by the First Amendment unless it would "materially and substantially interfere with the requirements of appropriate discipline in the operation of the school." The Court extended *Tinker* to postsecondary institutions in *Papish v. Board of Curators of the University of Missouri* (1973) when it overturned the expulsion of a student for publishing a political cartoon in a school newspaper.

In recent years, the Court's tendency has been to defer to school authorities. The Court has become far less protective of the rights of students to speak in the school environment. For example, in *Bethel School District No.*

403 v. Fraser (1986), a student was punished for nominating another student for a student government position in a speech filled with sexual innuendo that was delivered at a school assembly. The Court upheld the punishment. Chief Justice Burger, writing for the majority, emphasized the need for the Court to defer to the judgment of school officials. Further, he distinguished *Tinker* because *Tinker* involved curtailment of political expression, whereas the student's speech in *Fraser* did not.

The Court extended its deferential treatment of the determinations of school officials in *Hazelwood School District v. Kuhlmeier* (1988). In *Hazelwood*, a school principal would not allow a school journalism class to publish certain stories. Writing for the Court, Justice White quoted *Fraser* to explain that the "First Amendment rights of students in the public schools 'are not automatically coextensive with the rights of adults in other settings.'" He emphasized that the school newspaper was a nonpublic forum produced as part of the curriculum of the journalism class, and that schools have the power to control curricula. Thus, the principal had acted within his authority.

With respect to the ability of the school to control student access to "objectionable" materials, the Court has held that the First Amendment protects the right to receive information as well as the right to express it. In *Board of Education, Island Trees Union Free School District No. 26 v. Pico* (1982), the Court addressed whether a school library could remove "objectionable" books from its collection. The Court explained that such action by school authorities directly impacted the First Amendment rights of the students to receive information. Additionally, the unique characteristics of a school library—that it is part of a scholastic institution and is designed to provide student access to materials—make the First Amendment's protections especially applicable. However, if the school library can show a reason for removing or not purchasing certain materials that is not based on content, such as budgetary concerns or that the books were damaged and unreadable, the library would not violate the First Amendment.

Although it is clear that schools are restricted environments and public streets are public forums, when a school-sponsored event takes place on a street in front of a high school during school hours, the Court extends the restricted academic environment to the street. In *Morse v. Frederick* (2007), a student waived a "BONG HITS 4 JESUS" banner in the street, while the school was participating in the 2002 Olympic Torch Relay as it passed through Alaska. The Court gave little thought to alternatively giving the students more speech rights, especially because the principal had a legitimate interest in protecting the students from drug abuse.

d. Prisons

The need for order and discipline in a prison is substantially greater than that in public schools. As a result, the Court has held that the First Amendment does not protect speech by prisoners that is inconsistent with their status or would interfere with the legitimate penological interests of the prison system. The Court generally defers to the regulation of prisoners' speech by applying an analogue of the rational basis test. If the regulation is rationally related to the achievement of a legitimate penological interest, then the regulation will be upheld. As a result of the high deference this test provides, most restrictions of inmate speech are upheld. This deference has also generally extended to restrictions of access to prisoners by members of the press for interviews or to observe conditions in the prison.

In one instance, the Court has overturned a regulation on the content of mail sent by inmates to recipients outside the prison. In *Procunier v. Martinez* (1974), a prison prohibited inmates from mailing letters that either would "magnify grievances" or were "lewd, obscene, defamatory ... or otherwise inappropriate." The Court explained that this regulation was not rationally related to a legitimate penological interest because it was unrelated to maintaining order and discipline within the prison itself (the prison did not have a legitimate interest in preventing prisoners from airing their grievances to non-inmates or in censoring what prisoners wrote to those outside the prison). However, later decisions have called this holding into question. As a result, it is doubtful that *Procunier* is still good law (for example, in *Turner v. Safley*, (1987), the Court upheld a prison regulation restricting the ability of those in one facility to write to prisoners in another facility. The Court agreed that such correspondence could lead to comparisons between the two facilities that could cause dissatisfaction with a facility and cause unrest in the prison). Thus, the Court generally exhibits a high degree of deference to regulations of the speech of inmates in a prison facility.

e. The Military

The deference accorded to the military in regulating the speech of service members has generally exceeded even that of the deference accorded to prisoners. For example, in *Parker v. Levy* (1974), the Court upheld the conviction of an officer by a general court-martial for making statements that were critical of the Vietnam War to enlisted personnel. Furthermore, the officer had stated that black soldiers should refuse deployment in Vietnam because they were being used for the most hazardous duties. In upholding the conviction, Justice Rehnquist explained that the military establishment "is, by necessity, a specialized society separate from civilian society." Justice Douglas dissented reasoning that the officer's words and actions expressed his own deeply held personal beliefs and were not an attempt at subversion.

The extreme deference to the military in regulating the speech of service members has led to restrictions on the military that the Court would not sanction in most other contexts. These include political speech, actions intended as communication, and possession of child pornography, all of which are found to be prejudicial to good order and discipline. For example, in *Brown v. Glines* (1980), the Court upheld an Air Force regulation that prohibited the posting or distribution of printed materials on an Air Force base without the prior permission of the commanding officer. The Court upheld this prior restraint on publication because base commanders are charged with maintaining the essential military characteristics of "morale, discipline, and readiness." He must have authority over the distribution of materials that could affect adversely those characteristics.

B. Private Property

All of the foregoing discussion about government facilities, public forums, limited public forums, and nonpublic forums applies only to property owned by the government. There is no right to use private property for speech. This is because most protections of the Constitution, including free speech, require state action. When an individual person acts on his or her own accord, there is no state action because by definition such action is not by the government. Thus, the owner of private property can restrict the speech of others while they are on that owner's property without running afoul of the First Amendment.

In the past, the Court had found that some types of private property that were open to the public were subject to the Constitution's protections of speech. The Court held in *Marsh v. Alabama* (1946) that a company-owned town could not constitutionally prevent Jehovah's Witnesses from distributing literature within its borders. The Court found that, although the town was owned by a company and was private property, the company essentially acted as a government. The company had assumed the duties and functions of a government in its management of the town and therefore was a *de facto* government. Thus, the company's actions represented state action, and it was restrained by the First Amendment.

Following this decision, the Court compared a shopping mall to the company town in *Marsh* and found in *Amalgamated Food Employees Union Local 590 v. Logan Valley Plaza, Inc.* (1968) that the Constitution's speech protections extended to a labor dispute on the mall's property. The Court essentially considered the shopping mall, an important place where a substantial amount of the public gathered to conduct commerce, to be a microcosm of the town in *Marsh*.

However, the Court has retreated from the view that the First Amendment applies to shopping malls. Today, there is no constitutionally protected right to use shopping malls for speech. The retreat began in *Hudgens v. National Labor Relations Board* (1976), when the Court examined a prior decision that permitted a shopping mall to exclude speakers based on content and found that that was a content-based distinction that was not supportable under the First Amendment. Finding that it could not reconcile that decision with *Logan Valley*, the Court reversed its position and held that the First Amendment does not apply to privately owned shopping malls.

The Court later declared that shopping center owners do not have a constitutional right to exclude speakers. In *PruneYard Shopping Center v. Robins* (1980) the Court held that a state could create a state constitutional right to speak in shopping malls without violating the rights of the property owner under the federal Constitution. Specifically, the plaintiff contended that such a right created under a state constitution violated the plaintiff's rights under the First Amendment and also constituted a taking under the Fifth Amendment that required just compensation. The Court emphatically disagreed.

Today, *Marsh v. Alabama* (1946) remains good law but the Court has not extended that ruling beyond the situation of a company town. Otherwise, there is no right to speak on private property that is protected by the federal Constitution, though any state is free to create such a right under the state constitution (the federal constitution is a basement, not a ceiling for constitutional rights).

The Court has extended private property speech protections to homeowners in regard to picketing in front of a residence but not to prohibit solicitations at residences. In *Frisby v. Schultz* (1988), pro-life townspeople picketed in front of the home a doctor who performed abortions. In response, the Town Board enacted an ordinance that stated: "It is unlawful for any person to engage in picketing before or about the residence or dwelling of any individual in the Town of Brookfield." The town's justification for this ordinance was to ensure "that members of the community enjoy in their homes and dwellings a feeling of wellbeing, tranquillity, and privacy." The Town Board believed that a ban was necessary because it determined that "the practice of picketing before or about residences and dwellings causes emotional disturbance and distress to the occupants . . . [and] has as its object the harassing of such occupants."

Justice O'Connor, writing for the Court noted that the antipicketing ordinance operates at the core of the First Amendment by prohibiting individuals from engaging in picketing on an issue of public concern. Justice O'Connor noted that public streets are the archetype of a traditional public forum but also stated that "the First Amendment permits the government to prohibit offensive speech as intrusive when the "captive" audience cannot avoid the objectionable speech." The Court found that because the resident is "figuratively, and perhaps literally, trapped within the home, and, because of the unique and subtle impact of such picketing, is left with no ready means of avoiding the unwanted speech." The Court upheld the ordinance, but narrowly tailored it to protect unwilling listeners in their homes.

This decision contrasts with one made decades earlier where the Court struck down a city ordinance which made it illegal to distribute door-to-door any "handbills, circulars or other advertisements" in *Martin v. City of Struthers* (1943). Justice Black, writing for the Court, held that the First Amendment protects both "the right to distribute literature" and "the right to receive it" and stated that the distribution of literature is protected "even if it creates the minor nuisance for a community of cleaning liter from its streets."

The distinction between picketing and solicitation is that with solicitation, a private homeowner could place a sign on his door saying he would rather not be disturbed, while no such option exists for stopping a picketer outside the home. The picketing restriction is similar to the Court's decision in *Kovacs v. Cooper* (1949) where the court upheld a city ordinance that barred sound trucks from broadcasting in a loud and raucous manner on the streets. The Court saw plenty of alternative venues to discuss issues by human voice, newspapers, our pamphlets. The Court considered the city's need for reasonable protection in the homes or business houses from the distracting noises of vehicles equipped with such sound amplifying devices as sufficient justification.

Checkpoints

- **Impact of Location on Freedom of Speech**
  - Public Forum, Limited Public Forum and Nonpublic Forum
    - A regulation of speech in a public forum must be: (1) a reasonable, (2) content-neutral, (3) restriction on the time, place, or manner of speech, (4) that achieves an important government purpose.

- A limited public forum is a public space opened by the government specifically to be used for speech.
- A limited public forum is not created simply by opening a public space for use by the public; it must be opened specifically for speech.
- Additionally, the failure of the government to prevent speech in a public space does not create a limited public forum because the creation of a limited public forum requires the government affirmatively to open the public space for speech.
- Regulations of speech in limited public forums must meet the same test as regulations of speech in traditional public forums.
- A nonpublic forum is government property that is neither a public forum nor a limited public forum.
- The government may place reasonable and nondiscriminatory restrictions on expression in nonpublic forums.

- Private Property
  - There is no right to speak on others' private property protected by the federal Constitution.
  - However, a state is free to create such a right protected under that state's constitution without violating the property owner's First Amendment rights or effecting a taking under the Fifth Amendment.
- Restricted Environments
  - Government Workplace—Government as Employer and Founder
    - The government can regulate employee's participation in political activities and certain speech conducted in the workplace.
    - The test of whether a public employee has been improperly punished or discharged for engaging in speech in the workplace requires balancing the interest of the employee, as a citizen, in commenting on matters of public concern, versus the interest of the State, as an employer, in promoting the efficiency of the public services it performs through its employees.
    - Congress may regulate programs and organizations which promote a government message, but that does not mean Congress must then fund all speech on that topic.
    - The government cannot impose a condition on receipt of government funds in a government program that forces private groups to publicly express views it opposes. However, government can prohibit the use of government funds to cover speech that opposes the government's views (*USAID v. Alliance for Open Society International*, 2013).

- Public Schools
  - Public school officials may restrict student speech if that speech would materially and substantially interfere with the need for discipline in the school's operation.
  - The Court generally defers to the determination of school officials about what speech is a material and substantial interference with discipline in the school's operation.
  - However, that deference is not absolute, and the actions taken by the school officials must be reasonable in light of the speech.
  - Public school libraries have the ability to control their collections, but the First Amendment prevents them from removing materials from their collections based on the content of the materials.
  - The Court will allow school officials to prohibit speech that is vulgar and offensive in the interest of protecting minors, when the same speech would be normally be protected by the First Amendment.
- Prisons
  - The Court has developed a rational basis-like test for regulation of speech by prisoners: The regulation will be upheld if it is rationally related to the achievement of a legitimate penal interest.
  - Generally, the Court defers to the judgment of the facility concerning virtually all aspects of speech by prisoners, including between prisoners of different facilities and the access of the press to prisoners for interviews or to observe the conditions.
- The Military
  - Military service members are subject to greater regulation of their speech, including prior restraints on publication at a military installation, than are civilians or even prisoners because of the risk of prejudice to the good order and discipline of the military.
  - The Court generally evinces extreme deference to the judgment of the military because of the special, unique character of the military and its mission.

Chapter 4

Freedom of the Press

Roadmap

- **Freedom of the Press:** The press is subject to generally applicable laws and generally applicable taxes, but is not subject to taxes directed at the press.
  - The press is allowed to observe and report on judicial proceedings—any restrictions on this ability must pass intermediate scrutiny.
  - Broadcast media is subject to greater regulation then print media.
  - Cable companies and programming providers are less regulated than broadcast media.

I. Freedom of the Press

The First Amendment to the Constitution specifically mentions the freedom of the press separately from the freedom of speech: "Congress shall make no law . . . abridging the freedom of speech, or of the press." Although the Freedom of the Press Clause initially applied to only infringements by the federal government, the Court applied the Clause through the Fourteenth Amendment to state and local government in 1931. Freedom of speech and freedom of the press are complementary freedoms so protections afforded for speech are also afforded to the press and many of the protections afforded for speech were developed by laws and government acts restricting freedom of the press. However, the separate mention of the press in the First Amendment has given rise to two competing views of the amendment's protection of the press.

The first view is that the press is accorded greater protection than that provided by the Freedom of Speech Clause. This view is based on the critical role the press plays in a democratic society to create a marketplace of ideas and hold the government accountable to the people. A free media functions as a watchdog that can investigate and report on government wrongdoing. Under this view, restricting the press injures the republic by depriving the people of valuable information critical to the republic's functioning. Justice Powell expressed this viewpoint in his concurrence in *Branzburg v. Hayes* (1972). He argued that the press has a preferred position in our constitutional scheme and deserves additional protection because information is crucial to the proper functioning of our democratic republic. It is important to note that this view is not generally followed by the Court.

The second view argues that the Press Clause does not confer any additional protections beyond that of the Speech Clause for two main reasons. First, historical evidence indicates that the Founding Fathers generally viewed "speech" and "the press" synonymously. Second, it is difficult to provide a complete and accurate definition of the press as a separate group of persons. Any distinctions could easily run afoul of the Equal Protection Clause or work to deny protections afforded by the First Amendment. This second view was expressed by Chief Justice Burger in his concurrence in *First National Bank of Boston v. Bellotti* (1978). He explained that the historical record does not bear out that the Founders intended to afford any special protections to the "institutional press." This second view represents the position most often taken by the Court.

This section examines four topics and how they affect the press. First, it examines attempts to treat the press differently from the general public. Next, it examines the press's access to public facilities and documents. Then it addresses differences in the regulation of the broadcast media and the print media. Finally, it examines the Press Clause in light of new technologies, such as delivery over cable, satellite, and the Internet.

A. Efforts to Treat the Press Differently

The separate proclamation of protection for the press in the First Amendment has led to many attempts to treat the press differently from the general public. Issues have arisen in the context of taxation, providing additional protections for the press, and protection of confidentiality of reporters' sources. Generally, the Court has refused to sustain attempts to differentiate the press from the public, regardless of any benefits or detriments to the press.

On the issue of special taxes imposed on the press, the Court has consistently found such measures unconstitutional. Discriminatory taxes, even if apparently benign at first, could easily morph into either retaliatory measures or a form of censure, licensing or prior restraint. The Court has overturned two notable attempts at taxes aimed at the press. In *Grosjean v. American Press Co.* (1936), the Court invalidated a state's attempt to levy a tax on advertisements in publications with more than 20,000 issues circulated per week. The Court found that the tax could have the effect of chilling the press. Then in *Minne-*

apolis Star & Tribune Co. v. Minnesota Commissioner of Revenue (1983), the Court invalidated a state's attempt to tax paper and ink used for publications (but exempted the first $100,000 from the tax). Writing for the majority, Justice O'Connor explained that such a tax directed at the press would have a chilling effect and must be justified by a "counterbalancing interest of compelling importance" that the state could not achieve without the special tax. Thus, the press cannot be targeted absent a compelling reason (however, the press is within the reach of generally available taxes).

Interestingly, in the case of *Leathers v. Medlock* (1991), the Court upheld a tax that distinguished between members of the press. In this case, a trade organization composed of approximately 80 cable operators brought a class action challenging the extension of an Arkansas sales tax to cable television services. Cable petitioners contended that the exemption from the tax of newspapers, magazines, and satellite broadcast services, violated their constitutional rights under the First Amendment (and under the Equal Protection Clause of the Fourteenth Amendment). Justice O'Connor writing for the majority, first observed that the Arkansas sales tax is a tax of general applicability, applying to receipts from the sale of all tangible personal property and a broad range of services, unless within a group of specific exemptions. She then noted that a tax scheme that discriminates among speakers does not implicate the First Amendment unless it discriminates on the basis of ideas. Nothing in the record suggested that the choice to exempt certain media from the generally applicable tax was motivated by an interest in censoring the expressive activities of cable television.

The question of additional protection for the press has arisen in two different contexts. First, the press has attempted to stake a claim to greater speech protections than are available to the general public through exemptions from generally applicable laws. Second, it has tried to claim that the Press Clause provides journalists greater protection from searches and seizures. However, in both cases, the Court has refused to find that the press should be treated differently.

In *Cohen v. Cowles Media Co.* (1991), the Court stated authoritatively that the press is not exempt from generally applicable laws. *Cohen* was a breach of contract case (a newspaper revealed a source despite its promise to not do so). The newspaper argued that the First Amendment protected them from liability for breach of contract. The Court disagreed, explaining that the law governing contract breaches applies to all persons and is not intended to interfere with the activities of the press. Thus, enforcing generally applicable laws against the press does not offend the First Amendment, even if the enforcement incidentally affects the press' ability to perform its function.

Similarly, in *Zurcher v. Stanford Daily* (1978), the Court held that the press is not entitled to greater protections against searches and seizures than is the general public. In *Zurcher*, the police searched a student newspaper office pursuant to a valid warrant. The newspaper claimed that the search violated the newspaper's First Amendment rights, but the justices were not convinced. Writing for the Court, Justice White explained that the First Amendment lends newspapers no greater protection than what is generally applicable under the Fourth Amendment. Thus, the First Amendment conveys no new protections to the press from generally applicable laws than are available to the general public.

Finally, the press has tried to claim that it has a right to protect the confidentiality of its sources from discovery by the government. Members of the press frequently claim that the protection of their news sources is crucial to their ability to gather the information communicated to the public and that this immunizes them from complying with subpoenas requiring the disclosure of sources. However, the Court rejected this claim in *Branzburg v. Hayes* (1972). Justice White, writing for the majority, explained that the public's interest in effective law enforcement overrode the press's interest in protecting the identity of its sources. Justice White also explained that, were the Court to find that the press was so protected, determining who constituted the press would cause a definitional problem that would be difficult (if not impossible) to overcome. Thus, the First Amendment extends no special shield to the press protecting them from being lawfully compelled to reveal their sources.

In the absence of constitutional protection for the confidentiality of press sources, most states have recognized the importance of such protection by adopting a shield law or something similar. State shield laws protect reporters from being forced to disclose confidential information or sources in state court. There is no federal shield law and state shield laws vary in scope. The Court or federal law have recognized a variety of other privileges in government (i.e., executive, legislative and judicial privilege, privilege against compelled self-incrimination, without prejudice privilege (protecting communications made in the course of negotiations to settle a legal dispute)), and outside of government (i.e., attorney client privilege, spousal privilege, clergy privilege). A shield law creates a reporter source privilege pursuant to which the reporter cannot be forced by subpoena or other court order to testify about information contained in a news story or the source of that information.

B. Access to Government Property

The function of the press is crucial in a democratic republic, and this critical function is recognized by the First Amendment guarantee of the freedom of the press. The previous section showed that the First Amendment does not protect the press from generally applicable laws and taxes. However, freedom of the press also necessitates freedom of access to information, for without access to information the press's ability to perform its crucial function would be hindered or even exterminated. The Court has not yet addressed this question in the form of a general rule; however, it has addressed it in the specific context of access to judicial proceedings and access to prisons. In the former, the Court has found that the press enjoys considerable access to judicial proceedings; in the latter, the Court has found that the press is not entitled to greater access to prisons than is the general public.

Concerning access to judicial proceedings, the Court has found that the Sixth Amendment's guarantee of a fair and public trial requires that the press have access except in very limited circumstances. In *Globe Newspaper Co. v. Superior Court* (1982), the Court explained that restrictions imposed on the press's access to criminal trials are subject to strict scrutiny. In *Globe Newspaper*, Massachusetts prohibited the press and the general public from being present at a trial for certain sexual offenses where the victim was younger than eighteen. Justice Brennan, writing for the Court, explained that the press's access to criminal trials is constitutionally protected but not absolute. Any restriction on the press's access to such trials must be narrowly tailored to achieve a compelling state interest. However, the Court has yet to address whether the press's access is coextensive with that of the general public or whether the First Amendment affords the press greater access.

Contrary to the protection of access to judicial proceedings, the Court has held that the press has no greater right of access to prisons than does the general public. Here, the leading case is *Pell v. Procunier* (1974). In *Pell*, the California Department of Corrections prohibited the press from interviewing "specific individual inmates." The Court found that the press was generally not entitled to special access to information that was not generally available to the public. It extended this determination to access to prisons and found that the press's right of access to inmates was the same as that enjoyed by the public. Thus, because the press's right was no less than that of the general public, the California regulation did not infringe on any rights protected by the First Amendment.

C. Broadcast Regulation

The technology available to the press has advanced considerably since the time the First Amendment was ratified. In 1791, the technology was the printing press and the distribution was primarily through street vendors. In the intervening time, the broadcast media—radio and television—developed with the potential to reach far more people because of the technology and because it was free. Radio broadcasting became popular in the 1920s. The arrival of television in the 1950s forced radio into a niche role, as the leading companies moved into the much larger field of television. The popularity of television is reflected in the current 99% household ownership of television sets in the country.

The Court struggled to adapt First Amendment law to the newer technologies, which differ in two main ways from the traditional press. First, broadcast signals penetrate the homes and businesses of the public without being requested, making it harder to control who is exposed to broadcast information, especially young children. Second, there are only a limited set of channels available for broadcasting, and the Court found that the scarcity of channels required government regulators to ensure an efficient allocation and use of the broadcasting spectrum and to prevent one broadcaster from intruding onto another. Eventually, the Court determined that the differences between broadcast media and more traditional media required greater regulation of the broadcast media than is appropriate for the more traditional press.

In *Red Lion Broadcasting Co. v. FCC* (1969), the Court upheld the FCC's fairness doctrine, which required broadcasters (a) to "give adequate coverage to public issues" and (b) to present such issues fairly such that it "accurately reflects the opposing views." The Court analyzed the differences between the broadcast media and the print media and found that broadcast media is entitled to less protection than print media. Writing for the majority, Justice White explained that this different treatment is necessary because there are only a limited set of broadcast frequencies that the government has the responsibility to allocate. Without governmental assistance many would not have access to the frequencies to voice their viewpoints. Similarly, in *FCC v. Pacifica Foundation* (1978), the Court upheld the power of the FCC to regulate and punish the broadcast of indecent material over the airwaves, even if that material is not obscene. Writing for the majority, Justice Scalia explained that the specific regulation of broadcast media was appropriate because sending "patently offensive, indecent material" over the airwaves made that material "uniquely accessible to children" and invaded the public's right to be left alone.

D. Advancing Technology

Recent years have seen the emergence of new technologies for communication. Chief among them are cable television and the Internet. Just as it struggled to address the broadcast media when it was a new medium, the Court is currently struggling with the degree of constitutional protection to which these media are entitled. These media are different from the broadcast media in a few key ways. First, both cable and the Internet require intentional access to the information, either through a subscription to a service provider or by specifically requesting the information disseminated. Second, cable and the Internet are discrete communications media: there is no risk of interference as there is with the broadcast media. The Internet is also substantially easier and cheaper to establish a presence in than the other types of media and is frequently used to disseminate ideas that many find objectionable or are otherwise unpopular. These differences have caused the Court to reconsider its deferential attitude toward regulating new forms of media. The Court requires a regulation of cable to satisfy a form of intermediate scrutiny:

1. Content-neutral;
2. Narrowly tailored; and
3. Serve an important government interest.

However, the Court generally has been reticent to uphold any regulations of Internet content, essentially applying strict scrutiny to such regulations.

The Court's position on regulating cable is most clearly expressed in *Turner Broadcasting System, Inc. v. FCC* (1994). *Turner Broadcasting* involved a challenge to the Cable Television Consumer Protection and Competition Act of 1992, which required cable operators to carry local stations operating within the same market (called the "must-carry" provisions). On direct appeal, the Supreme Court vacated the district court's judgment upholding the must-carry provisions and remanded the case. Writing for the Court, Justice Kennedy explained that cable programming and operators are entitled to the protections of the First Amendment because they engage in speech. However, "the rational for a less rigorous standard of First Amendment scrutiny to broadcast regulation does not apply in the context of cable regulation" because "our distinct approach to broadcast regulation rests upon the unique physical limitations of the broadcast medium." The Court held that the must-carry provisions were not a content-based restriction but were intended to keep the broadcast media alive to ensure free access to television. Justice Kennedy explained that because they were content-neutral the regulations must be narrowly tailored to achieve a "substantial government interest." Concurring in part and dissenting in part, Justice O'Connor, joined by Justices Scalia, Ginsburg, and Thomas, found that the must-carry provisions were content-based because they indicated preferential treatment for certain content and were impermissible restraints on speech.

The Court first addressed Internet content restrictions in *Reno v. ACLU* (1997). *Reno* involved a challenge to the Communications Decency Act of 1996 (CDA), which prohibited the distribution of indecent material over the Internet. In a decision supported by seven Justices, the Court overturned the CDA. Writing for the majority, Justice Stevens explained that the statute was so vague and overbroad that it would prohibit "serious discussion about birth control practices, homosexuality ... or the consequences of ... rape." Recognizing that the government has a compelling interest in protecting children from exposure to sexually explicit materials, Justice Stevens explained that the government cannot prohibit communication of materials to adults to protect children. The Court distinguished the Internet from radio and cable broadcasting in three ways: (1) indecent messages on the Internet were not being exposed to children inadvertently; (2) the Internet was not invading the home without the individual who was exposed taking some affirmative step towards encountering those messages; (3) and Internet sites are not a scarce medium as are radio frequencies. The Court held that government regulation of the Internet would infringe on "the free exchange of ideas," and that the promotion of this exchange is an interest that outweighs any benefit of censorship.

> In response to *Reno*, Congress passed the Child Online Protection Act (COPA), which was challenged in *Ashcroft v. ACLU* (2004). The COPA required commercial Web site operators to restrict access to material which "the average person 'applying contemporary community standards, would find ... is designed to pander to, the prurient interest." On appeal, a divided Court explained that although the statute was not unconstitutionally vague and overbroad like the CDA, it was not the least restrictive means for achieving the compelling interest of protecting minors from sexually explicit materials. Writing for the majority, Justice Kennedy explained that filters could be more effective because they would not be limited to one method of content distribution, Web sites, but would cover email and forms of distribution yet to be developed.

Checkpoints

- **Freedom of the Press**
  - Differentiation between the Press and the General Public
    - Generally, the press is subject to generally applicable laws and is not entitled to any special exemption from them.

  - The press is not entitled to any specific protection from either searches pursuant to valid warrants or subpoenas requiring the divulging of news sources.
  - The press is also subject to generally applicable taxes and does not receive any specific protection from them.
  - However, the press is protected from taxes directed at the press, and such efforts to tax only the press are generally found to be unconstitutional.
- Access to Government Property
  - The Court has yet to provide a general rule on this question but has addressed it with respect to access to judicial proceedings and access to prisons.
  - The press enjoys a substantial ability to observe and report on judicial proceedings; any limitations on that ability must meet exacting standards. Any restriction on the press's access to criminal trials must be narrowly tailored to achieve a compelling state interest.
  - However, the press enjoys no greater access to prisons than the general public.
- Regulation of Broadcast Media versus Print Media
  - Generally, the broadcast media is subject to greater regulation than the print media because of (1) the scarcity of the broadcast frequencies; and (2) the government is responsible for allocating the channels and without government assistance some persons would not have access to the channels to express their viewpoints.
- Regulation of New and Emerging Technologies
  - Cable companies and programming providers are less regulated than are the broadcast media.
  - The Court has endorsed a form of intermediate scrutiny for regulations of cable companies and programming, requiring the regulation: (1) to be content-neutral; (2) to serve a substantial government interest; and (3) to be narrowly tailored to serve that interest.
  - The Court has generally been hostile to regulations of content on the Internet.
  - Regulations of content on the Internet must pass strict scrutiny else they are invalid.

Chapter 5

Freedom of Association, Political Parties, and Campaign Finance

Roadmap

- The First Amendment protects the right to associate, though it is not expressly stated in the Amendment.
- Limitations on the right to associate must pass intermediate scrutiny.
- Defining Association
  - The freedom of association does protect a group with discriminatory membership policies if:
    - The group is an intimate association, defined as a small, private gathering, or
    - The group is an integral part of an expressive activity.
- The Electoral Process and Campaign Finance
- States are free to regulate the electoral process how they see fit.
- Exacting scrutiny is the appropriate level of review when reviewing challenges to the electoral process.
- Congress is prohibited from fining or jailing an association of citizens for engaging in political speech, and may not impose restrictions on disfavored speakers.
- Corporations are protected by the First Amendment Freedom of Association Clause.

I. Freedom of Association, Political Parties, and Campaign Finance

The First Amendment contains no express protection of freedom of association. However, it does expressly protect the "right of the people peaceably to assemble." The Supreme Court has held that the right to associate is protected by the combination of the right to "peaceably to assemble" when read in the context of the other rights in the First Amendment and in conjunction with the Fourteenth Amendment's Due Process Clause. In so doing, the Court has determined that the right to associate is fundamental and protected by the First Amendment, especially when such association involves speech that is more effective when spoken collectively. Because of the fundamental nature of the right, any state action infringing on that right must pass strict scrutiny or fail.

The Court emphatically announced the right of freedom of association in *NAACP v. Alabama* (1958). At the time, Alabama required foreign corporations to qualify by registering with the state before conducting any business within the state. The attorney general of Alabama sought to enjoin the NAACP from conducting activities within the state and oust the organization, a nonprofit corporation organized under New York law, for failure to register. When the NAACP refused to comply with a court order to produce its membership rolls, the court held the NAACP in civil contempt and fined it. On appeal, the Supreme Court reversed the trial court's contempt citation and fine. Writing for the majority, Justice Harlan explained that, although Alabama had not taken any affirmative action to restrict the freedom of association, the production order "entail[ed] the likelihood of a substantial restraint" on the ability of the citizens of Alabama to exercise that right. Finding that the Fourteenth Amendment protected the right of the NAACP's members to associate freely, the Court held that the production order was state action infringing that right. Furthermore, because the state had not shown a "controlling justification" for the infringement, the Court invalidated the order, contempt citation, and fine.

A. Defining Association

The threshold question in analyzing the right of association is what associative activity is protected by the First Amendment. The Court has found that the right of association generally protects the right of a group of people to form an association and determine its membership, as long as its membership is not determined in a discriminatory manner. However, the Court has upheld discriminatory membership policies in one of two cases. First, it has permitted discrimination in determining the membership of an "intimate association," a small and private gathering. Second, it has permitted discrimination if the discrimination is integral to expressive activity.

The leading case announcing these minor exceptions to the nondiscriminatory requirement of the right of association is *Roberts v. United States Jaycees* (1984). In *Roberts*, the Jaycees, a national organization comprising young men between the ages of eighteen and forty, brought a right of association challenge to the Minnesota Human Rights Act. The Act proscribed discrimination based, *inter alia*, on race and gender. The Jaycees claimed that the freedom of association permitted the group to exclude women from its membership. The Court disagreed. In his opinion for the Court, Justice Brennan recognized that forcing a group to accept members that it does not wish to accept was the "clear[est] example of an intrusion into the internal structure or affairs of an association." However, he explained that the freedom of association was not inviolable and held that an infringement of that freedom was not unconstitutional if its reach is only so far as is necessary to accomplish a legitimate government purpose. However, the Court announced two exceptions to the general rule prohibiting discriminatory practices concerning association memberships. Discriminatory membership policies are permitted if the association (1) is an "intimate association," defined as a small and private gathering or (2) is an integral part of expressive activity. Because the Court found that the Jaycees were too large to be an "intimate association," and that the association was not an integral part of expressive activity, it determined that the discriminatory membership policy was not protected by the First Amendment and upheld the law.

Applying *Roberts*, the Court upheld discriminatory membership practices in *Boy Scouts of America v. Dale* (2000). The respondent, James Dale, was a Boy Scout who had risen through the organization to the rank of Eagle Scout and had become an assistant Scoutmaster. During college, he became involved with gay rights advocacy and was the co-president of the Gay/Lesbian Alliance at Rutgers University in New Jersey. After seeing an article that quoted Dale in his position with the Alliance, a Boy Scout official wrote to Dale and informed him that he could no longer participate in the Boy Scouts. Dale sued, claiming that the action violated the New Jersey law proscribing discrimination by places of public accommodation. The Boy Scouts claimed that their association had an antigay message, and the Court agreed in a five-to-four decision. Chief Justice Rehnquist's majority opinion found a sufficiently expressive message in the Boy Scouts' interpretation of its Scout Oath and its position taken during litigation. He explained that just because the message is not "trumpet[ed] ... from the housetops" does not mean the expression is unprotected by the First Amendment. Thus, the majority found that the Boy Scouts were an association tied to a message, and forcing them to permit homosexuals to be members would undermine that message. In his dissent, Justice Stevens noted that there was nothing in the Boy Scouts' literature to support this position.

Even nonmembers of a group can be so connected with a group that they are required to pay for the same services as members. In *Locke v. Karass* (2008), the Maine State Employees Association negotiated a new collective bargaining agreement in which nonmembers were required to pay a "service fee" to the union as its exclusive bargaining agent. This fee was used to fund national litigation efforts of the union. The nonmembers challenged the constitutionality of being forced to pay this fee. In a unanimous decision, the Court held the First Amendment was not violated. A local union can charge nonmembers for their share of its contribution to a national's litigation expenses if (1) the subject matter of the litigation is something that would be chargeable if the litigation were local and (2) the local chapter could ultimately benefit from the outcome of the national litigation.

B. Regulating Campaign Finance

Campaign finance regulations address the ways in which political campaigns are funded. This includes all spending done to promote or support candidates, ballot measures, political parties and more. Regulations can be applied to persons, corporations, political action committees, political parties and other organizations. They can come in the form of incentives, such as providing public financing to candidates who abide by spending limits, as well as restrictions, such as contribution limits on donors. Legislative efforts, judicial rulings and citizen initiatives have all played roles in shaping the regulation of political contributions.

Freedom of association issues arise with campaign finance regulations. Federal and state governments require some level of disclosure from candidates, committees and political parties of the amount and source of contributions and expenditures. States vary in the detail required in disclosures and in the frequency of reporting. A recent trend has been the use of electronic disclosure systems. Recognizing the potential to discourage contributions by forcing such disclosures, the Court has upheld the disclosure requirements as being narrowly tailored to stop corruption. However, the Court has found an exception where such disclosures may discourage contributions to a minor party candidate and will permit such groups to withhold the information.

In *Buckley v. Valeo* (1976), the Court reviewed the 1974 amendments to the Federal Election Campaign Act of 1971, a law passed in response to the abuses discovered in the Watergate investigation. A key part of the Watergate affair was a campaign finance scandal; including a slush fund to pay for illegal activity, attempts to keep illegal donations hidden, misappropriation of campaign donations and corporations wanting something in return for their donations and Nixon delivering. In order to increase transparency and to make sure that no one group of people could use their resources to have undue influence on the government, Congress enacted of a series of campaign finance reforms designed to restore the country's faith in government. The law imposed a ceiling on individual and group contributions to political campaigns for federal office, a limit on expenditures by a candidate's personal or family funds, a set of disclosure requirements, and a mechanism for public funding of presidential campaigns.

In *Buckley*, the Court upheld the requirement that all political candidates keep the names and addresses of financial contributors and make the information available for inspection for the public and the Federal Election Commission. The Court acknowledged that some potential donors might not donate to political campaigns in order to avoid disclosing their political affiliation; however, the Court found the government's interest in discouraging corruption through transparent disclosure was more substantial. However, the Court also found that disclosure could have particularly harmful effects on minor parties that have little chance of winning, because releasing the names of their financial contributors may discourage both contributions and associational activity. The Court applied this dicta in *Brown v. Socialist Workers '74 Campaign Committee* (1982), finding that the Socialist Party did not have to obey state disclosure laws. The Court based this determination on the fact that the party was a minor party and that, historically, it had been unpopular. Thus, the disclosure requirements would probably chill contributions to the party and would not serve a significant purpose because of the reduced likelihood of the party's electoral success. The Court has continued to uphold disclosure requirements in its recent cases, including *Citizens United v. Federal Election Commission* (2010).

The Court upheld a law facing a First Amendment freedom of association challenge that required the disclosure of names of those who sign petitions for ballot initiatives and referenda. In *Doe #1 v. Reed* (2010), a petition challenging the enactment of a bill which would expand the rights and responsibilities of domestic partners, including same-sex partners, was submitted. A group of intervenors then sought to obtain copies of the petition under the Washington Public Records Act (PRA). The petition sponsor and several other signers filed for injunctive relief to prevent the release of the petition. They argued the release of the signers' names would "subject these individuals to threats, harassment, and reprisals." Chief Justice Roberts, writing for the majority, identified the appropriate standard of reviewing challenges in the electoral context as "exacting scrutiny." Exacting scrutiny requires a substantial relation between the disclosure requirement and a sufficiently important governmental interest. "The strength of the government's interest must reflect the seriousness of the actual burden on the First Amendment." The plaintiffs mainly argued that the objective of seeking to prevent fraud in the electoral process by releasing the petition (and the names of its signers) did not outweigh the possible injury that would befall the signers when their names were released to the public. The Court acknowledged this issue was not before the Court in this case, but only the broad issue of whether the release of referendum petitions in general was constitutional. The Court held that the government's release of petitions does not as a general matter violate First Amendment rights because public disclosure promotes accountability in the electoral process by helping remedy the inadequacies of the verification and canvassing process. However, the Court did leave the door open to a different conclusion in an individual case if there was a showing of likely threats, reprisals and intimidation.

Contribution and spending limits of campaign finance laws have not encountered the same success as disclosure requirements. In *Buckley v. Valeo* (1976), the Court equated the spending of money in political campaigns with political speech deserving First Amendment protection and therefore invalidated expenditure limits but upheld contribution limits. The Court refused to apply the *O'Brien* test which the Court developed for symbolic or nonverbal speech, arguing the giving and spending of money for political campaigns "cannot be equated with" destroying a draft card (even if *O'Brien* applied, the Court held strict scrutiny would apply because this law was designed to suppress speech). The court saw expenditure limits as imposing substantial restraints on the quantity and quality of political speech because of the cost of media and the size of the audience. By limiting how much candidates could spend, the law limited how much candidates could say.

The court justified contribution limits because they cause little direct restraint on political communication and prevent both actual corruption and the appearance of corruption from large individual donations — the primary purpose behind the law's adoption.

The Court decided that independent expenditures to support a candidate (i.e. money spent by a political action committee) do not run the same risk of corruption or appearance of corruption. The Court found that the state could not restrict these expenditures to equalize political opportunity and influence. Limiting expenditures so that the wealthy cannot drown out the voices of those with less money in an election is not a compelling state interest.

The court upheld public funding of presidential campaigns because it increases speech and it upheld the expenditure limits public funding entailed because the government can include requirements on those who voluntarily accept public funds.

In *First National Bank of Boston v. Bellotti* (1978), the Court defined the free speech right of corporations for the first time in examining a Massachusetts law that prohibited bank and corporate donations in ballot initiatives unless the corporation's interests were directly involved. The Court held that corporations have a First Amendment right to make contributions to ballot initiative campaigns because "commercial speech is accorded some constitutional protection not so much because it pertains to the seller's business as because it furthers the societal interest in the 'free flow of commercial information.'" The Court asserted that "the inherent worth of the speech in terms of its capacity for informing the public does not depend upon the identity of its source, whether corporation, association, union, or individual." In deciding the case, the justices rejected the argument that the Fourteenth Amendment did not apply to corporations. The Court overruled *Pierce v. Society of Sisters* (1925), which stated that corporations "cannot claim for themselves the liberty which the Fourteenth Amendment guarantees," declaring the decision to be "untenable under decisions of this Court." Instead, the Court asserted that the due process clause extends freedom of speech and other First Amendment liberties to corporate entities.

In 1990, the Court ruled in *Austin v. Michigan Chamber of Commerce* that, even though the First Amendment did protect corporate expression, restrictions on independent expenditure were justified because of the compelling interest to prevent corruption or the appearance thereof in campaigns. The *Austin* majority quoted *Bellotti,* agreeing that political speech did not lose First Amendment protection "merely because the speaker is a corporation." However, the *Austin* majority held that the Michigan Chamber of Commerce, a non-profit corporation that wanted to publish a newspaper advertisement supporting a candidate, did not qualify for the non-profit exemption established in *Federal Election Commission v. Massachusetts Citizens for Life, Inc* (1986). The dissenting justices in *Austin* cited the statement in *Bellotti* that "the legislature is constitutionally disqualified from dictating the subjects about which persons may speak and the speakers who may address a public issue."

The holding of *Buckley* was challenged in *Randall v. Sorrell* (2006). Vermont passed a law limiting both expenditure and contribution limits during the election cycle. The Court held the expenditure limits imposed by the Vermont law were unconstitutional and were no different than the type previously struck down in *Buckley.* The Court also held the contribution limitations unconstitutionally low. Justice Breyer recognized the $200–$400 contribution limits during a two-year general election cycle as the lowest in the country and not indexed to inflation. Breyer concluded that this limit "inhibit[s] effective advocacy by those who seek election, particularly challengers," does not advance the purpose of preventing corruption in the electoral process and does more harm than good.

In *McConnell v. Federal Election Commission* (2003), the Court upheld most of the provisions of the "McCain-Feingold" Bipartisan Campaign Finance Reform Act of 2002 (BCRA) but later overturned much of it in *Citizens United v. Federal Election Commission* (2010). Due to the complexity and length of the decision, there are several majority opinions written by different justices. The law banned soft money donations to political parties ("Soft money" is money raised and spent by political parties that is exempt from the contribution limits to candidates or committees. Corporations and unions that could not contribute to candidates, used this route, as did individuals who had reached the contribution limit). The Court upheld the ban on soft money to prevent circumvention of the contribution limits the Court had upheld in *Buckley*.

The Court upheld BCRA's limitation on union, corporate and nonprofit organization political advertisements 30 days before primaries and 60 days before general elections as a constitutionally permissible way to prevent avoidance of campaign laws by issue advertisements. The Court also upheld BCRA's requirement that broadcasters keep publicly available records of politically related broadcasting. The Court said the government already regulates broadcasting and this requirement was not unduly burdensome.

In *Davis v. Federal Election Commission* (2008) the Court examined § 319(a) of the Bipartisan Campaign Reform Act which attempted to address the advantage of personal wealth in election campaigns. When a candidate spent more than $350,000 of his or her own money in the campaign, this provision allowed the opponent an increased contribution limit. Referred to as the "millionaire's provision," the court struck it down as a violation of the First Amendment. Justice Alito, writing for the majority, acknowledged that the Court has never upheld a law which imposes different contribution limits for candidates competing against each other. Alito agreed with *Davis* that this provision burdened his First Amendment right to spend his own money for his campaign.

In *Arizona Free Club Enterprise Club's Freedom Club PAC v. Bennett* (2011), past and future Arizona candidates and two independent expenditure groups challenged the constitutionality of the matching funds provision of the Arizona Citizens Clean Elections Act. The statute provided matching funds for publicly financed candidates if their privately funded counterparts made personal contributions or received funds from independent expenditure groups above a certain triggering amount. The Court found the statute went beyond its purpose of encouraging participation in public financing and decreasing corruption. Finding the statute more constitutionally problematic than that in *Davis v. Federal Election Commission* (2008), the Court held that the matching funds provision substantially burdens political speech without the compelling interest necessary to survive First Amendment scrutiny. The statute allowed publicly funded candidates to strategically allocate their money, while privately funded candidates and the groups that support them try to avoid triggering the matching funds provision of the statute.

In *McCutcheon v. Federal Election Commission* (2014), the court re-visited the 1974 Amendments to the Federal Election Campaign Act (FECA) that imposed aggregate limits on the direct contributions that individuals can make to national political parties and federal candidates in a calendar year. The constitutionality of the FECA amendments was challenged in 1976, which resulted in the court upholding the aggregate limits in *Buckley*. In 2002, the Bipartisan Campaign Reform Act (BCRA) was passed. The BCRA revised the aggregate limits, adjusted them to future (but not past) inflation, and changed the individual limitations from annual to biennial. The aggregate contribution ceiling on individuals during the 2011–2012 election cycle stood at $46,200 for federal candidates and $70,800 for national parties, or a $117,000 aggregate limit. Plaintiff Shaun McCutcheon, a businessman and contributor to various Republican candidates, wanted to exceed the federal aggregate limit. So he filed suit and was joined by the Republican National Committee.

In a 5–4 decision, the Court overturned limits on aggregate federal campaign contributions. The decision did not affect limits on how much individuals can give to an individual politician's campaign, which remain at $2,600 per election. Chief Justice Roberts, writing for the Court, said that "The government may no more restrict how many candidates or causes a donor may support than it may tell a newspaper how many candidates it may endorse."

Precedent was altered in the 5–4 decision of *Citizens United v. Federal Election Commission* (2010) as the Court overturned *Austin v. Michigan Chamber of Commerce* (1990), portions of *McConnell v. Federal Election Commission* (2003), and Section 203 of the Bipartisan Campaign Reform Act (2002) (which prohibited electioneering communications by corporations). In this case, Citizens United released a documentary criticizing Hillary Clinton during the 2008 primary elections, which violated the Bipartisan Campaign Reform Act, which "prohibits corporations and unions from using their general treasury funds to make independent expenditures for speech and that is an 'electioneering communication' or for speech that expressly advocates the election or defeat of a candidate" within 30 days of a primary or 60 days of a general election. The political documentary, which was meant to provide negative publicity for Democratic Party candidate Hillary Clinton, violated the primary time period. Writing for the majority in a 5–4 decision, Justice

Kennedy enhanced protection for an association's political spending in support or opposition of a party, finding that the force of the First Amendment prohibits Congress from fining or jailing an association of citizens for engaging in political speech. Citing *First National Bank of Boston v. Belloti* (1978), the Court reiterated that political speech is "indispensable to decision-making in a democracy," regardless of whether the speech comes from a corporation or an individual.

This decision overruled parts of two major Supreme Court cases, *Austin v. Michigan Chamber of Commerce* (1990) and *McConnell v. Federal Election Commission*, (2003), which upheld restrictions on the spending of corporations and unions supporting or opposing political parties. *Citizens United* found that, under First Amendment principles in the context of political speech, the Government could not impose restrictions on disfavored speakers, including corporations. The Court recognized that there were no sufficient government interests that would justify the suppression of political speech of corporations. The Court also expanded the definition of "we the people who are sovereign" to cover corporations. The majority argued that the First Amendment protects *associations* of individuals in addition to individual speakers, and further that the First Amendment does not allow prohibitions of speech based on the identity of the speaker. Corporations, as associations of individuals, therefore have speech rights under the First Amendment. Because spending money is essential to disseminating speech, as established in *Buckley*, limiting a corporation's ability to spend money is unconstitutional because it limits the ability of its members to associate effectively and to speak on political issues. The dissent criticized this expansion to be inconsistent with the Framer's intent to distinguish a corporation from a human being, saying that the Framers intended to "guard against corporate capture of elections."

The Court extended its ruling in *Citizens United* to state law in *American Tradition Partnership v. Bullock* (2012). There, the Court reviewed a Montana statute that regulated independent corporate expenditures on behalf of candidates. The law provided that a "corporation may not make . . . an expenditure in connection with a candidate or a political committee that supports or opposes a candidate or political party." The Court applied the reasoning from *Citizens* and held that the statute violated corporations' free speech rights.

Although the government is prevented from abridging an individual's freedom of speech, the Court does not confer an affirmative right to that individual to use the government's services in gaining funding for a political party. In *Ysursa v. Pocatello Educ. Ass'n* (2009), a public employee in Idaho was lawfully permitted to deduct a portion of his paycheck to remit to his union. However, this employee wanted this deduction to instead go to his union's political action committee. The Court ruled that the Idaho law permitting employee deductions to go to unions did not restrict political speech, but rather declined to promote political speech by not allowing the funds to go to a particular political action committee. The Court grounded the decision in the State's interest in avoiding the appearance that carrying out the public's business is tainted by partisan political affairs.

The Court has also examined whether a state's ban on the personal solicitation of campaign funds by candidates for judgeships violates the First Amendment. Florida is one of thirty-nine states in which the voters elect judges. To promote confidence in the integrity of the judiciary, the Florida Supreme Court adopted a canon for its Judicial Code of Conduct which provides that judicial candidates "shall not personally solicit campaign funds ... but may establish committees of responsible persons" to raise money for election campaigns. A judicial candidate, Lanell Williams-Yulee, who was disciplined by the Florida Bar for soliciting funds, raised a First Amendment challenge. In *Williams-Yulee v. Florida Bar* (2015), the Court upheld Florida's ban saying that a state has a vital interest in safeguarding public confidence in the fairness and integrity of the nations elected judges. Unlike the legislature or executive branches, the judiciary has no influence over either the sword or the purse so its authority depends largely on the public's willingness to respect its decisions. Chief Justice Roberts, writing for a five justice majority, distinguished politicians, who are expected to respond to the preferences of their supporters, from judges, who may not follow the preferences of their supporters or provide any special consideration to campaign donors, and concluded that judicial integrity is "a state interest of the highest order."

Checkpoints

- **Freedom of Association**
  - Generally, the First Amendment protects the right to associate, though it is not expressly stated in the Amendment.
  - The freedom of association has been incorporated against the states through the Fourteenth Amendment.
  - Infringements on the freedom must be narrowly tailored to achieve a legitimate government interest.
  - Defining Association
    - Generally, freedom of association does not protect a group that has discriminatory membership policies.

- However, the freedom of association does protect a group with discriminatory membership policies if:
    - The group is an intimate association, defined as a small, private gathering, or
    - The group is an integral part of an expressive activity.
    - A local union can charge nonmembers for their share of its contribution to a national's litigation expenses if (1) the subject matter of the litigation is something that would be chargeable if the litigation were local, and (2) the local chapter could ultimately benefit from the outcome of the national litigation.

- **The Electoral Process and Campaign Finance**
  - Generally, campaigns can be required to disclose lists of donors because of the government's substantial interests in preventing corruption and the appearance of corruption.
  - However, a minor party may refuse to comply with disclosure requirements because of the risk that the disclosure requirement could chill contributions to the party and because the party is unlikely to win at the ballot box.
  - It is unconstitutional to place expenditure limits on individuals running for office.
  - It is unconstitutional to place limits on contributions if there is no purpose for doing so.
  - Congress is prohibited from fining or jailing an association of citizens for engaging in political speech, and may not impose restrictions on disfavored speakers.
  - Corporations have a First Amendment right to make contributions to ballot initiative campaigns because commercial speech is accorded some constitutional protection because it furthers the societal interest in the 'free flow of commercial information.
  - The decision of *Citizens United v. Federal Election Commission* found that corporations, like individuals, have a First Amendment right to free speech.
  - In *American Tradition Partnership, Inc. v. Bullock* the Supreme Court extended the ruling in *Citizens* to the states.
  - "We the people who are sovereign" includes human beings and corporations; thus, corporations are protected by the First Amendment Freedom of Association Clause. However, the government has a justifiable interest in requiring corporations to disclose spending amounts, as such requirements do not subject corporations to danger, threats, or harassment.
  - Exacting scrutiny is the appropriate level of review when reviewing challenges to the electoral process.

- Exacting scrutiny requires a substantial relation between the disclosure requirement and a sufficiently important governmental interest.
- The strength of the government's interest must reflect the seriousness of the actual burden on the First Amendment.
- Limits on aggregate federal campaign contributions violate the First Amendment (*McCutcheon v. FEC*, 2014).
- States can ban judicial candidates from personally soliciting campaign funds because they have a vital interest in safeguarding public confidence in the fairness and integrity of the elected judges.

Chapter 6

The Establishment Clause

Roadmap

- Religion is not easily defined by the Court.
- The Religion Clauses apply to the states through the Fourteenth Amendment.
- Three analytical frameworks for Establishment Clause:
  - Strict Separation;
  - Neutrality; and
  - Accommodation.
- The three-part *Lemon* Test for analyzing Establishment Clause cases:
  - Whether the government act has a secular purpose;
  - Whether its primary effect neither advances nor inhibits religion; and
  - Whether it does not create an excessive entanglement between government and religion.
- Areas of Establishment Clause jurisprudence: school prayer, school curricular decisions, religious displays, equal access to public facilities, financial aid to religious institutions, and school vouchers
- The Court divides its analysis of financial aid to religion into two main groups:
  - Financial aid to primary and secondary schools
  - Postsecondary religious schools and for nonacademic activities at religious institutions

---

I. Introduction

Before the adoption of the First Amendment, it is important to know that the body of the Constitution contains a religious prohibition. Article VI, Clause 3 of the Constitution states:

> The Senators and Representatives before mentioned, and the Members of the several State Legislatures, and all executive and judicial Officers, both of the United States and of the several States, shall be

> bound by Oath or Affirmation, to support this Constitution; but no religious Test shall ever be required as a qualification to any Office or public Trust under the United States.

Under this "No Religious Test Clause," the government could not establish religion as a condition for holding federal office.

The First Amendment, which opens the hallowed Bill of Rights, begins with the often quoted words: "Congress shall make no law respecting an establishment of religion, or prohibiting the free exercise thereof." This portion of the First Amendment is commonly broken down at the comma into two Religion Clauses, the Establishment Clause and the Free Exercise Clause, respectively. These two clauses were designed to protect liberty of conscience, freedom of religious expression, religious equality and pluralism, and separation of church and state. In short, they protect the fundamental right to freedom of religion. Though these clauses appear to be simple and clear, in application, they are complex and vague and are some of the most contested words in the Constitution.

To fully appreciate the application of the Religion Clauses, it is crucial to understand two basic points. First, to comprehend when the First Amendment applies, one must know the Court's definition of what constitutes a "religion." Second, for most of the history of the United States, the Court did not apply the Religion Clauses to the states. In changing their applicability, the Court uses the Fourteenth Amendment to apply the Religion Clauses to the states.

A. Definition of Religion

What is "religion"? This preliminary question of what qualifies as religion increasingly requires a definition that can account for the growing variety of different religious beliefs and practices in the United States. This diversity, which any workable definition must embrace, shows that the apparently simple task conceals an extremely complex reality. Some commentators have suggested that providing a bright-line definition is unworkable because it is impossible to bring all religions within the scope of the definition without also encompassing practices that are not religious.

One theory called for two different definitions of religion, one for the Establishment Clause (which prevents the government from establishing a religion) and one for the Free Exercise Clause (which protects the freedom of to practice religion). The theory is that a narrow definition of religion for the Establishment Clause would restrict the limits on government, and a broader definition of religion for the Free Exercise Clause would increase the protections for religious conduct. The theory was illustrated in *Malnak v. Yogi* (3d Cir. 1979), where a school offered classes in transcendental meditation. A broad definition of religion for the Free Exercise Clause would protect transcendental meditation as a religious practice, but for a public school to provide the class, one would need a narrow definition of religion to prevent the class from running afoul of the Establishment Clause. This theory has never been accepted by the Supreme Court. In fact, Justice Wiley Rutledge expressly rejected this concept of a dual definition in his dissent in *Everson v. Board of Education* (1947). He stated that although the word *religion* appears only once in the First Amendment, the same word "governs two prohibitions and governs them alike."

Because of the diversity of beliefs and practices that any definition must encompass, the Court has directly addressed the issue in relatively few cases. The Court has successfully avoided the issue by deciding cases on independent grounds, which make reaching the question unnecessary. However, when the Court has dealt with defining religion, its rulings provide some insight, but little guidance.

In 1890, the Court, in *Davis v. Beason*, adopted a substantive definition of religion—a practice that involves "the belief in and the worship of a deity." The Court ruled that "the term 'religion' has a reference of one's views of his relations to his Creator, and the obligations they impose of reverence for his being and character, and obedience to his will."

In 1961, in *Torcaso v. Watkins*, the Court abandoned the substantive approach and moved toward a functional definition of religion. The case involved a provision of the Maryland Constitution, which had been used to deny a secular humanist an appointment as a notary public. The Court struck down the provision, unanimously holding "that the term religion did not apply solely to those beliefs which were based upon the existence of a deity." This ruling prevented the government from aiding a religion, even if that religion does not encompass a belief in a "God." Thus, the government could not avoid the prohibition of the Establishment Clause by claiming that the religion does not include "worship of a deity." Justice Hugo Black wrote: "Among religions in this country which do not teach what would generally be considered a belief in the existence of God are Buddhism, Taoism, Ethical Culture, Secular Humanism and others."

The Court has provided three different approaches to defining religion: First, it has attempted to outline who qualifies under the conscientious objector status. Second, it has required that a belief must be sincerely held, which is subject to examination by the court; and third, it has extended this class of people to include those with non-traditional beliefs that are associated with traditional religions. The Court reiterated the functional approach in *United States v. Seeger* (1965), which involved the interpretation of the Universal Military Training and Service Act of 1948. The Act allowed an individual to be a conscientious objector and avoid the military draft if such individual, "by reason of religious training and belief, is conscientiously opposed to participation in war in any form." Under the Act, the definition of "religious training and belief" was "an individual's belief in relation to a Supreme Being involving duties superior to those arising from any human relation, but not including essentially political, sociological, or philosophical views or a merely personal moral code." The trial court denied Daniel Seeger's claim of conscientious objector status because his belief was not based on a Supreme Being as required by the Act.

The crux of the issue focused around whether the term "Supreme Being" meant the orthodox concept of God or the broader concept of a power or being to which all else is subordinate. The Court chose the latter, formulating a functional definition of religion and citing theologian Paul Tillich's view of God not as a projection "out there" or beyond the skies but as the ground of our very being. The Court stated that a "person's belief can be classified as religious if such belief is 'sincere and meaningful . . . [and] occupies in the life of its possessor, a place parallel to that filled by God.'"

Thus, in *Seeger*, the Court abandoned the substantive definition of religion to prevent the judiciary from being in the position to decide the truth of a religious belief. As Justice William Douglas stated in *United States v. Ballard* (1944): "Men may believe what they cannot prove. They may not be put to the proof of their religious doctrines or beliefs. Religious experiences which are as real as life to some may be incomprehensible to others." In fact, the truth of religious views cannot properly be presented to the jury because doing so would open the door to converting prosecutions into religious persecutions. Courts are also not competent to determine whether a party has interpreted the tenets of his or her faith correctly. Since its early nineteenth-century decision in *Watson v. Jones* (1872), the Court has generally left these internal issues to the relevant religious tribunals, and courts must accept a religion's highest tribunal's interpretation of doctrine as binding. In *Gillette v. United States* (1971), Gillette did not oppose involvement in all wars but refused to submit to the draft and enter the armed forces for the Vietnam War because he thought that war was unjust. But the Court upheld the federal law that limited conscientious objector status to those people who objected to all wars. The court did not follow Gillette's argument that the law crippled freedom to exercise religion because most religions object only to particular wars (unjust wars) but instead followed the government's pragmatic argument that to allow objection to a particular war would make it too difficult for the country to ensure a ready military.

In response to the court's decision in *Seeger*, Congress amended the Universal Military Training Act and deleted the reference to a "Supreme Being." But the Act continued to provide that "religious training and belief" does not include "essentially political, sociological, or philosophical views, or a merely personal moral code." In *Welsh v. U.S.* (1970), the Court reexamined the Act and stated that purely ethical and moral considerations may be viewed as religious.

The first question in any free exercise claim is whether the plaintiff's beliefs are religious in nature, and whether those beliefs are sincerely held. This inquiry does not change when a challenger is incarcerated. The Court has clearly stated that its role is not in determining whether people are correctly observing the tenets of their faiths, but whether they are honest about their convictions associated with their faith (*Thomas v. Review Board of the Indiana Employment Security Division*, 1981). In *Thomas*, a Jehovah's Witness refused to continue his employment when he was assigned to a production line, which produced armaments, turrets, and other military materials. The petitioner believed that producing weapons violated the principles of his religion, even though other Jehovah's Witnesses working on the same production line did not have objections. The Court found that distinction irrelevant as the function of the courts is not as "arbiters of scriptural interpretation," and held it was unconstitutional to deny the petitioner unemployment compensation benefits. The Court recognized that religious beliefs do not need to be acceptable, logical, consistent, or comprehensible to others in order to warrant First Amendment protection. Only religious beliefs that are "so bizarre" and clearly nonreligious are not afforded First Amendment protection. The Court affirmed this interpretation in *Frazee v. Illinois Employment Security Department* (1989) when it held that the plaintiff who refused to work on Sundays, even if others practicing the same religion and similar other religions did not refuse, could object on religious grounds.

Organizations, foundations, and funds that operate exclusively for religious purposes are exempt from Federal income taxes. However, the IRS has struggled with defining "religion" because the First Amendment prohibits Congress from making laws regarding the establishment or free exercise of religion. The IRS in 1977 adopted *Seeger's* two-part test and found this test could be used to determine whether organizations are "religious" for purposes of tax exemption under the Code. This test is whether a belief is "sincere and meaningful" and occupies in the lives of the individuals holding them a place parallel to that filled by the belief in God of traditional religions. The IRS has used this test to deny tax-exempt status to many religious organizations. In *Retreat in Motion v. Comm'r*, the Tax Court held that a group that provided bus trips to Washington D.C., Disney World, and the Smokey Mountains in connection with youth ministry was not a religious organization to qualify for tax exempt status. Although the organization was formed to supply youths with a religious experience, the Tax Court found the fact that a majority of the trip was composed of recreational and not religious activity was enough for the organization to fail the statutory requirement that the organization be operated exclusively for a tax exempt purpose.

If an organization is found to be a church, the organization can receive significant additional tax benefits. These benefits provide an enormous incentive for religious organizations to obtain such classification. Achieving this status is more difficult than being deemed a religious organization. In *Vaughn v. Chapman* (1967), the Tax Court held that Congress intended the word "church" to have a much more restrictive definition than the term "religious organization." The Tax Court further explained in the subsequent case of *Church of Eternal Life & Liberty v. Comm'r* (1986), that religious purposes alone does not establish that a religious organization is a church. In *Eternal Life*, a "church" was defined as a coherent group of individuals and families that assemble to accomplish the religious purposes of mutually held beliefs. Small groups with one leader congregating normally at the leader's home have been found most commonly to violate the "church" requirements. In *Bubbling Well Church of Universal Love, Inc. v. Comm'r* (1980) a family constituting the sole members of a church claimed tax-exempt status. The 9th Circuit found that the use of money for house repairs and to pay salaries out of church funds were unreasonable because no part of the organization's net earnings can benefit a private person. The purpose of the regulation at issue is to ensure that the organization serves a public rather than a private purpose.

In *Wisconsin v. Yoder* (1971), Amish parents were convicted under Wisconsin's compulsory attendance laws for failing to send their children to school. The parents refused to send their children because the Amish way of life, as based on their religion, is incompatible with education beyond the eighth grade. The parents successfully challenged their convictions under the First Amendment. The Court characterized "a religious belief or practice entitled to constitutional protection" as "not merely a matter of personal preference, but one of deep religious conviction, shared by an organized group, and intimately related to daily living." The parties in *Seeger* and *Welsh* did not claim to be part of an organized religious group, yet the Court found that their beliefs fell within the definition of religion, so no one factor appears to be determinative for the court.

B. Applicability of the Religion Clauses to the States

For most of the nation's history, the Constitution's references to religion did not apply to the states. The language of the First Amendment refers only to the federal government: "Congress shall make no law respecting an establishment of religion, or prohibiting the free exercise thereof." The Court used the Fourteenth Amendment to apply the Religion Clauses to the states. It incorporated the Free Exercise Clause in *Cantwell v. Connecticut* (1940) and the Establishment Clause in *Everson v. Board of Education* (1947). This incorporation of the Religion Clauses into the Fourteenth Amendment for application against the states is the law today.

But does Article VI, Clause 3 of the Constitution, which prohibits religious tests for government office, apply to the states? In *Torcaso v. Watkins* (1961), the Court struck down a provision of the Maryland constitution that required a person to declare his or her belief in God before taking public office. But the court, reaffirming *Everson*, based its ruling on the establishment clause: "We repeat and again reaffirm that neither a State nor the Federal Government can constitutionally force a person 'to profess a belief or disbelief in any religion.'" In Footnote 1 of the opinion Justice Black wrote: "Appellant also claimed that the State's test oath requirement violates the provision of Art. VI of the Federal Constitution that 'no religious Test shall ever be required as a Qualification to any Office or public Trust under the United States.' Because we are reversing the judgment on other grounds, we find it unnecessary to consider appellant's contention that this provision applies to state as well as federal offices." The question of whether the no religious test clause binds the states remains unresolved. (Given the Court's First Amendment holding, that issue is largely academic).

II. The Establishment Clause

The First Amendment begins with the phrase: "Congress shall make no law respecting an establishment of religion." Although it is a prohibition directed at Congress, it has since been applied to the states through the incorporation doctrine of the Fourteenth Amendment. But what is a "law respecting an establishment of religion"? Clearly, the Establishment Clause prevents the government from aiding or formally establishing a government-sponsored religion. As Justice Black stated, a government may not set up a church or pass laws to aid one religion, all religions, or one religion over another (*Everson v. Board of Educ.*, 1947). However, even acting neutrally would "aid" religion in some manner, even if the government provided fire and police protection for religious buildings and nothing more. Thus, the government can completely avoid aiding religion only by actively acting against religion, but that is proscribed by the Free Exercise Clause, which is discussed in the next major section.

A. Three Major Analytical Frameworks: Strict Separation, Neutrality, and Accommodation

Three major analytical frameworks have developed to carry out the requirements of the Establishment Clause. Each has its promoters on the Court and each is visible in the Court's decisions. The first is commonly called the "wall of separation" or "strict separation." The second advocates the government taking a neutral approach to religion. The third advocates an accommodation approach to balance the relationship between government and religion.

1. *Wall of Separation or Strict Separation Approach*

The wall of separation approach maintains that the government should be separated from any and all religion as much as is practically possible. The phrase "wall of separation" was coined by Roger Williams, founder of the first Baptist church in America, when he wrote in 1644 of "[A] hedge or wall of separation between the garden of the church and the wilderness of the world." Thomas Jefferson, in an 1802 letter to the Danbury Baptist Association in Connecticut, adopted the phrase and wrote that the Religion Clauses of the First Amendment erected a wall of separation between the government and religion. The wall of separation approach requires the government to take an active stance to avoid interaction with religion as much as possible. Whether the motivation is to protect the state from the evils of religion, protect religion from the evils of the government, or create an environment where both flourish best, strict separationists will do their best to keep state and religion completely out of each other's realms. However, as mentioned before, some government functions, such as police and fire protection, cannot be denied to religious institutions without raising free exercise problems, even though, on some level, they can be viewed as aiding religion, without discriminating against religious institutions. Thus, even a strict separation approach cannot become an absolutist position without involving religious discrimination.

The Court first articulated the wall of separation doctrine in *Reynolds v. U.S.* (1878). Reynolds, a member of The Church of Jesus Christ of Latter-day Saints (LDS), was charged with bigamy under the Morill Anti-Bigamy Act after marrying Amelia Jane Schofield while still married to Mary Ann Tuddenham in the Utah Territory. He was secretary to Brigham Young and presented himself as a test of the federal government's attempt to outlaw polygamy. Reynolds argued that it was his religious duty to marry multiple times, and that the First Amendment protected his practice of his religion. The court examined the history of religious liberty in the US, determining that while the Constitution guarantees religious freedom, "the word 'religion' is not defined in the Constitution. We must go elsewhere, therefore, to ascertain its meaning, and nowhere more appropriately, we think, than to the history of the times in the midst of which the provision was adopted." The Court found that the leaders in advocating and formulating the constitutional guarantee of religious liberty were James Madison and Thomas Jefferson. Quoting the "separation" paragraph from Jefferson's letter to the Danbury Baptists, the court concluded that, "coming as this does from an acknowledged leader of the advocates of the measure, it may be accepted almost as an authoritative declaration of the scope and effect of the amendment thus secured." The Court also observed that the letter distinguished religious belief from action that flowed from religious belief. The former "lies solely between man and his God," therefore "the legislative powers of the government reach actions only, and not opinions." The court considered that if polygamy was allowed, someone might eventually argue that human sacrifice was a necessary part of their religion, and "to permit this would be to make the professed doctrines of religious belief superior to the law of the land, and in effect to permit every citizen to become a law unto himself."

The wall of separation language was next used 69 years later in *Everson* (1947). In that case, a school board in New Jersey had created a program to reimburse parents for the costs of using public transportation to send their children to Catholic schools. In his majority opinion, Justice Black wrote that the Establishment Clause constructs a wall that separates the government from religion, and that the "wall must be kept high and impregnable." He also said that the Court could not accept or permit any breach of the wall, no matter how small. However, the Court did not find that the reimbursement program breached that wall because providing public transportation was not related to religion but was a public function. Justice Black compared public transportation to other public functions, such as providing police and fire protection. Further, the Court said that, although providing the reimbursement did not violate the Establishment Clause, the Free Exercise Clause did not require the government to provide reimbursement for public transportation costs. The Court made it clear that even in a strict separation approach compromises must be made. So the question becomes where to draw the line, and strict separationists generally draw it in ways to keep religion out of the public sphere as much as possible.

Supporters of the neutrality and accommodation framework disagree with the notion of "separation of church and state," or at least the way the Supreme Court has interpreted the constitutional limitation on religious establishment. They think the phrase misrepresents the textual requirements of the Constitution and note that many aspects of church and state were intermingled at the time of the Constitution's ratification. Some of the intermingling between church and state includes religious references in official contexts and such other founding documents as the Declaration of Independence, which references the idea of a "Creator" and "Nature's God" (though these references did not ultimately appear in the Constitution). Critics of the wall of separation approach argue that a clear dividing line between religious expression and government expression is impossible and, therefore, the wall metaphor is unhelpful. Critics also argue that many strict separationists are hostile to religion, seeking to confine it to a private sphere, which is contrary to the elevation of the fundamental right to freedom of religion guaranteed by the First Amendment.

2. *Neutrality Approach: The Endorsement Test*

The second major framework focuses on maintaining neutrality between government and religion. This means that the government cannot give or indicate a preference of religion over secularism or another religion. The neutrality approach is supported by the Court's decision in *Everson*, which prohibited state power from being used to either handicap or favor religions. Other supporters of neutrality argue that it requires the government to keep its promotion or discouragement of religious observance, belief, or activity to a minimum.

The difficulty arises in evaluating whether a government program or activity violates the neutrality requirement. In *Lynch v. Donnelly* (1984), Justice O'Connor expressed the view that the neutrality approach mandates that every government act be examined under the totality of the circumstances to determine whether it amounts to an endorsement or disapproval of religion. The difficulty of measuring the neutrality of government action led to the development of an "endorsement test"—whether the government action endorses either a specific religion or its symbols or endorses religion over secularism in general. This test has been promoted by several Justices (in addition to Justice O'Connor).

In *Capitol Square Review & Advisory Board v. Pinette* (1995), the Court addressed (without a majority opinion) which government actions violate the endorsement test and when it should be applied. Seven Justices agreed that, if the state government had allowed the Ku Klux Klan to place a large cross in a ten-acre public park across from the statehouse in Columbus, Ohio, it would not have violated the Establishment Clause. In separate opinions, the Justices articulated three different approaches to applying the test. Justice Antonin Scalia, writing for the majority, opposed applying the test when the issue is private speech delivered on public property. Justice O'Connor, joined by two other Justices, concurred, stating that the endorsement test is applied from the perspective of a reasonable person, similar to that in tort law, but possessing some knowledge that may not be held by the general public. This removes the focus from examining (1) whether a particular person would be offended by the potential religious character of the government's action and from (2) whether a reasonable person would think that the action endorses religion. Justices John Stevens and Ruth Bader Ginsburg advocate the third approach, agreeing with Justice O'Connor that endorsement depends on the perception of a reasonable person, but without any special knowledge and simply from the perspective of a passerby. Thus, the government could allow the Ku Klux Klan to place/ burn the cross, without endorsing the Klan or its symbols (the cross) and without endorsing the Klan over another religion or secularism.

3. *Accommodation of Religion Approach*

The third major framework, accommodation of religion, is based on the belief that the Establishment Clause recognizes the social importance of religion. Supporters of accommodation argue that the presence of religion in society should be welcomed, as long as the government does not directly aid a religion in its religious function. Under the accommodation framework, government action only violates the Establishment Clause if it establishes a state religion, forces people to participate in religion, or favors one religion over another. Anything else would not run afoul of the Establishment Clause.

Justice Stanley Reed applied this approach in his dissent in *Illinois ex rel McCollum v. Board of Education* (1948). *McCollum* involved a program releasing public school students from class for a short period to attend optional religious classes on the school premises. The Court held that this program was unconstitutional because the classes occurred on public school premises (thus, the state's laws compelling student attendance at school were used to teach religion). In his dissent, Justice Reed argued that the Founding Fathers, including Jefferson and Madison, had approved of requiring students at the University of Virginia to attend religious services. Thus, because education was a public function, and not a religious one, Justice Reed said that the requirement did not support a religion itself.

The Court addressed a similar situation in *Zorach v. Clauson* (1952). In this case, the program was upheld because the religious classes were not taking place on public school property. The Court stated, "When the state encourages religious instruction or cooperates with religious authorities by adjusting the schedule of public events to sectarian needs, it follows the best of our traditions. For it then respects the religious nature of our people and accommodates the public service to their spiritual needs." Justice William Douglas's majority opinion stated that complete separation between church and state would interfere with many social traditions based on religion, such as chaplains in legislatures, religious holidays off from school, and oaths in the courtroom. The dissenting opinions, by Justice Robert Jackson and Justice Black, criticized the majority's distinction based merely on the location of the religious classes. They argued that it would not violate the Establishment Clause only if the religious instruction occurred outside of school hours. Justice Black also reiterated his wall of separation view and explained that the majority's decision represented a balancing test that strayed too far into the realm of religion and that a categorical approach is more appropriate.

B. The *Lemon* Test for Analyzing the Establishment Clause

In 1970, the Court implemented a tripartite test for deciding cases under the Establishment Clause, and held that a law is constitutional if it:

1. Has a secular purpose;
2. Primary effect neither advances nor inhibits religion; and
3. Does not create an "excessive entanglement" between government and religion.

Lemon v. Kurtzman (1971) involved a challenge to Rhode Island and Pennsylvania statutes that subsidized salaries for teachers in private schools. Chief Justice Warren Burger, writing for the majority, reasoned that the Establishment Clause not only forbade establishing an official religion but also prohibited government actions that were steps in that direction. Chief Justice Burger acknowledged that the Court's prior decisions did not call for a total separation between church and state, and that the "wall" of separation had become "a blurred, indistinct, and variable barrier." The Chief Justice then created what has been called the *Lemon* test. This test provides that a law that allows for "sponsorship, financial support, [or] active involvement" in religious activity violates the Establishment Clause, unless it has a secular legislative purpose, its primary effect neither advances nor inhibits religion, and it avoids creating "excessive entanglement" between government and religion. The analysis under the excessive entanglement prong involves these three factors:

1. The "character and purposes" of the particular religious institutions;
2. The nature of the governmental aid; and
3. The relationship between the two that results from the aid.

The Court applied its new test and held the state statutes unconstitutional because they violated the Establishment Clause. The state laws required substantial oversight and intervention of "an intimate and continuing" character to ensure that the schools receiving the government aid did not violate the neutral stance on religion mandated by the First Amendment. This oversight and intervention would require entanglement between the government and the institution of the character and nature prohibited by the Religion Clauses.

Although the *Lemon* test was announced in the context of financial aid to religious institutions, it is used as a general framework for analyzing laws under the Establishment Clause, and its very terms indicate that it has broader application. It is important to note that the Court is not restricted to the *Lemon* test. It has since decided several cases without using it. The test is a favorite of those Justices who favor the wall of separation framework, including both of its subcategories of strict separation and neutrality; whereas Justices who favor the accommodation framework have pushed for the Court to overrule the *Lemon* test. Recent developments have called the vitality of the test into question even though it has never been expressly overruled. Some fairly recent decisions have even invoked the test with approval. However, several Justices on the Court (if not a majority) disapprove of the test and have advocated replacing it with other alternative approaches.

C. Other Tests Proposed, but Not Adopted

The symbolic endorsement test is a reformulation of the *Lemon* test. Over the past few decades, several Justices have adopted it. Most recently, Justice O'Connor applied it in her concurrence in *Lynch v. Donnelly* (1984), which is discussed shortly. Nevertheless, it has remained a minority test and has never been adopted authoritatively by the Court. The symbolic endorsement test examines whether the challenged government act expresses government endorsement or disapproval of religion. This endorsement or disapproval can either be direct (intent to endorse or disprove) or indirect (the act's effect is endorsement or disproval). The test differs from the *Lemon* test by deemphasizing the secular purpose prong and reformulating the other two prongs into an analysis of the endorsement or disapproval of religion.

The "endorsement test" was applied in *Salazar v. Bueno* (2010). Under this test, the Court views the challenged religious display, which arguably excessively entangles government and religion, through the eyes of a hypothetical reasonable viewer who is aware of all pertinent facts and history surrounding the display. In 1934, a Latin cross was placed on a rock outcropping to honor fallen soldiers in World War I. Over time, the cross had deteriorated, and a new one was erected in its place on the Mojave National Preserve. A retired Park Service employee challenged the constitutionality of this religious symbol on national lands. Under the endorsement test the Court held this monument would be reasonably viewed as commemorating fallen soldiers, not endorsing a religious viewpoint. The Court reasoned that the cross had been deemed by Congress to be a monument honoring our national heritage, had been continuously repaired by the community and was a place where the community regularly gathered to pay homage to these fallen individuals.

Another alternative to the *Lemon* test is the "coercion test." This test has also received substantial support from some Justices, with Justice Kennedy applying it in several cases, including *County of Allegheny v. ACLU* (1989) and *Lee v. Weisman* (1992). The coercion test examines the government action for the coercive effect it has on participation in state-sponsored or state-initiated religious activity. It is typically applied in the context of primary and secondary schools but has been applied in other situations as well. The coercion examined can be obvious or subtle. Subtle coercion, such as peer pressure, is more insidious because it is harder to detect. Similar to the symbolic endorsement test, the coercion test has remained a minority approach, and the Court has never expressly supported it.

D. Government Support for Religious Beliefs

1. *School Prayer and Other Government-Sanctioned Prayer*

Since the 1960s, a common Establishment Clause battleground has been prayer in public schools. The Supreme Court has held that prayer in public schools is unconstitutional if it is initiated or sanctioned by school officials. The Court reached this decision in *Engel v. Vitale* (1961), where a New York school district wrote a prayer and required the students to recite it at the beginning of each school day. The Court held that this was a clear violation of the Establishment Clause. Relying on historical arguments, Justice Black, writing for the majority, explained that the First Amendment precludes the government from prescribing any official prayer in any program of state-sponsored religious activity. Justice Douglas concurred, relying on the neutrality framework and reasoning that government interference in spiritual matters would be a divisive force.

In his dissent, Justice Potter Stewart advocated the accommodation framework. He wrote that denying children the ability to pray interferes with the nation's spiritual heritage. This heritage includes several government-sponsored invocations of religion such as the Supreme Court's invocation of God's protection at the beginning of every day's session, the provision in the Pledge of Allegiance that the United States is "one nation under God," and the National Day of Prayer, which Congress established in 1952. He reasoned that students praying in school is similar to *Zorach* (students allowed to leave school for religious classes) because the school district's prayer is merely an expression of our national heritage. Several constitutional amendments have been proposed to authorize prayer in public schools. However, none of these amendments have received the required two-thirds vote to pass Congress.

Similarly, in *Abington School District v. Schempp*, the Court struck down a state law that required public school students to read Bible verses at the beginning of the day and recite the Lord's Prayer. Unlike *Engle*, the state did not write the content of the prayer. Yet the Court held that the school requirement was an inherently religious activity and violated the Establishment Clause. The Court was careful to limit its holding: it did not extend the decision to preclude the study of any religion's scripture in literature or religion courses.

The Court's holdings in *Engle* and *Abington* make it clear that the Establishment Clause prohibits government-prescribed prayer in public school. In *Wallace v. Jaffree* (1984), the Court expanded this holding to an Alabama statute that provided for prayer led by teachers for *willing* students only. But what about a period of silence in public schools that can be used for meditation or prayer? In *Wallace v. Jaffree* (1985), the Court considered two other Alabama statutes that authorized a one-minute period of silence for meditation (1978 statute) and a period of silence for "meditation or voluntary prayer" (1981 statute).

The majority took a stance reminiscent of the neutrality framework in its analysis of the statute before the Court. Justice Stevens, writing for the majority, applied the *Lemon* test and held that the statute violated the first prong, which requires the legislative act to have a secular purpose. The Court held that the law lacked a secular purpose because the legislature intended to return voluntary prayer to Alabama public schools. The Court further reasoned that the only purpose was religious because the statute had the same effect as the 1978 statute, except that it added prayer as an accepted activity. This statute therefore was an endorsement of a religious activity.

Justice O'Connor, in her concurrence, also took a neutrality stance while balancing the competing values of the Religion Clauses. She reasoned that nothing in the Constitution prohibits students from engaging in completely voluntary prayer. A state law that provides for a moment of silence, without mentioning prayer, was sufficient to protect the students' rights to voluntary prayer and to avoid impermissible government involvement in religion.

Chief Justice Burger dissented and advocated the accommodation framework. He argued that the statute merely stated that prayer was a permitted activity, and because it did not require prayer, it was not an endorsement of prayer. Justice Byron White agreed with this position, reasoning that the statement was necessary, otherwise a teacher would not be able to confidently say that prayer was permitted, if a student so inquired.

In *Lee v. Weisman* (1992) the Court considered the issue of prayer at graduation ceremonies. It held that public schools could not invite clergymen to deliver invocations and benedictions at middle school and high school graduations. The majority opinion, written by Justice Kennedy, stated that the government may not coerce the support of religion or participate in the exercise of religion. It may also not act in a manner that establishes or tends to establish a state religion. The Court held that the law violated the Establishment Clause because it permitted school principals to select and invite clergymen to pray at school-sponsored graduations, and control the content of the prayer by telling the clergymen that it must be nonsectarian. The Court also found that peer pressure could force unwilling students to participate. Justice David Souter concurred, expressing the concern that students participating in the graduation ceremony would be a captive audience to any prayer delivered. He distinguished presidential proclamations and addresses because they are not targeted at any person in particular, and the audience is free to leave.

The Court also examined prayer at school-sponsored activities that are not academically related. In *Santa Fe Independent School District v. Doe* (2000), the Court held that student-led nondenominational prayer at high school football games was unconstitutional even though the students voted on whether to have the prayer and which student should deliver it. Justice Stevens wrote the majority opinion, stating that this was not private speech because the public school endorsed and facilitated the prayer. It endorsed the prayer by encouraging it and following the tradition of praying at football games. The school facilitated prayer by providing the facilities where they were delivered and permitting their broadcast over the school's public address system. Additionally, the fact that the students voted to have the prayer did not make it constitutional because fundamental rights cannot be removed by majority vote. Justice Stevens noted that the proper question was whether an objective observer would perceive the prayer as state endorsement of religion, similar to the "symbolic endorsement" test offered by Justice O'Connor and others.

In *Elk Grove Unified School District v. Newdow* (2004), the Court had an opportunity to address whether the phrase "under God" in the Pledge of Allegiance constituted prayer in school. The Elk Grove Unified School District's policy required elementary school teachers to lead their students in reciting the Pledge. The father of a student sued on the grounds that the policy violated the Establishment Clause. However, the Court sidestepped the issue and unanimously disposed of the case on standing grounds stating that because the plaintiff did not have legal custody of his daughter, he could not sue on her behalf.

Justice Stevens wrote the plurality opinion for the Court and concluded that the Pledge is a common pronouncement of the ideals represented by the flag of the United States. Stevens noted that the Pledge was originally created over 100 years ago, that Congress adopted it in 1942, and in 1954 Congress amended the Pledge to include "under God."

Three Justices, Chief Justice William Rehnquist, Justice O'Connor, and Justice Clarence Thomas, wrote concurring opinions. Chief Justice Rehnquist believed that the Court should not sidestep the issue. Rather, it should hold that reciting the Pledge, including the phrase "under God," does not violate the Establishment Clause. For Chief Justice Rehnquist, the phrase is not sufficient to transform reciting the Pledge into a religious exercise because it only recognizes the founding history of the country.

Justice Thomas reiterated his argument that the Establishment Clause is a federal provision and thus is not incorporated into the Fourteenth Amendment. He argued that, regardless, the school district's policy did not create, maintain, or lend governmental authority to establish any religion. Justice O'Connor again advocated the endorsement test and its application to speech and public displays sponsored by the state. She considered the Pledge to be "ceremonial deism," which is ceremonial references to the divine in certain circumstances without offending the First Amendment. Other examples include the imprint of "In God We Trust" on the currency, traditional patriotic songs, and the Court's invocation of God before beginning each session. Justice O'Connor explained that the phrase "under God" is a generic reference to the divine, not a specific reference to any certain deity or religion. Furthermore, even if some of the members of Congress who approved the phrase had religious purposes, those purposes are not controlling because they also had valid secular purposes.

Engel, *Jaffree*, *Lee*, and *Doe* clearly indicate that prayer in public schools is generally not permitted if the schools or any other level of government, sanction or endorse it in any way. This includes student-led, nondenominational, and voluntary prayer if the school sanctions the prayer, the organization, or its delivery. Allowing the students to vote on whether to have the prayer does not remove the government's impermissible entanglement, which arose from the school sanctioning the prayer. However, it is an open question as to whether prayer at a public school activity, such as graduation, would be permitted if it was entirely originated by students and if the school had no part in organizing, delivering, or managing the prayer. The Court has yet to decide this issue, despite an existing split in the circuit courts.

2. Issues Involving School Curriculum Decisions

School prayer is only one way that a state may violate the Establishment Clause of the First Amendment. Another is a public school's inclusion of religious doctrine or ideas in its curriculum. A primary example of this is the struggle between teaching creationism and evolution. Until Charles Darwin's theory of evolution, articulated in his 1859 book *On the Origin of Species*, became accepted in the scientific community, schools taught the Genesis creation narrative as the origin of the universe. As schools switched to teaching evolution, a backlash ensued, the most significant of which occurred after World War I when several states passed laws banning the teaching of evolution. The famous Scopes Trial involved the prosecution of John Scopes, a high school science teacher, for violating Tennessee's Butler Act which had made it unlawful to teach evolution in any state-funded school. Although the trial addressed whether modern science could be taught in public schools, the backdrop was a theological contest between Modernists who said evolution was consistent with religion, and Fundamentalists who said it was not. Scopes lost his case and additional states passed laws banning the teaching of evolution.

In 1928, Arkansas passed a law modelled after Tennessee's Butler Act that prohibited any teacher in a public school or publicly funded university from teaching evolution. The statute specifically forbade teaching "the theory or doctrine that mankind ascended or descended from a lower order of animals" or adopting or using a textbook that taught such a theory. A violation of the statute was a misdemeanor and punishable by the teacher's removal from his or her position. In 1966, Susan Epperson, a biology teacher in Little Rock, Arkansas, decided to teach evolution but did not want to lose her job. So she filed a lawsuit seeking to overturn the law and to obtain an injunction against her being dismissed for teaching the evolutionary curriculum. The case eventually arrived at the Supreme Court and in *Epperson v. Arkansas* (1968), the Court held the Arkansas law unconstitutional for violating the Establishment Clause.

Writing for the Court, Justice Abe Fortas recognized that a state has plenary power to prescribe its school curriculum, but held that this power does not extend to prohibiting the teaching of a scientific theory without violating the Establishment Clause. Although the Arkansas law did not expressly support religion, Justice Fortas reasoned that it was based on the same religious purposes as Tennessee's Butler Act which was the subject of the *Scopes* trial. The Court said that a legislature cannot circumvent the Establishment Clause simply by omitting religious language from a law that excludes a scientific theory from school curriculum when the basis for the exclusion is to further religious doctrine.

Justice Black's concurrence stated that the Court was misguided by overturning the law because it determined that the law was motivated by religion. He wrote that it was simply too difficult to determine the legislature's actual reason for passing the law, and that the Court should defer to the legislature's stated purpose. He also considered the majority's position to be dangerous because it required public schools to teach a theory that many consider to be anti-religious and the Establishment Clause does not permit preferring non-religion over religion.

After the Court's decision in *Epperson v. Arkansas*, creationists lobbied states to adopt laws that required teachers to teach creationism. The Court considered this issue in *Edwards v. Aguillard* (1987). *Aguillard* involved a Louisiana statute that forbade teaching evolution in public schools unless the school also taught creationism. The statute allowed schools to teach neither concept; but if a school taught one, then it was required to teach the other. The trial and appellate courts both found that the law violated the Establishment Clause.

Justice Brennan, writing for the majority, explained that the Court is especially vigilant in monitoring the compliance of elementary and secondary schools with the Establishment Clause because of the tender age and impressionability of the students. The Court applied the *Lemon* test and found that the law was unconstitutional because it violated the first prong of the test (law must have a secular purpose). Generally, a court must defer to the legislature's stated reason for enacting a law, unless the stated purpose is inaccurate and is a pretext to conceal the true purpose. Louisiana claimed that its secular purpose was to protect academic freedom. However, the Court observed that the law restricted the teaching of evolution and the law's sponsor preferred that schools teach neither creationism nor evolution. The Court found the stated purpose to be a pretext because teaching neither doctrine would in fact hamper academic freedom and undermine providing a comprehensive education in the sciences. The effect of the law failed to foster academic freedom because no law prohibited the teaching of any scientific theory. Rather, it removed the teachers' freedom to teach only evolution. The Court found that "because the primary purpose of the Creationism Act is to endorse a particular religious doctrine, the Act furthers religion in violation of the establishment clause."

Creationists then sought to remove the overt religious component to their theory and re-name it "intelligent design." They argue that intelligent design is "an evidence-based scientific theory about life's origins" that challenges the dominant view of modern science. They lobbied school districts to require the teaching of intelligent design. The Supreme Court has not heard a challenge to such a requirement but in *Kitzmiller v. Dover Area School District* (2005), a U.S. District Court ruled that a public school district policy that required the teaching of intelligent design violated the Establishment Clause.

Another question the Court has confronted is whether a state may require public schools to offer activities that are arguably religious if the state claims that they have secular purposes. In *Abington School District v. Schempp* (1963), the Court addressed a state law that required public schools to begin each school day with a reading of at least ten Bible verses without commentary. Abington Senior High School began its school day by reading the verses and reciting the Lord's Prayer. This activity was led by a student, who selected the verses and the version of the Bible to use. The school provided a copy of the King James Version, but the student could use another version if she provided it herself. Pennsylvania claimed that the law served secular purposes, including promoting morality, counteracting materialism, preserving our institutions, and teaching literature. The Court said that the religious nature of the activity could not be ignored and held that the activity violated the Establishment Clause. It explained that the law was not constitutional simply because students could excuse themselves from participating in the activity.

Writing for the majority, Justice Tom Clark recognized that the Court cannot endorse a "religion of secularism" because doing so would permit the government to either establish or act hostilely toward religion. However, he explained that holding this law unconstitutional does not prohibit the Bible from being studied for its literary and historic value or from being used in a comparative study of religion, and the Establishment Clause does not mandate such a course of action. However, a state requiring its government-sponsored schools to participate in religious exercises violates the concept of neutrality embodied in the Establishment Clause.

Justice Brennan concurred, recognizing that the exercises mandated by the law may have permissible goals, such as fostering harmony and tolerance and enhancing the teacher's authority. However, because these benefits were not derived from the content of the activity but from the solemn and communal nature of the exercise, the same goals could be reached with "less sensitive materials." For example, schools could achieve the same effect by reading the speeches of great Americans, reading from historical documents, or even reciting the Pledge of Allegiance. Justice Brennan refuted the argument that the law was constitutional because it does not prefer one Christian or Jewish sect over another because many others would find the forced reading of the Judeo-Christian Scriptures patently offensive. Similarly, any attempt to create a "common denominator religion," divorced from any particular institution, is doomed to fail.

From these cases, it is clear that the Court interprets the Establishment Clause as prohibiting the states from infusing religion into public school curricula. The state cannot condition the teaching of a scientific theory on the teaching of a competing religious doctrine. It also cannot require public schools to provide religious exercises, even if the legislature claims a secular purpose for the activity or permits the students to choose to not participate. Regardless of whether participation is voluntary, the Establishment Clause is violated by infusing religion into government-sponsored school curricula, either in courses taught or activities provided.

3. *Equal Access, Religious Displays, and Official Acknowledgment of Religion*

Reconciling the need for government neutrality with the notion that public spaces should be open to at least some religious expression is a difficult balancing act for the courts. How much space should the state give to religion to accommodate it, without violating the Establishment Clause? This issue arises in several different contexts, including religious groups' access to public facilities, public displays of religion and official acknowledgment of religion.

a. Equal Access to Public Facilities

One example of access to public facilities that frequently arises is equal access to facilities at public schools or state universities. The Court addressed this in *Widmar v. Vincent* (1981), in which it struck down a Kansas state university regulation that prohibited student-run religious organizations from using the university's facilities. The Court rejected the argument that religious worship and teaching were not speech protected by the free speech clause. Justice Powell, writing for the Court, said "the question is not whether the creation of a religious forum would violate the Establishment Clause." The question is whether the University, by opening its facilities for use by student groups and excluding groups because of the content of their speech, can meet the test of strict scrutiny. He recognized the state's compelling interest in complying with the Establishment Clause; however, an "equal access" policy would not be incompatible with that Clause if it meets *Lemon's* three-pronged test: (1) It has a secular legislative purpose; (2) its principal or primary effect would be neither to advance nor to inhibit religion; and (3) it does not foster "an excessive government entanglement with religion." Justice Powell explained that an open-forum policy (permitting access to all registered student groups) has a secular purpose, and because all groups were permitted, it would not give rise to excessive entanglement with religion. Additionally, the effect prong would be satisfied because the primary effect of such a policy would not benefit religion, and any benefit to religious groups would be incidental to and encompassed by the benefits to all other student groups, religious and secular alike.

This issue arose nine years after *Widmar*, in *Board of Education v. Mergens* (1990). *Mergens* presented the question of the constitutionality of the federal Equal Access Act, which required secondary schools that received any federal financial assistance to provide equal access to student groups. Per the Act, if a school allowed any noncurricular student groups to meet at the school during non-instructional time, it created a "limited open forum" and could not discriminate based on the ideas of any group. Westside High School denied a request by some students to form a Christian club with membership open to all students. The Court, in an eight-to-one decision, upheld the Act, finding that it did not violate the Establishment Clause.

Justice O'Connor wrote an opinion that was in part a majority opinion and in part a plurality opinion. The majority interpreted the term "limited open forum" in the federal statute and held that it differed from the concept of a limited public forum in the Court's First Amendment jurisprudence. The limited open forum in the statute applied to any noncurricular group, including a chess club or a volunteer service organization, and prohibited discrimination against a group based on the religious or political content of the group's beliefs or expression. Although the Act limited the participation of school officials in the meetings of any religious groups, it permitted the school to monitor the activities of a group.

Despite an overwhelming vote in favor of the constitutionality of the Equal Access Act, the Court could not agree on the reasons that it did not violate the Establishment Clause. Justice O'Connor, in her plurality opinion, found that the statute passed the *Lemon* test. She explained that the purpose of the law was secular because it was an antidiscrimination measure, its primary effect was not to advance religion, and it did not create any excessive entanglement because the school officials were restricted from participating in the group's activities. In his concurrence, Justice Thurgood Marshall did not challenge the use of the *Lemon* test but reasoned that any school that permitted a religiously oriented student group to operate would have to take measures to avoid the appearance that the school endorsed the group's views.

Justice Kennedy, also concurring, did not join Justice O'Connor's use of the *Lemon* test. Instead, he argued that the Court should find that the Act violated the Establishment Clause only if (1) it directly benefited religion so as to establish or tend to establish a state religion or (2) the government coerced student participation in religious activities. Because neither condition was met, the Act was constitutional. Justice Kennedy also refused to apply the *Lemon* test in such a manner that would significantly restrict the ability of the government to accommodate religion. The sole dissenter, Justice Stevens, found that only extracurricular student groups advocating partisan religious, political, or ethical beliefs were noncurricular groups within the statutory meaning. Further, the Court's construction of the Act was perilously close to requiring schools to permit organized prayer and possibly some religious ceremonies.

In *Lamb's Chapel v. Center Moriches Union Free School District* (1993), the Court unanimously upheld the general rule that government cannot discriminate against a speaker by punishing speech or denying the right to speak based on the religious content of one's speech. In that instance, the Court overturned a school district's regulation that prohibited a religious group from using available school property, even though social, civic, or recreational groups were permitted. Justice White, writing for the Court, held that this discrimination was unconstitutional in violation of the Free Exercise Clause. However, the Court also held that permitting the religious group access to school property when it was not being used for school purposes was not an establishment of religion. Although he did not use it in his analysis, Justice White expressly stated that the *Lemon* test was still viable. He stated, without analysis, that permitting religious groups access to school property after school hours was not an establishment of religion under *Lemon*. This decision was upheld in *Good News Club v. Milford* (2001), where the Court held that the exclusion of a Christian children's club from meeting on school premises after school hours was impermissible viewpoint discrimination.

b. Employment of Chaplains by Legislatures

Apart from the realm of the public school and the state university, the Court has also addressed state involvement with religious practices in other contexts. In these non-educational contexts, the Court has been substantially more accommodating of the involvement of government in religious activities. The Court has upheld the practice of many legislatures, including Congress, of employing chaplains and opening its sessions with prayer. It has also found that displays of city-owned religious symbols on private property do not violate the Establishment Clause.

The Court addressed legislative employment of chaplains to deliver prayer in *Marsh v. Chambers* (1983). *Chambers* involved a challenge to Nebraska's legislature, which had chaplains on its payroll and opened each legislative session with a state-sanctioned prayer. The state legislature had employed a Presbyterian minister for eighteen years. The Court held that this was not a violation of the Establishment Clause. Writing for the majority, Chief Justice Burger explained that, in light of the long tradition of opening legislative meetings with prayer, history weighed against finding this practice unconstitutional. Without considering application of the *Lemon* test, the Chief Justice relied solely on history and found that based on "the unambiguous and unbroken history of more than 200 years," the practice had become such a part of society that its constitutionality could not be seriously contested. He also stated that the compensation of the chaplain from the public treasury similarly did not raise a constitutional issue. In fact, he noted that the same Congress that enacted the First Amendment had a paid chaplain. Although *Marsh* stands for the proposition that if the historical argument is so clear and strong the *Lemon* test need not be used, the Chief Justice failed to explain why history proved so decisive and how it could displace the test.

In his dissent, Justice Brennan argued that the Court had abandoned the criteria that the Court had developed since *Everson*. Justice Brennan articulated the view that the Constitution is a living, evolving document that should not be stifled by historical calcification. He argued that the diversity of religion in the United States required a new interpretation of the Establishment Clause; the issue should turn on whether state sponsorship of a religious practice would offend the sensibilities of today's Americans, considering their increased diversity.

In *Town of Greece v. Galloway* (2014), a 5–4 majority held that the town's practice of opening its town board meetings with a prayer offered by members of the clergy does not violate the Establishment Clause when (1) the practice is consistent with the tradition long followed by Congress and state legislatures, (2) the town does not discriminate against minority faiths in determining who may offer a prayer, and (3) the prayer does not coerce participation from non-adherents. Although the ideological split was predictable, the court was surprisingly unanimous in the view that some legislative prayers are constitutionally permissible. In *Marsh* (1983), there were three dissenters, but in *Town of Greece* even the dissenters agreed with *Marsh*. As Justice Kagan wrote, "I believe that pluralism and inclusion in a town hall can satisfy the constitutional requirement of neutrality; such a forum need not become a religion-free zone."

So the division between the majority and dissent centered on how to accommodate religious diversity. Justice Kennedy's majority opinion found that neutrality and equal treatment of religious diversity is best achieved by allowing each particular faith to express itself in its own uniqueness. Christians can mention Jesus when it is their turn, Muslims can mention Mohammed when it is their turn, and so on. Although each particular prayer may be sectarian, the scheme as a whole is not: the scheme as a whole recognizes religious diversity. Each person gets his or her turn to represent his or her faith. This approach also respects equality in that religious citizens are citizens too, and part of recognizing them as equal citizens is to allow their beliefs and their practices to frame and even solemnize governmental occasions.

Justice Kagan's dissent seeks religious speech that finds common denominators between faiths so that all faiths are placated and none exalted. In her view, each speaker must tone down their particular faith as a sign of respect of other faiths. Her approach is to avoid having those who do not share the speaker's beliefs, feel isolated, alienated, or separated from their government. She is not as concerned about coercion as she is that they will feel like outsiders to their own government because they do not share in the faith of those who are governing them. Justice Kennedy tries to deflect this worry by saying that if there emerges a "pattern of prayers that over time denigrate, proselytize or betray an impermissible government purpose," then this may rise to a Constitutional violation. But the standard is vague and hard to define: what constitutes a pattern? Kennedy later refers to "a course and practice over time"— but over *how long* of a time? When does a prayer tip over into proselytization?

Justice Kagan's alternative to letting each religion pray uncensored is to try to find a kind or type of prayer that everyone will find acceptable, a kind of common denominator theism. But what kind of prayer is acceptable to the range of religions and atheists? Those who dislike their faith being watered down to a generic God might also be offended and there is the problem of enforcement. As Justice Kennedy explained, "to hold that invocations must be nonsectarian would force the legislatures that sponsor prayers and the courts that are asked to decide these cases to act as supervisors and censors of religious speech." Better, Kennedy went on, is the Town of Greece's "current practice of neither editing nor approving prayers in advance nor criticizing their content after the fact."

c. *Religious Displays*

The Court considered the display of religious symbols in *Lynch v. Donnelly* (1984). *Lynch* involved a Christmas nativity scene that the city owned but displayed on private property held by a nonprofit organization. The display included a Christmas tree, colored lights, reindeer, Santa's sleigh, and a nativity scene. The Court held that this did not violate the Establishment Clause. Chief Justice Burger, writing for the Court, analyzed this issue under the accommodation framework. He explained that it is not feasible to obtain a total separation between church and state. The metaphor of a "wall" does not accurately portray the complex relationship that exists between religion and government, which have been intertwined throughout history, as exemplified by the phrase "In God We Trust" on U.S. currency.

The Chief Justice then applied the *Lemon* test and found that the display was not unconstitutional. He explained that the purpose prong of the *Lemon* test was only violated if the challenged act was unquestionably motivated by religious consideration alone. Because the display was designed to celebrate the secular holiday of Christmas and depict the origins of that holiday, then the display was not solely motivated by religious considerations, and it did not violate the purpose prong of the test. Chief Justice Burger explained that the primary effect prong was difficult to analyze and resorted to analogies. He determined that the nativity scene did not benefit religion any more than reimbursing private schools for public transportation or endorsing the Christmas holiday, which was a contraction of its old name, "Christ's Mass." Finding that any benefit was incidental and too attenuated to be substantial, the Court held that the nativity display did not violate the primary effect prong. It also found that the entanglement prong of the *Lemon* test was not violated; although the city owned the display, it did not design it and paid minimal costs for upkeep. Furthermore, the Court determined that political divisiveness was not sufficient to constitute excessive entanglement.

Justice O'Connor concurred in the judgment and advocated a new approach to analyzing cases under the Establishment Clause: this new approach is called the "endorsement test." Under this test, the Establishment Clause is not violated as long as there is no excessive entanglement or government endorsement or disapproval of religion. It is a naturalistic approach. Further, to be unconstitutionally excessive, entanglement must either threaten to interfere with the independence of religious institutions, or it must provide religious groups with greater access to government than nonreligious groups. Thus, Justice O'Connor essentially would remove the secular purpose prong of the *Lemon* test and transform the other two prongs into a question of whether the intent or effect of the challenged act was to endorse or disapprove of religion. Although the Court has never expressly adopted this approach, since *Lynch*, the test has gained some traction and influence. Justice Brennan dissented and criticized the majority's approach for failing to address the clearly religious message of the nativity scene and for focusing instead on the secular holiday context of the display.

Although it upheld the nativity display in *Lynch*, a divided Court struck down a display in a later case, *County of Allegheny v. ACLU* (1989). In a portion of Justice Harry Blackmun's plurality opinion, which five Justices supported, the Court cited *Lynch* and applied Justice O'Connor's establishment test. The Court found that endorsement could be shown by demonstrating that the government has either taken a position on religious questions or made religion relevant to one's standing in "the political community." Justice Blackmun explained that based on *Lynch*, whether a religious display impermissibly endorses religion depends on the context of the display. Accordingly, he analyzed the entire context of the display at issue in *Allegheny*, including the placement of the nativity scene in the display, the fact that carols were sung in front of it, and the display of a sign indicating that a religious organization owned the nativity portion. Contrasting this display with the one in *Lynch*, where the nativity was included among several other figures, he determined that this display was unconstitutional. However, a different majority of six Justices determined that display was not an endorsement of religion and was therefore constitutional because it included a Christmas tree, a Hanukkah menorah, and a sign stating that the city was saluting freedom during the holidays.

Justice O'Connor concurred, agreeing that the secular Christmas tree and the religious menorah were constitutional because they celebrated religious diversity and pluralism. Justice Brennan, joined by Justices Marshall and Stevens, believed that both displays were religious and unconstitutional. Justice Brennan explained that the Establishment Clause does not permit an otherwise religious display simply because it celebrates pluralism. Justice Stevens wrote his own opinion, which Justices Brennan and Marshall joined, warning of the potential for social unrest from any governmental display of religious symbols. Justice Kennedy, in a dissent joined by Chief Justice Rehnquist and Justices White and Scalia, explained that the endorsement test fails because it is too difficult to apply. They preferred an accommodation approach, reasoning that the Establishment Clause is not violated as long as the action is not coercive by the government, and it does not benefit religion more directly than other practices, which are already considered part of the American heritage. Thus, to the dissenters, the entire display, including the nativity scene, was constitutional because it was merely a passive recognition of religious holidays; it was not coercive, nor did it seek to gain converts.

In *Pleasant Grove City, Utah v. Summum* (2009), a private group donated a monument containing the Ten Commandments to the city and objected when it refused to erect the monument. The Court recognized a governmental entity's entitlement to "say what it wishes," citing *Rosenberger v. Rector and Visitors of Univ. of Va.*, (1995), and select the views that it wants to express (*Rust v. Sullivan*, 1991). It can ordinarily exercise this freedom when it receives private assistance to deliver a government-controlled message. However, the government speech must comply with the Establishment Clause, which limits its ability to advocate for a particular religious belief.

Rather than conducting a full Establishment Clause analysis, this case was decided implementing the Free Speech clause and the government's unrestricted right to speak. Here, the Court decided that a permanent monument displayed on public property constitutes government speech. Thus, because the issue is not whether the government is exercising view-point discrimination by restricting an individual's speech on government property, the government has much more discretion. The Court recognized a history of city officials being able to select which monuments it wanted to erect on governmental property, which were often donated by private individuals like in this case. Justices Scalia and Thomas concurred, stated that it was obvious that from the start that this case has been "litigated in the shadow" of the Establishment Clause because the whole reason for the controversy is the city's reluctance to associate itself with the Ten Commandments and to continue instilling a wall of separation between church and state. Citing *Van Orden v. Perry* (2005), discussed below, the concurrence reassured the city that it can safely exhale, as constructing the monument would not violate the Establishment Clause. Interestingly, the benefactor organization in both *Pleasant Grove City* and *Van Orden* was the Fraternal Order of Eagles.

d. *Official Acknowledgment of Religion*

The struggle over the display of religious symbols on public property has been fierce, particularly over state-mandated displays of the Ten Commandments of the Judeo-Christian heritage. At issue is how much the government may accommodate religion. In *Stone v. Graham* (1980), the Court held that a Kentucky law that required public schools to display the Ten Commandments in each classroom was unconstitutional, even though the displays were purchased with private money. The Court determined that the statute had no secular purpose. Therefore, it violated the Establishment Clause (however, under the accommodation framework, a display that officially acknowledges religion is permissible. Factors relevant to this analysis include the history, purpose, location, and context of the display).

To illustrate the continuing tension, consider the recent case of *Van Orden v. Perry* (2005), in which the Court addressed the placement of a monument containing the Ten Commandments around the Texas state capitol. It was one of thirty-eight monuments and historical markers in the twenty-two acres of land surrounding the capitol and was designed to commemorate the "people, ideals, and events" of the unique identity of the state of Texas. The monument, at six feet tall and three feet wide, was placed to the north of the capitol. In addition to the Ten Commandments, it contained several other images, including an eagle holding the American flag, an eye inside a pyramid, two stars of David, and the Greek letters rho and chi. A private civic group donated the monument and paid for its erection. The state was involved only in accepting the monument and in designating its location. After encountering it frequently over a six-year period, the plaintiff(s) challenged the monument, claiming that it violated the Establishment Clause. The Court disagreed and held, without a majority opinion, that the monument did not violate the Establishment Clause primarily because of its location and private commissioning.

Chief Justice Rehnquist, joined by Justices Scalia, Kennedy, and Thomas, issued a plurality opinion, which exhibited a decidedly accommodationist tone. He recognized the inherent antagonism between the Establishment Clause and the Free Exercise Clause but said that the Court must maintain the division between church and state while simultaneously not showing hostility to religion by ignoring our religious heritage. He noted that the Court has selectively applied the *Lemon* test, and that the plurality declined to apply it here. Instead, it focused on the monument and the Commandments' place in the nation's history—that is, its presence in the courtroom of the Supreme Court building and its role in the executive and legislative branches. He then distinguished *Stone v. Graham* (1980), which involved a law mandating the appearance of the Ten Commandments in classrooms and had had a religious purpose. By contrast, the monument here served a historical purpose, and it was a passive display, because people were not required to encounter it every day.

Justice Stephen Breyer concurred, noting that one cannot find a simple mechanical test to apply in Establishment Clause jurisprudence. Instead, he explained that one must use a case-by-case analysis while adhering to the purposes of the Establishment and Free Exercise Clauses. He argued that the Constitution does not require everything that is religious to be purged from the public arena. Relying on the monument's history and its location, he reasoned that the state likely allowed the monument for its secular (rather than its religious) effects. After examining the nature of the monument, the fact that it is one of many monuments and markers, and its location, which is not on public school grounds, Justice Breyer reasoned that if the Court found the monument to be unconstitutional, it would indicate hostility toward religion, which the relationship between the Establishment and Free Exercise Clauses forbids.

The dissenters would have held the monument unconstitutional under the Establishment Clause. Justice Stevens took a strict neutrality approach and found that if the Court is to preserve any fragment of Jefferson's wall of separation metaphor, the monument must be struck down. He agreed that the Establishment Clause permits official recognition of religion, in light of our nation's heritage, but he thought that this monument went too far. He argued that times had changed since the monument was erected, and he expressed concern that the monument would make those who did not subscribe to the Judeo-Christian beliefs feel as if they were outsiders. He explained that the Court's reference to government speeches that invoke religion was inapposite because the speakers are individuals and not the government itself. He concluded that the monument was inherently discriminatory and that the wall of separation should be preserved.

Justice Souter also dissented. Although he agreed that government is required to remain neutral, he did not believe that a display of the Ten Commandments, which are religious on their face, could possibly be nonreligious. He suggested that a similar monument could be constitutional, if it included a secular explanation of its place in the nation's heritage and was accompanied by other historical monuments. The fact that there were other historical monuments scattered across the twenty-two acres around the capitol did not correct the failure to have a secular reference point inscribed on the monument. He also rejected the argument that, because the constitutional challenge came forty years after the monument's erection, it was therefore constitutional. He argued that the mere passage of time is irrelevant in constitutional analysis. He said that a citizen should be able to come to his or her state's seat of government without having to confront religion in the process.

In contrast with the decision in *Van Orden*, the Court struck down the display of the Ten Commandments in two county courthouses, largely because of their location and prominence. In *McCreary County v. ACLU* (2005), the Court found a predominantly religious motivation to these displays. The displays were large and prominently placed, and there had been three different versions of the display, the last included each commandment framed and hung individually. Writing for the Court, Justice Souter explained that the government must be neutral when it comes to religion. He appeared to apply the

Lemon test and found that the predominant purpose behind the displays was religious and not secular, which violated the first prong of the test. He compared this display with the one in *Stone* (Ten Commandments displayed in classrooms) and found that they had two distinct characteristics in common: (1) They both contained the actual text of the Commandments, rather than a symbolic representation, such as stone tablets with illegible writing on them and (2) the display was separate and not part of any secular display involving a historical context. Because the displays were not part of a general display of law givers, as in the courtroom of the Supreme Court, and they bore a facially religious message, the Court held that they were unconstitutional.

In dissent, Justice Scalia, joined by Chief Justice Rehnquist and Justices Thomas and Kennedy, argued that the displays were constitutional. In addition to pointing to several historical facts to illustrate his point, he argued against the *Lemon* test. He claimed that the Court had misused the test by contorting the first prong. Instead of requiring any secular purpose, the Court has required an act to have a secular *primary* purpose. The Court's reliance on the purpose behind the displays, rather than on the displays themselves, was improper. Further, Justice Scalia noted that the displays at issue here were included among and no more prominent than other historical documents and portraits throughout the courthouses.

Aside from physical representations, the Court has held that a government action cannot symbolically endorse a religion (*Board of Education of Westside Community Schools v. Mergens*, 1990). More specifically, it has distinguished unconstitutional laws that solely benefit religion from constitutional statutes that provide exemptions for religion. In *Estate of Thorton v. Caldor* (1985), the Court struck a statute that prohibited employers from requiring employees to work on their Sabbaths because it gave individuals unqualified excuses not to work on religious grounds, and favored religious beliefs. On the other hand, in *Corporation of Presiding Bishop of the Church of Jesus Christ of Latter-Day Saints v. Amos* (1987), the Court allowed a religious organization's right to be exempt from Title VII laws on employment discrimination based on religion because doing so would alleviate the government's interference with religious organizations and their missions. Based on these cases, it seems clear that the Court considers the context of the official acknowledgment to be key.

When a religious display is accompanied by other displays that are of other religious traditions, or includes an explanation of the historical importance of the display, the Court tends to permit the display. However, when the religious aspect of the display is emphasized and singled out, the Court is hesitant to uphold the display. The Court has also indicated that it feels the need to police the public school classroom more closely than statehouses or courthouses because of the impressionability of children's minds. Additionally, it sometimes ignores the *Lemon* test in Establishment Clause jurisprudence, which may call the test's continuing vitality into question. Some Justices prefer the endorsement test, and others look solely to history as a guide. However, the Court has never rejected the test expressly, nor has it accepted a different test as being more workable. Thus, if the religious display passes the *Lemon* test, or if its secular aspects, including demonstrating religious plurality, are emphasized over its religious content, then the Court seems willing to permit it.

4. *Financial Aid to Religious Institutions*

Government programs that provide either direct or indirect aid to religious groups and institutions are challenged frequently under the Establishment Clause. Since different Justices embrace different tests and since there is inherent difficulty in applying those tests, the jurisprudence in this area has been muddled. As late as 2000, the Court was divided on this issue but nonetheless allows the government to give financial assistance to parochial schools as long as the money is not used for religious education (*Mitchell v. Helms*, 2000).

a. Analysis before the Lemon *Test*

The seminal case on this issue, *Everson v. Board of Education* (1947), was already discussed to introduce the wall of separation framework. At issue in *Everson* was a New Jersey law that reimbursed parents for public transportation costs incurred to send their children to private religious schools. The Court held that the law did not violate the Establishment Clause and therefore was constitutional.

Justice Black, writing for the majority, explained that the Establishment Clause prevents states from using tax revenues to support any institution "which teaches the tenets and faith" of any religious group. However, the Free Exercise Clause similarly forbids any state from interfering with the free exercise of religion. Thus, no state can exclude any person from benefiting from tax revenues that are spent on the general welfare merely because of their faith or lack thereof. Justice Black took a decidedly neutralist approach and wrote that, although the government cannot help religion, neither can it hinder it. Without this aid to the parents, some students would not be able to attend the parochial schools; however, the same could be said if the state cut off "such general government services as ordinary police and fire protection, connections for sewage disposal, public highways and sidewalks." For Justice

Black, it was important that the funds went to the parents, not the schools. This law did nothing more than help parents transport their children to their schools, regardless of religious affiliation. Thus, this law did not penetrate the wall of separation. If the state had refused to reimburse the parents due to the religious affiliation of the schools, then that would have been antagonistic toward religion and would have violated the Free Exercise Clause.

Justice Jackson dissented, finding that the law discriminated against non-Catholics and was unconstitutional. He reasoned that the law was essentially a religious test because it limited reimbursement to parents that sent their children to private nonprofit schools, and only Catholic schools operated completely on a nonprofit basis, whereas Protestant schools and public for-profit schools did not qualify. He compared this to providing police or fire protection only to Catholic schools.

In his dissent, Justice Rutledge took a wider view of the law and would have held that it used the state's taxing power to directly benefit a religion. For him, the issue was not about the reimbursement of bus fares but about the state's invasion into the private realm of a person's relationship with his God. Taking a strict-separation approach, Justice Rutledge wrote that the Establishment Clause commanded a strict separation that "necessarily entails hardship" on those who choose to use services that the state cannot provide in lieu of those it can. Thus, withholding the reimbursement would not make the state antagonistic toward religion but would remain faithful to the Establishment Clause.

b. Analysis under the Lemon *Test*

Although *Everson* is the seminal decision in this area, the Court did not state any specific test for analyzing financial aid to religious institutions. In *Lemon v. Kurtzman* (1971) (states subsidized teachers' salaries in private schools), the Court set out a three-prong test, under which a law does not violate the Establishment Clause if it:

1. Has a secular purpose (or a secular primary purpose);
2. Principal or primary effect does not advance or inhibit religion; and
3. Does not foster an excessive entanglement between government and religion.

This test applies to cases involving financial aid to religious schools and other religious institutions.

i. Direct and Indirect Aid to Schools

The Court has addressed direct and indirect financial aid to religious schools in several cases. Generally, it has been hesitant to permit financial assistance to primary and secondary religious schools if doing so would violate the *Lemon* test or if the aid would further the mission of a religious school. In *Meek v. Pittenger* (1975), the Court prohibited a state from loaning "instructional material and equipment" (which included maps, charts, audio-visual materials, and laboratory equipment) to private schools because such aid could conceivably advance a religious school's overall religious mission. The Court held that it violated the second prong of *Lemon* test—the principal effect of the government aid advanced religion. Furthermore, it violated the third prong because providing these "auxiliary services" could require the government to supervise and manage the use of the money, which would result in excessive entanglement.

The Court has similarly struck down other statutes that could be construed to aid the religious mission of a parochial school. This includes providing instruction for remedial or accelerated students, guidance counseling, and even testing and services for students that have hearing and speech impairments. However, in *Wolman v. Walter* (1977), the Court upheld a law that provided for diagnostic speech, hearing, and psychological services because the services had only a *de minimis* educational content, if any, and thus were not related to the mission of nonpublic schools. Further, nonpublic employees were not involved in the delivery of the services, and the services were offered off-site at neutral locations. In *Zobrest v. Catalina Foothills School District* (1993), the Court allowed the government to provide sign language interpreters for parochial school students. It cited the program as one that dispenses aid to individual handicapped children, not to schools, and viewed it as a neutral service that does not offend the Establishment Clause, nor is skewed toward religion.

The Court has also held that money for field trips, and building repair and maintenance is related to the school's mission. For example, in *Wolman*, the Court invalidated a law authorizing state funds to pay for field trips "to governmental, industrial, cultural, and scientific centers designed to enrich the secular studies of students." It found this to be direct aid to religious education, which could lead to excessive entanglement. The Court also struck down a statute that authorized direct grants to qualified nonpublic schools for maintenance and repair of school facilities and equipment. The state's secular purpose was to safeguard the health, safety, and welfare of the students. However, because the grants were not limited to facilities used only for secular purposes but were also given to religious buildings, the Court found that the law's effect was to further the parochial schools' religious mission. The Court followed the same rationale in a case where a New York statute authorized the use of public funds to reimburse church-sponsored and nonpublic schools for resources expended on testing (*Committee for Public Ed. And Religious Liberty v. Regan*, 1980). The statute was not a violation of the Establishment clause because the three tests in question dealt with pupil evaluation, comprehensive achievement tests, and scholarship and college qualification tests, which could not easily be used to support a religious purpose. Although the state aided a religious school and consequently freed up funds to potentially spend on religious purposes, there is no constitutional violation nor a primary effect to advance religion.

The Court has also found that state funding of salaries for teachers, who provided remedial instruction on school premises to disadvantaged students in parochial schools, was unconstitutional in *Aguilar v. Felton* (1985). The Court applied the *Lemon* test and held that it violated the third prong; the extensive supervision the state had to exercise over the program constituted extensive entanglement. The Court held similarly in *School Dist. Of Grand Rapids v. Ball*, 473 U.S. 373 (1985) because it feared that teachers involved in the publicly funded program would intentionally or inadvertently further religious mission while teaching courses. However, over a decade later, in *Agostini v. Felton* (1997), the Court retreated from *Aguilar* and indicated that providing such remedial education on the campuses of parochial schools did not violate the Establishment Clause. In doing so, it liberally applied the *Lemon* test and found that *Aguilar* was no longer good law. Writing for the majority, Justice O'Connor found that the *Aguilar* Court had made four assumptions that have since been undermined: (1) Any public employee, working on the premises of a parochial school, presumptively includes religion in his or her work; (2) public employees working on the grounds of religious schools symbolically established a state religion; (3) any funding that directly aids the educational mission of religious schools impermissibly aids religious indoctrination, even if the funding reaches the schools "on the basis of neutral, secular criteria ... made available ... on a nondiscriminatory basis"; and (4) public employees who provide such instruction necessarily create an excessive entanglement because of the degree of supervision required. Thus, the Court will uphold a program that funds public employees who provide remedial instruction to disadvantaged students on the grounds of parochial schools if it meets certain requirements: (1) The employees cannot participate in religious indoctrination and (2) the program receives funding on the basis of neutral, secular purposes.

The Court has upheld other instances of aid to nonpublic schools under the *Lemon* test if the aid could not reasonably benefit a school's religious mission. In *Wolman*, the Court permitted state aid to nonpublic schools to administer and score standardized tests. To qualify, the schools had to administer the same test that was given to the public school children. Nonpublic employees could not be involved in preparing or scoring the tests. By contrast, in *Levitt v. Committee for Public Education* (1973), the Court held that the state could not subsidize non-standardized tests that teachers created for their own classes because there was no way to ensure that the tests were devoid of any religious aspects.

The Court has also decided several cases that involved aid to institutions of higher learning that were affiliated with a religious institution. Generally, the Court is more accepting of aid to these institutions because the Court considers the students to be more sophisticated and less susceptible to religious indoctrination. However, any such programs must still survive the Establishment Clause, usually measured by the *Lemon* test.

For example, in *Tilton v. Richardson* (1971), the Court found that a federal law that provided funds to religious colleges for construction of new buildings passed the *Lemon* test and did not run afoul of the Establishment Clause. The law excluded any buildings used for religious purposes, and the federal government retained an interest in the buildings for twenty years. The Court explained that the law's purpose was secular — to aid the expansion of facilities to accommodate the increasing numbers of students entering higher education. Furthermore, it did not have the effect of promoting religion because the grants included strict restrictions concerning the use of the facilities. Last, the aid would not foster excessive entanglement because in contrast to parochial primary and secondary schools, religious indoctrination was not a substantial purpose of the colleges and universities. Additionally, many religious schools enjoyed a "high degree of academic freedom," which encouraged free thinking and critical responses to professors. However, the Court invalidated the portion of the law that permitted the buildings to be converted to religious use after the twenty-year period. The Court reasoned that under the effects prong, the conversion would advance religion.

Following the rationale in *Tilton,* the Court in *Hunt v. McNair* (1973) permitted religious institutions of higher learning to benefit from state revenue bonds. The use of the bonds did not violate the Establishment Clause because, similar to the grants in *Tilton*, the money was restricted to buildings that were not used for religious purposes. Furthermore, the money was also available to nonreligious private colleges and universities. The Court further distinguished colleges and universities from elementary and secondary schools in *Roemer v. Board of Public Works* (1976). *Roemer* involved a Maryland program that provided direct financial aid to private institutions of higher learning.

The program did not exclude private religious institutions except for seminaries. The state provided funds based on the student population at the religious institution, calculated at 15 percent of the amount it spent per student in the public colleges and universities. The Court approved the program by a vote of five to four but without a majority opinion. Justice Blackmun's plurality applied the *Lemon* test and upheld the aid because (1) the purpose was to support private higher education as an alternative to the public system; (2) the effect was not to promote religion because the law prohibited use of the funds for "specifically religious" activities; and (3) the minimal state oversight of the program did not involve excessive entanglement. Justices White and Rehnquist concurred in the judgment. However, they criticized the plurality's use of the *Lemon* test. Instead, they found that the program was constitutional because the measure was not religiously motivated and it did not advance religion.

With respect to state financial aid to religiously affiliated schools, the Court draws a distinction between parochial primary and secondary schools and colleges and universities. In the former, the Court is much less tolerant of financial aid, direct or indirect, to such schools, primarily because the students are impressionable at this age, and the schools are more likely to emphasize religious indoctrination. In the latter, the Court is substantially more tolerant because neither of those considerations are as prevalent. The Court's distinction seems to create a presumption against the constitutionality of financial aid to primary and secondary schools that are affiliated with a religious institution; however, there does not appear to be any such presumption for religious colleges and universities.

To survive the *Lemon* test, aid to religious primary and secondary schools must have a clearly secular purpose. Furthermore, the aid cannot be used to provide religious education or to conceivably further the religious mission of the schools. Additionally, to avoid excessive entanglement, the aid generally may not involve any public employees, unless it is a program for remedial instruction of disadvantaged students with sufficient safeguards. In contrast, the Court will generally uphold aid to colleges and universities that are affiliated with religious institutions, as long as the money is not used for any religious purposes. The Court has even permitted direct aid to postsecondary schools to offset the per-student cost if the school is not solely aimed at religious education, as is the case with religious seminaries.

ii. Aid to Students at Religious Schools and School Vouchers

The issue of school vouchers has come to the forefront of public concern and thus to the attention of the courts. States create these programs, which provide funds for children to attend a school other than the one to which the state assigns them. The purpose is to create "school choice" for students, so that the public schools will have to compete for students, either among themselves or against private schools, which will improve the quality of public education. However, many voucher programs permit state funds to be used to attend parochial schools, which leads to challenges that the programs violate the Establishment Clause. These programs are distinguishable from those in *Everson*, *Wolman*, and *Meeks* because voucher programs directly subsidize the educational mission of the schools by providing state funds to the schools by way of the students.

Until recently, the Court had addressed the issue of state funding of parochial schools but had not laid out clear guidance on the issue, finding some programs unconstitutional and others constitutional. For example, in *Committee for Public Education and Religious Liberty v. Nyquist* (1973), the Court used the *Lemon* test to strike down a program, that provided partial tuition reimbursements and tax benefits to the parents of students that attended nonpublic primary and secondary schools. The Court explained that the program ran afoul of the effects prong of the *Lemon* test because there was no effective way to ensure that the money was used solely for "secular, neutral, and non-ideological purposes" and thus, direct aid was unconstitutional, regardless of its form. Similarly, in *Sloan v. Lemon* (1973), the Court struck down a Pennsylvania program that provided similar benefits and specifically prohibited the state from having any supervision or control over any private schools.

Approximately ten years later, the Court became more receptive to school voucher programs. In *Mueller v. Allen* (1983), it upheld a Minnesota law that permitted parents to deduct educational expenses from their state income tax. Even though the law made no distinction between religious and nonreligious private schools, the Court found that it did not violate the Establishment Clause.

Nearly twenty years after *Mueller*, the Court upheld Ohio's voucher program in *Zelman v. Simmons-Harris* (2002). In a contested decision, the Court held that the program did not violate the Establishment Clause. The Ohio voucher program specifically stated that its aim was to provide school choice for families residing in the Cleveland City School District. It was designed to permit low-income and minority children to attend any school other than the inner-city school to which they were assigned, even if the school was parochial. (Ohio enacted the law because Cleveland's public schools had repeatedly been ranked among the poorest performing schools in the United States. It designed the program to improve that statistic by providing tuition for students who attended private schools and by financing tutoring for students who remained in public schools.) Writing for the majority, Chief Justice Rehnquist did not apply the *Lemon* test. Rather, he applied *Agostini* (remedial instruction to disadvantaged students) and explained that the Establishment Clause only prohibits states from making laws that "have the 'purpose' or 'effect' of advancing or inhibiting religion." The Chief Justice explained that Ohio's program served a valid secular purpose—educational assistance those who needed it the most, that is, the poor in a public school system that was failing to meet the needs of its students. The Court also had distinguished programs that directly aided religious schools from programs that only aided religious schools because of independent, private choice. Here, the program did not encourage students to choose a religious school over any other private or public school; thus, it fell into the latter category and did not have the effect of advancing or restraining religion. Thus, its neutrality toward religion made the voucher program constitutional.

Justice Souter, dissenting, attacked the program and the majority's reasoning on two main grounds. First, the voucher program was skewed in favor of religious schools because students predominately choose religious schools over other, secular private schools. The financial incentives resulted in students choosing religious schools, not out of free will but due to financial reasons. He found it significant that most students (1) elected to attend religious schools, (2) chose schools of a different faith than their own, and (3) based the decision on financial reasons (because, for example, Catholic schools were substantially cheaper than other private schools).

Second, Justice Souter thought that the Ohio voucher program undermined the very purpose of the Establishment Clause because it violated three of its objectives: (1) respect for freedom of conscience, (2) the prevention of corruption of religion by establishing a state religion, and (3) the social conflict that religion has produced throughout history. The voucher program was contrary to the Establishment Clause because the state financial aid did not reach religious schools as a product of genuine free choice.

Similarly, Justices Stevens and Breyer would have found the program unconstitutional. In his dissent, Justice Stevens explained that this program removed "a brick from the wall that was designed to separate religion and government," would lead to the very religious strife that the founding fathers wished to prevent, and could undermine our form of government. Justice Breyer's dissent recognized that, although the Establishment Clause permits states to provide limited forms of assistance to religious schools, this program went too far. For Justice Breyer, the doctrine of separation is even more important today because of the great diversity of religions in the United

States. This type of voucher program would lead to religious strife because the public may feel that certain religious schools are too extreme, or it would cause various religions to compete for the state money. Additionally, the amount of supervision required to ensure that schools complied with the program's standards would require an unconstitutional excessive entanglement of government and religion.

Thus, the Court will permit a school voucher program, even if it benefits religious schools, as long as it meets certain requirements:

1. Does not provide financial incentives for students to elect religious schools over other private or public schools;
2. Is effectively neutral toward religion and permits genuine, individual choice in determining which school to attend; and
3. Provides benefits to a wide array of people, limited only by financial need and residence in a particular school district.

States may also permit parents to deduct some of their children's private school educational expenses from their income taxes, even if the schools are religious. Yet the Court indicated in *Zelman* that its decision did not grant blanket approval to voucher programs; thus, there will undoubtedly be future challenges to the constitutionality of such programs.

iii. Aid to Non-scholastic Religious Organizations

If one were to plot the Court's view of financial aid to religious organizations on a continuum, the aid to non-scholastic religious institutions is on the opposite side of the spectrum from the Court's close scrutiny of aid to primary and secondary schools. The Court clearly views financial aid to religious primary and secondary schools with a watchful eye, and as presumptively invalid. Although the Court is generally more accepting of aid to religious postsecondary educational institutions, it is even more tolerant of such aid to non-scholastic religious institutions. In these situations, the Court is generally deferential to legislative judgment.

Although there are few cases addressing the issue of aid to non-scholastic religious organizations, the Court's jurisprudence dates back over a century. In 1899, the Court addressed an Establishment Clause challenge to government funding for a new facility in a hospital affiliated with the Roman Catholic Church. In *Bradfield v. Roberts* (1899), the Court upheld the funding because the hospital did not discriminate based on the religion of those seeking treatment, and the fact that a religious group operated the facility was "wholly immaterial" to the constitutionality of the aid.

In *Bowen v. Kendrick* (1988), the Court upheld the constitutionality of government grants to provide counseling and health care for pregnant adolescents and their parents. The Adolescent Family Life Act provided grants to religious and nonreligious groups for counseling adolescents against engaging in sexual activity. Yet the program specifically prohibited the use of federal funds for any abortion-related services, including counseling and other family planning services. Writing for the majority, Chief Justice Rehnquist applied the *Lemon* test and found that the law had a secular purpose—to reduce or eliminate teenage pregnancy, teen sexual activity, and teen parenthood, as well as the socioeconomic problems they caused. The program did not have the effect of advancing or hindering religion because the Act was neutral, and the aid was more important than who provided the services. Furthermore, it did not create an excessive entanglement between religion and government because the Act did not require the government to monitor the recipients of the grants. The Court pointed out that it had found excessive entanglement in cases that involved primary and secondary schools with a substantial purpose of religious indoctrination, and it distinguished *Bowen* on those grounds.

Justice Blackmun dissented and found the Act to be unconstitutional. The program essentially subsidized religious teachings because the religious groups performed counseling without any constraints on sectarian content. He also disagreed with the Court's assertion that the religious groups at issue were not as pervasively sectarian as the primary and secondary schools for whom government aid was found to be unconstitutional. He likened the groups' mission to the pervasively sectarian and inculcatory motives of the primary and secondary schools to which the government generally cannot provide financial aid and distinguished them from the religiously affiliated postsecondary institutions to which government aid was generally upheld. Justice Blackmun argued that the law advanced religion, in violation of the *Lemon* test, because the government essentially paid for religious groups to indoctrinate teenagers. Under Justice Blackmun's analysis, the majority placed too much emphasis on the fact that the Act was facially neutral and disregarded the same policy reasons that supported striking down financial aid to primary and secondary religious schools.

The Court has struck down tax exemptions that violate the Establishment Clause. In *Texas Monthly, Inc. v. Bullock* (1989), the Court considered a sales tax exemption for religious periodicals, which were entirely composed of writings promoting religious teachings. In a plurality opinion, authored by Justice Brennan, the Court struck down the exemption. The exemption directly benefited religion and was not merely incidental, because the tax benefits were only given to publishers of religious periodicals, and nonreligious organizations were excluded. By providing tax exemptions, the government was forcing the taxpayers to be "indirect and vicarious donors" to the religious organizations. As a result, more extensive entanglement occurred than if the government imposed a tax of general application. In his dissent, Justice Scalia argued that the exemption might be necessary to avoid possible interference with the free exercise of religion. He took an accommodationist view and found a middle ground that would not implicate either the Establishment Clause or the Free Exercise Clause.

In another tax-related case, *Jimmy Swaggart Ministries v. Board of Equalization* (1990), the Court unanimously upheld a state sales and use tax on products purchased out of state because it applied generally. California could apply the tax to religious groups because if it exempted religious groups from these taxes, except for serving meals, then it would violate the Establishment Clause. Justice O'Connor delivered the majority opinion and found that the tax did not foster an excessive entanglement with religion. These tax-related decisions show that the Court will defer to the legislature's balancing of values, but when the balance weighs too much in favor of religion, as in *Texas Monthly*, the Court's deference disappears and the law is stricken.

Court has further explained that tax exemptions that benefit religion are constitutional so long as they benefit other institutions, such as charitable and educational organizations (*Walz v. Tax Commission*, 1970). In *Walz*, a property owner sought an injunction to prevent the New York City Tax Commission from allowing religious organizations tax exemptions on property used solely for religious worship. The statute in question also benefited hospitals, libraries, playgrounds, scientific, professional, historical, and patriotic groups, thus the Court did not see it as an excessive government entanglement and did not find that it constituted an establishment. The Court also pointed out that the government was not contributing to revenue of churches and by not forcing the church to pay taxes, created a wall of distance between church and state. Eliminating the exemption would increase the government's involvement with religion by creating a stronger legal relationship between the entities by way of tax valuation of church property, tax liens, tax foreclosures, and other potential conflicts. Recognizing that Congress has granted tax exemptions for churches since 1802, and in 1870 specifically exempted churches and appurtenant grounds from "any and all taxes or assessments, national, municipal, or county," the Court opted to leave history unchanged.

5. *Conclusion*

As discussed, the Court tends to divide its analysis of financial aid to religion into two main groups. On one hand, financial aid to primary and secondary parochial schools is generally presumed to violate the Establishment Clause. To be constitutional, the aid must be solely for secular purposes, not to advance the mission of the religious school, and any services funded by the aid may need to occur off school grounds. On the other hand, the Court generally defers to laws that provide financial aid to postsecondary religious schools and religious institutions for nonacademic activities. The Court does not feel the need to watch government financial aid in postsecondary schools as closely as it does aid to religious elementary and high schools because there is less emphasis on religious indoctrination and college students are less impressionable. Similarly, in the nonacademic context, the Court is more tolerant of financial aid to religious groups and generally defers to legislative judgment.

Checkpoints

- **Definition of Religion**
  - A "religion" is any deep, sincere belief that occupies a place in that person's life analogous to that of God in commonly recognized religions.
  - The Court has provided three different approaches to defining religion: First, it has attempted to outline who qualifies under the conscientious objector status; second, it has required that a belief must be sincerely held, which is subject to examination by the court; and third, it has extended this class of people to include those with non-traditional beliefs that are associated with traditional religions.
  - In determining whether a belief constitutes a religion, the courts cannot inquire into subjective aspects, such as the truth of religious views, or of the correct interpretation of matters of faith, including doctrines, tenets, and dogma.
  - When evaluating a person's sincerity, the inquiry cannot include whether a belief system is generally recognized, whether it has a certain minimum number of believers, or what constitutes the particular beliefs of the system.
- **Applicability of the Religion Clauses to the States**
  - The Court first incorporated and applied the Free Exercise Clause to the states in 1940 and applied the Establishment Clause to the states in 1947.

- **Analytical Frameworks for the Establishment Clause**
  - There are three primary frameworks used to analyze Establishment Clause cases.
  - Strict separation: There is a "wall of separation" between the government and religion, and the Court should not tolerate a breach of that wall, no matter how *de minimis* the breach may be. Government should never directly support religion and cannot provide aid to individuals that indirectly benefits religion.
  - Neutrality: The government should approach religion neutrally. This means that the government should neither actively aid nor actively inhibit religion. The government should keep its promotion or discouragement of religious observance, belief, or activity to a minimum.
  - Accommodation: The government should accommodate religion. This framework allows for the most intermingling of state and religion. The Establishment Clause is violated only if the government establishes an official religion, coerces religious participation, or favors one religion over another. Coercion occurs only if the government requires or punishes the failure to engage in religious practice. Social pressure is not coercion.
- **Tests for Analyzing Establishment Clause Questions**
  - The *Lemon* test consists of three prongs, all of which must be met to comply with the Establishment Clause:
    - Law must have a valid secular purpose (sometimes the Court says that the law's primary purpose must be secular);
    - Law's primary effect must neither advance nor inhibit religion; and
    - Law must not create an "excessive entanglement" between government and religion.
- **Other Tests Proposed but not Adopted**
  - The symbolic endorsement test, espoused by Justice O'Connor in *Lynch v. Donnelly*, examines whether the challenged government act expressed government endorsement or disapproval of religion. This endorsement or disapproval can either be direct (intentional) or indirect (by effect, rather than intent). The test changes the *Lemon* test by deemphasizing the secular purpose prong and reformulating the remaining two prongs.
  - The endorsement test views the challenged religious display through the eyes of a hypothetical reasonable viewer who is aware of all pertinent facts and history surrounding the display.
  - The coercion test examines the coercive effect of the government action on participation in state-sponsored or state-initiated religious activity. The

coercion can be either obvious or subtle, such as through peer pressure, and the latter is more insidious because it is harder to detect. Justice Kennedy applied this test in *County of Allegheny v. ACLU* and *Lee v. Weisman*.

- **Categories of Establishment Clause Cases**
  - School Prayer and Other State-Sanctioned Prayer or Religious Activity
    - The Court typically applies the *Lemon* test when prayer in public schools is involved.
    - Generally, prayer in public schools is not permitted if a public school or any level of government sanctions the prayer in any way. This includes student-led nondenominational prayer that is voluntary if the school sanctioned the prayer, its organization, or its delivery. This general prohibition cannot be circumvented by permitting the students to vote on whether to have the prayer and on who shall deliver it.
  - School Curriculum Decisions Involving Religion
    - Through application of the *Lemon* test, the Establishment Clause prohibits the states from infusing religion into their public school curricula.
    - The states cannot condition the teaching of a scientific theory on the teaching of a competing religious theory. Furthermore, states cannot require public schools to participate in religious exercises, even if the state espouses a secular purpose or allows students and teachers to voluntarily participate.
  - Equal Access to Public Facilities
    - If a public facility is open to the public, then the government cannot deny a group access solely because that group is religious in nature.
  - Prayer in Legislatures
    - Town boards may open with prayer as long as it does not coerce participation and does not discriminate against minority faiths in determining who can offer the prayer (*Town of Greece v. Galloway*, 2014).
  - Religious Displays on Public Property
    - The Court permits placement of religious symbols on public property, as long as the placement does not convey symbolic endorsement of a particular religion, or endorsement of religion in general, and as long as the symbols are included among other secular and religious symbols in equal fashion.
    - The Court has found ways around the Establishment Clause when dealing with the obstruction of monuments donated by private groups. This alternative is to call the display a form of government speech, which is not subject to a view-point discrimination analysis.

- Official Acknowledgment of Religion
  - Official acknowledgment typically occurs when a religious display or other religious expression is made by the government or included in a governmental building.
  - The Court is generally suspicious of such governmental religious displays when they are not balanced by secular displays. However, the Court generally finds no violation of the Establishment Clause if the religious displays are accompanied to an equal degree by secular displays.
  - The Court distinguishes between governmental acts and independent acts by government officials, such as presidential speeches.
  - If a solely religious display is intended to emphasize religious pluralism or another secular purpose, it will likely be upheld by the Court.
  - The Court is generally very suspicious about religious displays and expression in the context of primary and secondary schools.
  - The government cannot symbolically endorse a religion or uphold laws that solely benefit religion.
- Financial Aid to Religious Institutions
  - The Court is generally suspicious of and does not permit government-based financial aid to religious primary and secondary schools. However, if the aid can be separated from the school's primary mission, and it can be provided solely by state employees, the Court may permit it. The Court feels a greater need to monitor the primary and secondary schools because of the youth and impressionability of the children, as well as the greater emphasis on religious indoctrination in those schools.
  - In contrast, the Court is generally more accepting of government-based financial aid to religious colleges and universities, as well as nonscholastic institutions, because they tend to place less emphasis on indoctrination and the students are able to critically analyze and choose their own beliefs.
- Aid to Nonscholastic Religious Organizations
  - Tax exemptions that benefit religion are constitutional so long as they benefit other institutions, such as charitable and educational organizations

Chapter 7

Freedom of Religion: The Free Exercise Clause

Roadmap

- The Free Exercise Clause
  - Laws impacting the free exercise of religion are divided into two groups:
    - Laws that facially discriminate
    - Laws that are facially neutral, but have an adverse effect on religion
  - Prisoners are still afforded the right to freedom of religion, but are subject to a lower level of scrutiny.
  - Religious groups can sometimes receive tax exemptions. Employees claiming religious rights are more protected, but not in all circumstances.
- The two Religion Clauses take complementary approaches to preserve the freedom of religion and conscience, however tension between the two becomes evident when the government prohibits acts that are required by one's religion.

I. The Free Exercise Clause

The First Amendment not only contains a direct command that "Congress shall make no law respecting an establishment of religion," but also expressly forbids Congress from "prohibiting the free exercise" of religion. Similar to the Establishment Clause, the second clause, called the Free Exercise Clause, is stated in seemingly simple terms. Prior to 1940 when the Supreme Court first applied the Free Exercise Clause to the states, the Court utilized other Constitutional provisions to protect religious freedoms. For example, in *Pierce v. Society of Sisters* (1925) the Court used the fundamental right of parents to control the upbringing of their children to strike a statute prohibiting parents from sending their children to private or parochial schools.

The Court has stated repeatedly that the Free Exercise Clause prevents the government from punishing religious beliefs or from compelling them.

Through this clause, the Constitution prohibits the government from legislating thoughts or beliefs; however, it permits the government to legislate conduct. In *Braunfeld v. Brown* (1961), Chief Justice Warren stated that the people have an absolute freedom to hold whatever religious beliefs they choose. However, since its first decision interpreting the Free Exercise Clause, *Reynolds v. United States* (1878), the Court has clearly and unequivocally declared that "Congress was deprived of all legislative power over mere opinion, but was left free to reach actions." Because the Free Exercise Clause only permits the government to regulate actions, the clause is implicated, according the Court in *Lyng v. Northwest Indian Cemetery Protective Association* (1988), when a law burdens a person's ability to observe his or her religious requirements or obligations in one of two ways: (1) It prohibits conduct that is required by a religious belief; or (2) it requires conduct that is forbidden by a religion.

The Free Exercise Clause cannot be read so broadly that any conduct a person claims to be part of the "free exercise" of his or her religion is or could be protected from governmental interference. Otherwise, no law could have any effect because a person could always claim that the conduct it prohibited was required by his religious beliefs. As an example, in *Reynolds*, the Court upheld a law that prohibited polygamy, despite the fact that Mormons claimed that their religion required them to practice polygamy. Therefore, the Court is forced to draw a "line in the sand" to separate what is protected under the Free Exercise Clause and what the government can prohibit.

Similar to other freedoms protected by the First Amendment, the freedom to exercise one's religion is a fundamental right. Thus, laws impacting the free exercise of religion are generally divided into two categories. First, there are laws that facially discriminate against religion, either by discriminating against all religions or by discriminating against a specific subset, or even a single, religion. Second, there are laws that are facially neutral, but have an adverse effect on all, some, or even one religion. Each of these categories is discussed in turn.

A. Laws Discriminating against Religion

Facially discriminatory laws are those that expressly interfere with a person's ability to observe the requirements of his or her religion or expressly require a person to act in a manner that is inconsistent with his or her religion. Generally, a law that facially discriminates against religion must pass strict scrutiny to be constitutional. A law is facially discriminatory if it is not neutral and is not of general applicability. Although governments rarely overtly discriminate against religion, when they do so, the law may violate the Free Exercise Clause, if it fails strict scrutiny.

Under the Court's decisions, laws that are neither neutral nor generally applicable—are facially discriminatory. Under the test the court created in *Employment Division v. Smith* (1990), a law is not neutral if it specifically forbids conduct of a religious but not a nonreligious nature, or if it forbids beliefs of a religious nature but not similar nonreligious beliefs. Furthermore, a law is not generally applicable if it is so substantially underinclusive that it does not prohibit nonreligious conduct that is substantially similar to the prohibited religious conduct. A law that is facially discriminatory based on one's religious beliefs, not one's conduct, is absolutely unconstitutional under the Free Exercise Clause. A facially discriminatory law that only reaches conduct must meet strict scrutiny, that is, narrowly tailored to achieve a compelling government purpose. Whereas, laws facially discriminating against religious beliefs always violate the Free Exercise Clause.

One example of a facially discriminatory law was the statute at issue in *McDaniel v. Paty* (1978). Tennessee disqualified religious ministers and other members of religious orders from membership in the state legislature. The Court unanimously declared that the Tennessee constitutional provision violated the Free Exercise Clause. The plurality, written by Chief Justice Burger, explained that the disqualification was not directed at belief but at the "status, acts, and conduct" of a person. The Chief Justice pointed to historical evidence that a religious minister is no more likely to work toward establishment of religion than any other person. Other Justices found that the law at a minimum violated the "freedom to act" branch of the Free Exercise Clause.

The Court reaffirmed the strict scrutiny requirement for laws that facially discriminate against religion in its decision in *Church of the Lukumi Babalu Aye, Inc. v. Hialeah* (1993). The Church of the Lukumi Babalu Aye purchased land in the city of Hialeah, Florida, and planned to build "a house of worship as well as a school, cultural center, and museum." The church practiced a religion called Santeria, a fusion of traditional African religion and Roman Catholicism. Santeria teaches that the spirits require animal sacrifices to survive and believers should make sacrifices at significant events, such as a birth, marriage, or death. In response to the planned construction, the City passed an ordinance that prohibited animal sacrifice by any individual or a group that "kills, slaughters, or sacrifices animals for any type of ritual, regardless of whether or not the flesh or blood of the animal is to be consumed."

The Court unanimously declared that the Hialeah ordinance was unconstitutional. Justice Kennedy, writing for the majority, explained that the city clearly passed this ordinance because it disapproved of the Santeria religion. The ordinance was facially discriminatory because it outlawed certain activities, specifically in reference to religion. Further, it was not of general applicability because it only applied to individuals and groups who sacrificed animals for religious purposes; thus, its purpose was not protect the public health and or prevent cruelty to animals. Thus, failing the *Smith* test, the Court concluded that the law was facially discriminatory. To survive strict scrutiny, the means must be narrowly tailored to meet a compelling government interest. Even if the law could fairly be said to support the policies just noted, the Court explained that its application was so substantially under inclusive that it could not be narrowly tailored to achieve those ends. The Court also noted the ordinance clearly violated the policy of religious toleration underlying the Free Exercise Clause. Justice Scalia, in his concurrence, explained that the First Amendment does not permit the Court to investigate into the legislature's intent, and the Court may only consider the effects of laws in First Amendment inquiries. Here, the ordinance had unconstitutional effects on the free exercise of religion, regardless of legislative intent.

B. Neutral Laws Adversely Affecting Religion

Facially neutral laws are those that place a burden on a person's ability to fulfill his or her religious obligations, even though they may not require an act inconsistent with a person's religion or may not prohibit an act that is required by a person's religion. Although the government may be attempting to remedy a social problem that is completely unrelated to religion, it may violate the Free Exercise Clause either by requiring action in a manner that is inconsistent with a person's religious beliefs or by forbidding action that is required by a person's religious beliefs. In these cases, the courts must weigh the strength of society's need to remedy the secular social problem against the need to avoid impacting a person's ability to act in accord with her religion. Today, the Court gives great deference to the legislature's judgment when laws are generally applicable and target only conduct, not belief. Thus, the Court will generally only apply the rational basis test. However, in certain instances, Congress has statutorily required the Court to apply strict scrutiny.

1. *Early Cases Deferred to the Government Concerning Actions but Not Beliefs*

The Court's jurisprudence concerning facially neutral laws has undergone several changes, from great deference to the legislature, to slowly restricting the power of government, to applying strict scrutiny, and finally back to according great deference. In its early decisions, the Court accorded great deference to the government and generally upheld the challenged act, as long as the enactments regulated conduct. If the government infringed on a person's right to freedom of religious belief, the Court generally struck down the government's actions. The seminal case, *Reynolds v. United States* (1878), dealt with a Latter-Day Saint (commonly called a Mormon) who practiced polygamy in violation of a federal law. The Mormons claimed that their religion required them to marry multiple spouses and that they could not submit to the federal ban on the practice. Finding that the law was aimed solely at conduct, the Court upheld the law. The Court determined that the Constitution granted the government broad authority to regulate conduct because laws are made to govern actions. To hold otherwise would be to abdicate the foundations of civilized government and to place a man's beliefs above the law of the land, permitting "every citizen to become a law unto himself," which would lead to anarchy.

However, the Court has not strictly adhered to the distinction between belief and conduct. In *Cantwell v. Connecticut* (1940), the Court refused to defer to the judgment of the state legislature. A man and his two sons, who were ordained ministers of the Jehovah's Witness religion, were arrested and convicted of attempting to sell religious literature without a license. The Court overturned their convictions and struck down the statute as violating the Free Exercise Clause. It was especially bothered by the unfettered discretion of the licensing officials, which constituted an unconstitutional prior restraint on both free speech and the free exercise of religion. The Court explained that the Free Exercise Clause protects both the freedom to believe, which is absolute and may not be infringed, and the freedom to act, which the government has the power to regulate if it does not unduly burden religion. This new test placed a slightly greater limit on the power of government than existed in *Reynolds*.

The Court followed similar reasoning in *Braunfeld v. Brown* (1961), a case in which Jewish merchants challenged a law that required businesses to close on Sundays. The merchants argued that their religion already required them to close on Saturdays; thus, the new law permitted them to be open only five days per week, whereas their competitors could be open for six days. The Court found that the law only indirectly burdened the free exercise of religion. It did not directly prohibit a particular religious practice, and the law was not directed at Jews in particular. Rather, it was of general applicability, and the burden on the Jewish merchants was an unintended consequence of the law. The Court suggested that the state could enact legislation to exempt followers of religions that mandated closing on another day from being subject to the Sunday closing law. Furthermore, the Court placed another limitation on the government's ability to regulate the free exercise of religion. It said that the law would have violated the Free Exercise Clause if the state could have accomplished its goal in another way that did not burden any religious practice.

2. Strict Scrutiny Becomes the Test

Following its decision in *Braunfeld*, the Court began to view government acts that infringe on the free exercise of religion with an increasingly narrow lens and applied heightened scrutiny. For example, in *Torcaso v. Watkins* (1961), the Court struck down a provision of the Maryland state constitution that required a person to declare his or her belief in God before taking public office. Although the Court noted that the federal Constitution forbade religious tests as a prerequisite to federal office it based its ruling on the establishment clause: "We repeat and again reaffirm that neither a State nor the Federal Government can constitutionally force a person 'to profess a belief or disbelief in any religion.'" It then reasoned that the Free Exercise Clause, as applied to the states by the Fourteenth Amendment, placed a similar limitation on the states by prohibiting them from benefiting or burdening a person because of religious beliefs. The argument that the requirement was only a regulation on conduct, not belief, failed because in effect it amounted to forcing a person to profess a particular religious belief, which violated freedom to believe and act according to one's religion.

With its decision in *Sherbert v. Verner* (1963), the Court stated that it required laws burdening the free exercise of religion to pass strict scrutiny. There, a woman who practiced the Seventh-Day Adventist faith was fired because she refused to work on Saturdays. After being unable to find other gainful employment because of her religious scruples, she filed for unemployment compensation under South Carolina law but was denied benefits because her refusal to work on Saturdays did not constitute "good cause." The Court held that the requirement that a worker either accept employment in violation of her religious practices or lose eligibility for unemployment compensation was an unconstitutional burden on her ability to practice her religion. Justice Brennan, writing for the Court, pointed out that South Carolina only denied benefits to those who held a day other than Sunday to be a holy day of rest. The Court reasoned that the rational basis test would not sufficiently protect the liberty guaranteed by the Free Exercise Clause. The Court expressly distinguished *Braunfeld* (law required businesses to close on Sundays) because the state's interest was not in a secular day of rest for the benefit of workers but an interest in preventing fraudulent unemployment claims. Applying strict scrutiny, the Court found that this was not a sufficiently compelling interest and the means chosen were not narrowly tailored.

In *Wisconsin v. Yoder* (1972), the state of Wisconsin required all children to continue their education until after the age of sixteen. The state prosecuted and convicted Amish parents who refused to send their children to school after the eighth grade. They adhered to the Old Amish faith and believed that salvation required them to live and work in a church community that is apart from the world and all worldly influence. Attendance in school beyond eighth grade violated their faith because it exposed the children to contrary teachings. After their children have learned basic skills in reading, writing, and arithmetic, they are required to learn to enjoy physical labor, manual work, and self-reliance, which cannot be taught in the classroom.

The state argued that any burden placed on the ability of the Amish to practice their faith was incidental and subordinate to the state's interest in preventing violations of its child labor laws. The Court held that the state's interests inconsequential compared to the interference with the Amish religious practices. Therefore, Wisconsin's law violated the Free Exercise Clause.

Although the Court held that a law burdening the free exercise of religious practices must pass strict scrutiny, it did not always follow this test, and most laws challenged on free exercise grounds after *Sherbert* were upheld. The cases in which the Court invalidated a law under strict scrutiny generally fell into two categories: Either they were denials of government benefits to individuals who quit their jobs on religious grounds, or they involved the application of a state law compelling attendance at school by Amish children, as in *Yoder*. Every other challenge was derailed by the Court's deference to the government.

3. *Modern Cases Interpreting the Free Exercise Clause*

Although the Court expressly adopted (even if it did not consistently apply) strict scrutiny in challenges under the Free Exercise Clause, in 1990 it decided a watershed case where its jurisprudence essentially came full circle back to *Reynolds*. In the seminal case of *Employment Division v. Smith* (1990), the Court overruled the strict scrutiny test as applied in *Sherbert* and replaced it with extreme deference to the government's judgment. *Smith* involved a challenge to an Oregon law that prohibited "the knowing or intentional possession of a 'controlled substance'" unless it was obtained by a valid prescription. Oregon included the hallucinogenic drug peyote on the "controlled substances" list. The challengers had been dismissed from their jobs with a private drug rehabilitation center because they took peyote in a sacramental ceremony of the Native American Church.

Writing for the Court, Justice Scalia examined the Court's jurisprudence beginning with *Sherbert* (denied unemployment compensation because of refusal to work on Saturdays). Justice Scalia stated that the Free Exercise Clause protects the right to believe and profess whatever religion one chooses. However, he acknowledged that practicing one's religion requires more than belief and profession; it often involves actions and conduct. However, he limited the conduct protections of the Free Exercise Clause only to governmental acts that were targeted at a religion and were not generally applicable. Hence, he wrote that the clause prevented the government from banning "the casting of 'statutes that are to be used for worship purposes,' or to prohibit the bowing down before a golden calf." The Court stated that the Free Exercise Clause does not extend to generally applicable laws that required conduct forbidden by a religion or forbade conduct required by a religion.

Pointing to the initial case of *Reynolds*, he explained that from the beginning, the Court did not exempt conduct-regulating laws from the Free Exercise Clause, if the law was generally applicable. He then distinguished prior decisions, such as *Cantwell*, *Sherbert*, and *Yoder*, on the grounds that none of those cases were pure Free Exercise Clause cases but were mixed with other constitutionally protected rights, such as freedom of speech and the right of parents to direct the upbringing of their children. The Court then explained that *Smith* was a pure Free Exercise Clause case and was controlled by the line of cases beginning with *Reynolds*. It expressly rejected applying strict scrutiny to generally applicable laws that merely burden religion. Justice Scalia explained that the reason for applying strict scrutiny in cases such as racial discrimination or regulation of content-based speech were inapplicable here. In those situations, strict scrutiny operated to restrict the government and to "enhance equality of treatment and an unrestricted flow of contenting speech," both of which were "constitutional norms." However, in this situation, application of strict scrutiny amounted to the creation of a personal right to nullify laws by claiming that they violated one's religion, which he described as a "constitutional anomaly."

Justice O'Connor concurred in the judgment but disagreed with the Court's reasoning. Justices Brennan, Marshall, and Blackmun partly joined in her opinion, but they did not concur in the judgment. Justice O'Connor applied strict scrutiny and found that the Oregon law banning the ingestion of peyote was constitutional. The state's interest in banning peyote as a controlled substance was compelling, and the law was narrowly tailored. She explained that the First Amendment was enacted to protect the free exercise of religion for those who practiced religion different from the majority. Thus, strict scrutiny was appropriate for analyzing the constitutionality of free exercise challenges because it balanced the interests between the First Amendment's preservation of religious liberty and the state's interests in enforcing its laws of general application. She argued that a law should not be immune from the First Amendment simply because it is generally applicable and that the majority had misread the Court's precedent.

Responding to *Smith*, Congress passed the Religious Freedom Restoration Act (RFRA) in an attempt to overturn the Court's decision and restore strict scrutiny as the test in Free Exercise Clause challenges. However, in its decision in *City of Boerne v. Flores* (1997), the Court struck down the RFRA as applied to state and local governments. It concluded that although Congress's power under the Fourteenth Amendment's Enforcement Clause was broad, it had overstepped that power in enacting the Act because it violated the separation of powers and threatened to upset the balance of power among the branches of the government.

In 2006 the Court applied RFRA in a federal context and ruled in favor of the freedom to exercise religion. In *Gonzales v. O Centro Espirita Beneficente Uniao Do Vegeral* (2006), the UDV, a Christian spiritist sect based in Brazil that receives communion through a sacramental tea made from two plants unique to the Amazon, one of which contains a hallucinogen (DMT) that is banned by the Controlled Substance Act, sought to block federal enforcement against it on free exercise grounds. The government conceded that the challenged application would substantially burden a sincere exercise of religion; however, it advanced what it thought were three compelling interests: (1) protecting UDV members' health and safety; (2) preventing the diversion of this sacramental tea from the church to recreational users; and (3) complying with the 1971 UN Convention on Psychotropic Substances. The Court was not persuaded by these interests, stating that the government was required by the RFRA to demonstrate that the compelling interest test is satisfied through application of the challenged law to the particular claimant whose sincere exercise of religion is being burdened. The Court also found no indication that Congress considered the harms of DMT involved in this religious use and said it was analogous to peyote, for which the President and Congress carved out an exception in the Controlled Substances Act to allow for religious use by Native Americans.

In *Church of the Lukumi Babalu Aye, Inc. v. Hialeah* (1993) (unconstitutional to ban animal sacrifice), the Court reaffirmed *Smith* and stated that a neutral law of general application does not need a compelling justification that is narrowly tailored. In *Cutter v. Wilkinson* (2005), the Court interpreted the statute similar to the RFRA, called the Religious Land Use and Institutionalized Persons Act of 2000 (RLUIPA). The RLUIPA, which Congress enacted under the Spending and Commerce Clauses, prohibited any government from imposing "a substantial burden on the religious exercise of a person residing in or confined to an institution," unless the burden meets strict scrutiny. The Court held that the law was constitutional. Justice Ginsburg, writing for the Court, explained that the law does not impermissibly advance religion because it does not advance any particular religion, or religion itself over non-religion, but is merely an accommodation of religious practices. She traced the struggle between Congress and the Court in the RFRA battle and reasoned that the RLUIPA was distinguishable because Congress had expressly relied on the Spending and Commerce Clauses. The Court then explained that RLUIPA was merely an accommodation of religious observances but did not protect that accommodation over the need for order and safety in an institution and did not distinguish among "bona fide faiths."

Post-*Smith* when the government imposes a substantial burden on free exercise, the Court will first decide whether Smith applies. If it does, then the Court will examine whether the law in question is "neutral" and "generally applicable," and whether the case involves other constitutional rights in addition to the Free Exercise Clause, before applying the rational basis test. However, if federal laws such as RFRA or state laws or constitutions with stronger free exercise protections apply, the Court will apply strict scrutiny.

In *Burwell v. Hobby Lobby Stores, Inc.* (2014) the court held that, as applied to closely held corporations, the Department of Health and Human Services (HHS) violated the Religious Freedom Restoration Act (RFRA) when it promulgated regulations pursuant to the Affordable Care Act (ACA) that required employers to provide employee access to certain contraceptives with abortifacient properties, where those employers had religious objections to the practice of abortion. It is the first time that the court has recognized a for-profit corporation's claim of religious belief, but it is limited to closely held corporations.

The court found that RFRA applies to regulations that govern the activities of closely held for-profit corporations like Conestoga, Hobby Lobby, and Mardel. HHS argued that the companies cannot sue because they are for-profit corporations, and that the owners cannot sue because the regulations apply only to the companies. But Justice Alito, writing for the majority wrote that would leave merchants with a difficult choice: give up the right to seek judicial protection of their religious liberty or forgo the benefits of operating as corporations. According to Alito RFRA's text shows that Congress designed the statute to provide very broad protection for religious liberty and did not intend to put merchants to such a choice. It employed the familiar legal fiction of including corporations within RFRA's definition of "persons," but the purpose of extending rights to corporations is to protect the rights of people associated with the corporation, including shareholders, officers, and employees. Protecting the free-exercise rights of closely held corporations thus protects the religious liberty of the humans who own and control them.

The court reasoned that because HHS has already devised and implemented a system that seeks to respect the religious liberty of religious nonprofit corporations while ensuring that the employees of these entities have precisely the same access to all FDA-approved contraceptives as employees of companies, so too it could devise such a plan for closely held corporations.

The dissent argued that RFRA does not cover Conestoga, Hobby Lobby, and Mardel because they cannot "exercise ... religion" and " the exercise of religion is characteristic of natural persons, not artificial legal entities ... Religious organizations exist to foster the interests of persons subscribing to the same religious faith. Not so of for-profit corporations. Workers who sustain the operations of those corporations commonly are not drawn from one religious community." The dissent pointed out that the majority opinion denies legions of women who do not hold their employers' beliefs access to contraceptive coverage that the ACA would otherwise secure.

a. Prisoner's Right to Free Exercise of Religion

Although prisoners are still protected by the Free Exercise Clause, prisons are subject to a lower level of scrutiny. In a case where the Court also extended prisoners the fundamental right to marry, partially based on the Free Exercise Clause, it held that when a prison infringes on prisoner's constitutional rights, the regulation is valid if it is "reasonably related to legitimate penological interests" (*Turner v. Safley*, 1987). This standard is tied to the government's interest in regulating security in prisons and adopting solutions to prison administration—activities that the court is "ill suited" to regulate (*Procunier v. Martinez*, 1974). The Court has further refused to allow a more rigorous level of scrutiny, and has turned down allowing this high level paired with an exception for instances when prisoners are conducting "presumptively dangerous" activities (*Turner v. Safley*, 1987).

Consider a case where prison officials prohibited a Buddhist state prisoner from the right to hold religious services, but simultaneously provided facilities for Protestant, Jewish, and Roman Catholic believers (*Cruz v. Beto*, 1972). Inmates were awarded points of good merit for participating in the services which would help enhance the prisoners' eligibility for class and job assignment promotions, and parole. The Court began its analysis with a reminder of the judiciary's role as constitutional enforcers, not prison supervisors. The Court found this unconstitutional and emphasized that while prisons do not have a duty to provide chapels and religious leaders for every corresponding orthodox religion, they still must provide reasonable opportunities for prisoners to exercise religious freedom under the First Amendment, without threat of penalty. Contrast this case with *O'Lone v. Shabazz*, 1987, where the prison officials were deemed to have acted reasonably. Here, the Court acknowledged their reasonable concerns that accommodating certain practices would present a higher risk of security in the prison. In this case, Muslim prisoners wanted to be excused from their jobs on Fridays to attend their weekly service that, by Muslim practice, must be held every Friday after the sun reaches its zenith and before the Asr, or afternoon prayer. The Court gave deference to the prison officials' judgment regarding security risks, and testimony given before the trial court that to restructure work schedules based on beliefs would "be a drain on scarce human resources" at the prison.

b. Rejecting Exemptions Based on the Free Exercise Clause

While some groups may be exempt from paying Federal income taxes because of religious belief, this assertion does not automatically provide tax exempt status. In *Jimmy Swaggart Ministries* (1990), a case challenging a state sales and use tax on products purchased out of state, the Court held that the generally applicable sales tax did not impose a constitutionally significant burden on an organization's religious practices, and thus did not violate the Free Exercise Clause. The Court in *Hernandez v. Commissioner* (1989) also rejected a free exercise challenge when petitioners from The Church of Scientology tried to claim charitable deductions on payments required by the church. Recognizing that the required payments were not gifts or contributions, the Court distinguished the *quid pro quo* situation from a circumstance where someone of a different religion contributed to a church free of requirements. The latter is one that was intended to benefit from the exemption. The Court has also held that parents who provide monetary support for their children during mission trips may not claim charitable exemptions for funds placed in the children's checking accounts because the church lacks control of the funds (*Davis v. U.S.*, 1990). In *Bob Jones University v. United States* (1983), the Court placed its duty to refrain from assisting a discriminatory organization above its duty to impose restrictions on an organization's free exercise of religion. In this case, the Court refused to allow a tax exemption to private schools that racially discriminated, recognizing a "fundamental, overriding interest in eradicating racial discrimination in education [that] substantially outweighs whatever burden denial of tax benefits places on petitioners' exercise of their religious beliefs." The need to eliminate discrimination constituted a compelling government interest and the Court held that "no less restrictive means" were available. In *Bowen v. Roy* (1986), the Court wrote that virtually all actions the government takes are potentially susceptible to Free Exercise objections. Using a hypothetical example of someone who practices spiritual beliefs on par with Norse mythology and the holding of Wednesday as Woden's Day, the Court pointed out that this person could object to filing tax returns on Wednesdays. To allow this free exercise challenge would make it impossible for the Government to enforce any generally applicable rules absent a compelling government interest.

Employment compensation, however, is more closely protected. The Court has refrained from invalidating government actions based on *Sherbert* in all cases except in cases denying unemployment compensation, and in recent years has refrained from applying the *Sherbert* test outside the unemployment compensation context (*Employment Division v. Smith,* 1990). In a case containing issues of employment benefits and tax exemptions, the Court applied tax exemptions to self-employed members of religious groups, but not to employees or employers (*U.S. v. Lee,* 1982). In *Lee,* an Amish employer sued for the refund of taxes on behalf of himself and his Amish employees. Writing for the Court, Chief Justice Burger held that the tax exemptions were available only to the self-employed individuals, and was thus not available to the Amish employer and employees. It recognized that the payment of taxes conflicted with Amish religious beliefs, but nonetheless held that a religious belief that conflicts with taxes provides no basis for resistance and must be applied uniformly to all, except as provided by Congress.

4. *Conclusion*

The modern constitutional standard grants deference to the judgment of the government when laws restrict religious conduct. This was established in *Smith* and reaffirmed in *Lukumi Babalu Aye.* However, Congress successfully reestablished strict scrutiny in cases involving government burdens on the religious exercise of institutional persons by passing RLUIPA and by granting for-profit corporations religious exemptions under RFRA. This reestablishment is by statute and is not constitutionally required. Hence, in that limited situation, the free exercise of religion is protected by statute from neutral, generally applicable laws that burden religion.

II. Resolving Conflict between the Establishment, Free Exercise, and Free Speech Clauses

As we have seen, the two Religion Clauses take complementary approaches to preserving freedom of religion and conscience. First, the Establishment Clause prohibits the establishment of religion by the federal government and extends that prohibition to state governments through the Fourteenth Amendment. Depending on the framework applied, this means that the government must (1) scrupulously honor the "wall of separation" between the government and religion; (2) act neutrally toward religion; or (3) accommodate religion without preferring one religion over another. Second, the Free Exercise Clause affords an absolute right to believe in any religion of one's choice, but it minimally protects the right to practice one's religion without interference from the state. This essentially amounts to strict scrutiny for facially discriminatory laws but only a rational basis test for laws of general application that burden the ability to practice one's religion, either by requiring acts in violation of one's religion or by prohibiting acts required by one's religion. Sometimes, only one clause is implicated, but it is far more common for both clauses to be implicated by the same situation. The tension between the two clauses becomes evident when the government prohibits acts that are required by one's religion.

When a government tries to accommodate religion by respecting a religion's peculiarities, similar to that in *Yoder*, it sometimes goes too far and indicates a preference for a particular sect over another. The Court found that this was the effect of the New York law in *Board of Education of Kiryas Joel Village School District v. Grumet* (1994). In that case, a particular Jewish sect purchased an undeveloped subdivision and petitioned the state to form a village. New York granted the petition and drew the village's boundaries around the subdivision that the Jewish sect exclusively inhabited. The two schools in the village were entirely private and were segregated based on gender. Neither school provided for the education of special needs students; thus, those children had to attend public schools in a neighboring school district. The parents withdrew their special needs children from the public schools because the students there were very different from them. In an effort to solve the problem, New York created a public school district exclusively for the Village of Kiryas Joel. The Court held that the new school district, which contained only members of the Jewish sect, was an unconstitutional establishment of religion. Writing for the majority, Justice Souter found that this single-religion school board violated the neutrality that the Establishment Clause required. New York's attempt to meet the needs of the Jewish sect and accommodate their faith went too far and effectively established a religion by law in the Village of Kiryas Joel. In dissent, Justice Thomas explained that the Court's decision was antagonistic toward the Jewish sect because it prohibited the government from vesting political power in a group of citizens if they all belong to the same religion. He wrote that accommodation of religion particularly that of a minority, "follows the best of our traditions."

The Court also addressed the conflict between the clauses in *Locke v. Davey* (2004), which involved a state constitutional provision that prohibited granting state scholarships to students who pursued degrees that were of a devotional nature or were "designed to induce religious faith." The state of Washington provided the Promise Scholarship Program to enable academically qualified students with financial need to attend college at a religious or other private school, as long as students did not pursue a degree in theology. Chief Justice Rehnquist wrote the majority opinion, in which the Court recognized that although the Religion Clauses "are frequently in tension," the program at issue here struck the appropriate balance between the two clauses. Washington permitted students to use the scholarship money at religious institutions, which offset the single restriction that the scholarships could not be used toward theology degrees. He found that the state's accommodation of religion (attending religious schools) did not violate either the Establishment Clause or the Free Exercise Clause. Furthermore, the state had a substantial interest in not funding students pursuing devotional degrees that put only a minor burden on the recipients of the scholarship. In his dissent, Justice Thomas thought that the program violated the Free Exercise Clause. It was facially discriminatory because it provided a generally applicable program and then carved out a single exception that targeted religion. Sometimes, the accommodation of religion implicates the Freedom of Speech Clause, instead of the Establishment Clause. The Court resolves this conflict in favor of permitting religious speech. In *Widmar v. Vincent* (1981), the Court held that to avoid content-based and viewpoint-based discrimination of speech, state universities must give student religious groups the same access to university meeting rooms that other student groups receive. The Court has extended this to the use of public school buildings by religious groups after school hours.

In *Trinity Lutheran Church of Columbia, Inc. v. Comer* (2017), a 7–2 court held that a Missouri program that denied a grant to a religious school for playground resurfacing, while providing grants to similarly situated non-religious groups, violated the free exercise clause. Denying a public benefit to an otherwise eligible recipient solely on account of its religious status is "odious to our Constitution." The court distinguished Locke v. Davey (2004) where the State of Washington did not allow state scholarships for pursuing a devotional theology degree. Washington chose not to fund a distinct category of instruction so Davey was denied a scholarship not because of who he was, but because of what he wanted to do. Here Trinity Lutheran is denied a grant simply because of what it is—a church. Missouri could not rely on *Locke* because devotional theology is an essentially religious endeavor while playground resurfacing is not. The Court found that the discrimination against the church failed strict scrutiny because Missouri did not have a compelling government interest.

In *Rosenberger v. Rector and Visitors of the University of Virginia* (1995), the Court addressed whether the University of Virginia's Student Activities Fund could deny funds for printing a Christian student publication. In an opinion written by Justice Kennedy, the Court first found that the program violated the Free Speech Clause. It then found that the fund was neutral toward religion because it was not "a tax levied for the direct support of a church or group of churches." Rather, the fund was financed by a fee charged to the students. The fund was distributed to a variety of student publications for the purpose of reflecting the diversity of the campus student body. The Establishment Clause did not require the school to deny eligibility to a student publication because of the viewpoint that the publication expressed. In dissent, Justice Souter argued that the Establishment Clause prohibited the Christian student publication from using money from the fund. The student activities fee, used to finance the fund, was similar to a tax and permitting the student religious group to use the funds results in the use of public money to subsidize religious proselytizing. For Justice Souter, this struck at the heart of the policy behind the Establishment Clause.

Checkpoints

- **The Free Exercise Clause**
    - The Court generally interprets this Clause as preventing the government from either punishing religious beliefs or from compelling religious beliefs. The Clause protects both the freedom to believe, which is absolute and may not be infringed, and the freedom to act, which the government has the power to regulate, if it does not unduly burden religion.
    - Laws Discriminating against Religion
        - Under the *Smith* test, a law is facially discriminatory if the law is not:
            - Facially neutral toward religion; and
            - Generally applicable to everyone, regardless of religion.
        - When a law facially discriminates against religion, the Court generally requires the law to pass strict scrutiny.
    - Facially Neutral Laws
        - A law that is enacted to remedy a social problem and that is not discriminatory toward religion may still have a discriminatory impact. Application of the *Smith* test renders a law not facially discriminatory if the law is:
            - Facially neutral toward religion; and
            - Generally applicable.
        - The Court applies a rational basis test to facially neutral laws. The Court greatly defers to the government, even if it burdens religion, because to do otherwise would allow person to nullify or escape application of the law by claiming that it conflicted with his or her religious beliefs.
        - In the twentieth century, the Court began to chip away at the deference, and in early 1960, it applied strict scrutiny to facially neutral laws that

burdened religion. However, in 1990, the Court returned to its early determination that government actions deserved great deference.

- Note, however, that Congress opposed returning to the rational basis test and attempted to restore strict scrutiny as the test. The Court struck down the Religious Freedom Restoration Act as applied to state and local governments because Congress had overstepped its power under the Enforcement Clause of the Fourteenth Amendment. The Court upheld the Religious Land Usage and Institutionalized Persons Act because Congress had express relied on its power under the Commerce and Taxing and Spending Clauses.
- Prisoners are protected by the Free Exercise Clause, but are subject to a lower level of scrutiny. When a prison infringes on prisoner's constitutional rights, the regulation is valid if it is reasonably related to legitimate penological interests.
- Under the Affordable Care Act, requiring closely held for-profit corporations to provide their female employees with no-cost access to contraception violated the Religious Freedom Restoration Act (*Burwell v. Hobby Lobby Stores, Inc.*, 2014).

- **Resolving Conflicts between the Establishment, Free Exercise, and Free Speech Clauses**
  - The Establishment and Free Expression Clauses frequently conflict because they protect opposing freedoms.
  - When the Establishment Clause and the Free Speech Clause conflict, the Court has protected the freedom of speech.

Master Checklist

Chapter One: First Amendment Theory and Methodology

- ❑ **Interpreting the First Amendment**
  - ❑ Despite the language of the First Amendment, "Congress shall make no law … abridging the freedom of speech," the court had never adopted a literal interpretation.
  - ❑ The First Amendment was likely a reaction to the English suppression of the press and speech through licensing (prior restraints) and the crime of seditious libel.
  - ❑ Until the early twentieth century, the First Amendment was only applied to the Federal Government. This changed with *Gitlow v. New York* (1925), when the Court held that the freedom of speech and press are within First Amendment protection and "among the fundamental personal rights and 'liberties' protected by the Due Process Clause of the Fourteenth Amendment from impairment by the states."
  - ❑ Free speech is vital to democracy because it allows the voters to hear and discuss a variety of viewpoints and hold public officials accountable.
  - ❑ Free speech is necessary to evaluate the truth of ideas. We arrive at the truth most accurately and efficiently when we allow ideas to openly compete in the marketplace.
  - ❑ Free speech is necessary to achieve personal autonomy and self-fulfillment.
  - ❑ Free speech offers a safety valve for releasing pent-up frustration in a lawful activity.
  - ❑ Free speech promotes tolerance of different viewpoints which engenders a respect for others, an important component to a pluralistic society.

- ❑ **Defining Speech**
  - ❑ Clearly oral and written communication of information, ideas and emotions is speech.
  - ❑ Conduct is speech when (1) the actor intended to communicate a particularized message, and (2) the circumstances are such that there is a great likelihood that the message would be understood by those who viewed the conduct.
  - ❑ Under O'Brien, government regulation of expressive conduct is permissible if:
    - ❑ The government has the power to regulate the field;
    - ❑ The regulation furthers an important or substantial government interest;
  - ❑ The government interest is unrelated to the suppression of free expression; and
  - ❑ The restriction on First Amendment freedom "is no greater than is essential" to further the government interest.
  - ❑ If the conduct at issue is speech (thus invoking the First Amendment), and the state's regulation was unrelated to suppression of free expression, then the O'Brien test applies. If the regulation is related to suppressing expression then strict scrutiny applies.
  - ❑ A federal statute that criminalizes "knowingly providing material support or resources to a foreign terrorist organization" passes the O'Brien test because it serves the governmental interest of preventing terrorism (*Holder v. Humanitarian Law Project*, 2010).
- ❑ **Vagueness and Overbreadth**
  - ❑ Vagueness and overbreadth both permit a person to facially challenge a law rather than to challenge based on a specific application, and both operate as an exception to the standing doctrine by allowing a person to challenge a law without having to suffer a personal injury.
  - ❑ When determining whether a law is overbroad and vague, the Court first determines how deep the enactment interferes with constitutionally protected communication. Second, the Court examines whether the statue is facially vague, at which time the complainant must show that the law is vague in all of its applications.
  - ❑ A law is void for vagueness if a reasonable person reading the law would not know what speech is illegal.

- ❑ A law regulating speech is unconstitutionally overbroad if it regulates substantially more speech than the constitution permits.
- ❑ Even if found overbroad, the Court can save the statute if (1) it can be given a limited construction; or (2) has a severability clause.

❑ **Content-Based Regulation and Prior Restraints**

- ❑ Except for several categories of speech which are unprotected or less protected, government regulation of speech based on its content must pass strict scrutiny.
- ❑ A prior restraint is a judicial order or administrative scheme which prevents speech from occurring.
- ❑ The Court requires that "a law subjecting the exercise of First Amendment freedoms to the prior restraint of a license" contain "narrow, objective, and definite standards to guide the licensing authority."
- ❑ Protective orders that the court issues during discovery does not amount to an unconstitutional prior restraint.

❑ **Compelled Speech**

- ❑ The right not to speak is afforded the same First Amendment protection as the right to speak.
- ❑ The government cannot force citizens to engage in speech.
- ❑ A union requiring nonmembers to pay a substantial assessment for a political fund is compelled speech that fails strict scrutiny (*Knox v. Service Employees*, 2012).

Chapter 2: Unprotected and Less Protected Speech: Permissible Content-Based Restrictions

❑ **Unprotected and Less Protected Speech**

- ❑ Advocacy of Illegal Action — Modern Test
    - ❑ The speech must be (1) directed at producing imminent lawless action and (2) the likely to bring about the imminent lawless action.
- ❑ Fighting Words and the Hostile Audience
    - ❑ Speech that is so patently offensive or insulting that it would provoke a violent reaction from even a reasonable person constitute fighting words.

- ❑ Under the hostile audience doctrine speech must cause or be imminently about to cause a disturbance of the peace.

❑ True threats of illegal, violent harm are not protected by the 1st A. (*Watts v. U.S.*, 1969).

❑ Hate Speech can only be restricted if it falls under an existing category of restricted speech.

❑ **Sexually Oriented Speech**

- ❑ The Court has created three categories of sexually oriented speech: (1) obscenity; (2) child pornography; and (3) profanity and indecency.
- ❑ Obscenity and child pornography are unprotected speech and laws prohibiting them need only pass the rational basis test.
  - ❑ Under *Miller*, material is obscene if:
    - ❑ The average person would find that the work appeals to the prurient interests when viewing the work as a whole and applying contemporary community standards;
    - ❑ The work describes or depicts sexual conduct defined by the applicable law in a patently offensive way; and
    - ❑ As a whole, the work lacks serious literary, political, scientific, or artistic value.
  - ❑ Under *Stanley*, one has a constitutionally protected right to possess obscene materials.
  - ❑ However, under *Reidel*, no one has a constitutionally protected right to produce, distribute, or sell obscene materials.
  - ❑ Under *Ferber*, the government may regulate or proscribe child pornography without applying the *Miller* test when the material depicts minors in sexual acts and actual minors were used.
  - ❑ However, under *Ashcroft v. Free Speech Coalition*, where the material purports to depict children engaging in sexual acts, but no actual children were used, the *Miller* standard applies.
- ❑ Profane and indecent speech are protected by the First Amendment, thus laws punishing this speech must pass strict scrutiny.
- ❑ However, the Court has identified limited exceptions to this protection for such speech in schools and on the broadcast media.

- ❑ But the Court has refused to extend those exceptions to First Amendment protections to telephones, cable television, and the Internet, thus they are protected under the First Amendment.
  - ❑ Public libraries and schools are neither traditional nor designated public forums so Congress can condition federal assistance for Internet access to them on the installation of software that blocks obscene or pornographic images.

❑ **Defamation**

- ❑ The First Amendment requires that a public official or a public figure cannot recover for defamation without proving that the publication was made with actual malice, defined as knowing that the publication was false or acting with reckless disregard of its falsity.
- ❑ A public official is a public employee who controls, or is perceived to control, the conduct of governmental affairs.
- ❑ Under *Damron*, a criminal charge against a public official, no matter how remote in time or place, is always "relevant to his fitness for office."
- ❑ There are two kinds of public figures:
  - ❑ A person who, by virtue of her position, generates public interest in her, is a public figure for all purposes and in all contexts; and
  - ❑ A person who injects himself in the forefront of a public controversy becomes a public figure for the limited purposes of that controversy and related issues.
- ❑ A private person still enjoys protection from defamation under the traditional definition, except that states cannot permit a private person to recover on a strict liability theory.
- ❑ Further, a private person may not recover presumed or punitive damages without meeting the amplified actual malice standard.

❑ **Speech-Related Torts Other Than Defamation**

- ❑ The New York Times standard applies to the ability of public figures and public officials to recover for intentional infliction of emotional distress and for false light invasion of privacy.
- ❑ The First Amendment prevents recovery for publication of true information that is private, once that information is released to the public, such as through publication in court documents, and is obtained lawfully.

- ❑ **Speech by Public Employees**
  - ❑ The government can prohibit participation in political activities by government employees.
  - ❑ The government may prohibit its employees from speaking on matters of public concern if its interest in efficient operations outweighs the employee's interest in such speech.
  - ❑ This prohibition is lawful when the speech contains matters of public concern yet is made in furtherance of the employee's job.
- ❑ **Government Speech**
  - ❑ Speech on behalf of the federal government is generally immune to constitutional challenges.
  - ❑ The government may promote one idea or activity at the exclusion of another without being viewpoint discriminatory.
  - ❑ The government is prohibited from enacting restrictions or conditions on funding that interferes with private speech or the judicial function.
  - ❑ The government cannot force a private organization to publicly profess a viewpoint that mirrors the government's view but is not held by the organization itself.
    - ❑ Government may compel the payment of subsidies to be used in funding government speech.
    - ❑ Specialty license plate designs constitute government speech and therefore states are entitled to reject a proposal for plates based on its message.
- ❑ **Commercial Speech**
  - ❑ Commercial speech is (1) an advertisement; (2) that refers to a specific product; and (3) is motivated by economic motives.
  - ❑ The First Amendment protects commercial speech, but it protects it less than noncommercial speech. Not all advertisements constitute commercial speech, and paid editorial advertisements fall within the protection of the First Amendment.
  - ❑ The Court applies a four-part test to determine the validity of regulations of commercial speech. This test requires: (1) a substantial interest in regulating the speech; (2) the regulation must directly advance the interest; (3) the regulation must be no more extensive than necessary to serve the interest; and (4) the speech must not be misleading and must concern lawful activity.

- ❏ The last two prongs of the test are understood only to require that the regulation be narrowly tailored, not the least restrictive means, to achieve the government interest.
- ❏ The First Amendment does not protect commercial speech that is misleading, deceptive, or false or concerns illegal activities. Thus, a regulation of such speech need only pass rational basis scrutiny.
- ❏ It is unconstitutional to put a complete ban on legal service advertisements.
  - ❏ Attorneys may engage in truthful advertisement of their services as long as the advertisement is not deceptive, subject to regulation.
  - ❏ Any solicitation by targeted, direct mail is protected, but may be regulated to some degree.
  - ❏ In-person solicitations by attorneys are not protected when they are motivated by profit, but are protected when the representation will be for free.
- ❏ The use of trade names by a business is not protected by the First Amendment.
- ❏ States generally cannot limit commercial speech where the laws were enacted under the theory that people will be better off without the information.
  - ❏ However, the Court has upheld some restrictions on commercial speech that is truthful advertising of legal activities when the restrictions are aimed at addressing other problems, like traffic safety.
- ❏ The Court has struck down regulations of certain activities or products with the goal of reducing participation in the activities or consumption of the products.
- ❏ But the Court has permitted states to regulate gambling advertisements to reduce gambling in the state.

Chapter 3: Level of Free Speech Protection Differs Based on Location of Speaker

- ❏ **Impact of Location on Freedom of Speech**
  - ❏ Public Forum, Limited Public Forum and Nonpublic Forum

- ❑ A regulation of speech in a public forum must be: (1) a reasonable, (2) content-neutral, (3) restriction on the time, place, or manner of speech, (4) that achieves an important government purpose.
- ❑ A limited public forum is a public space opened by the government specifically to be used for speech.
- ❑ A limited public forum is not created simply by opening a public space for use by the public; it must be opened specifically for speech.
- ❑ Additionally, the failure of the government to prevent speech in a public space does not create a limited public forum because the creation of a limited public forum requires the government affirmatively to open the public space for speech.
- ❑ Regulations of speech in limited public forums must meet the same test as regulations of speech in traditional public forums.
- ❑ A nonpublic forum is government property that is neither a public forum nor a limited public forum.
- ❑ The government may place reasonable and nondiscriminatory restrictions on expression in nonpublic forums.

❑ **Private Property**

- ❑ There is no right to speak on others' private property protected by the federal Constitution.
- ❑ However, a state is free to create such a right protected under that state's constitution without violating the property owner's First Amendment rights or effecting a taking under the Fifth Amendment.

❑ **Restricted Environments**

- ❑ Government Workplace — Government as Employer and Founder
  - ❑ The government can regulate employee's participation in political activities and certain speech conducted in the workplace.
  - ❑ The test of whether a public employee has been improperly punished or discharged for engaging in speech in the workplace requires balancing the interest of the employee, as a citizen, in commenting on matters of public concern, versus the interest of the State, as an employer, in promoting the efficiency of the public services it performs through its employees.

- ❑ Congress may regulate programs and organizations which promote a government message, but that does not mean Congress must then fund all speech on that topic.
- ❑ The government cannot impose a condition on receipt of government funds in a government program that forces private groups to publicly express views it opposes. However, government can prohibit the use of government funds to cover speech that opposes the government's views (*USAID v. Alliance for Open Society International*, 2013).

❑ **Public Schools**

- ❑ Public school officials may restrict student speech if that speech would materially and substantially interfere with the need for discipline in the school's operation.
- ❑ The Court generally defers to the determination of school officials about what speech is a material and substantial interference with discipline in the school's operation.
- ❑ However, that deference is not absolute, and the actions taken by the school officials must be reasonable in light of the speech.
- ❑ Public school libraries have the ability to control their collections, but the First Amendment prevents them from removing materials from their collections based on the content of the materials.
- ❑ The Court will allow school officials to prohibit speech that is vulgar and offensive in the interest of protecting minors, when the same speech would be normally be protected by the First Amendment.

❑ **Prisons**

- ❑ The Court has developed a rational basis-like test for regulation of speech by prisoners: The regulation will be upheld if it is rationally related to the achievement of a legitimate penal interest.
- ❑ Generally, the Court defers to the judgment of the facility concerning virtually all aspects of speech by prisoners, including between prisoners of different facilities and the access of the press to prisoners for interviews or to observe the conditions.

❑ **The Military**

- ❑ Military service members are subject to greater regulation of their speech, including prior restraints on publication at a military installation, than are civilians or even prisoners because of the risk of prejudice to the good order and discipline of the military.

- ❑ The Court generally evinces extreme deference to the judgment of the military because of the special, unique character of the military and its mission.

Chapter 4: Freedom of the Press

- ❑ **Freedom of the Press**
  - ❑ **Differentiation between the Press and the General Public**
    - ❑ Generally, the press is subject to generally applicable laws and is not entitled to any special exemption from them.
    - ❑ The press is not entitled to any specific protection from either searches pursuant to valid warrants or subpoenas requiring the divulging of news sources.
    - ❑ The press is also subject to generally applicable taxes and does not receive any specific protection from them.
    - ❑ However, the press is protected from taxes directed at the press, and such efforts to tax only the press are generally found to be unconstitutional.
  - ❑ **Access to Government Property**
    - ❑ The Court has yet to provide a general rule on this question but has addressed it with respect to access to judicial proceedings and access to prisons.
    - ❑ The press enjoys a substantial ability to observe and report on judicial proceedings; any limitations on that ability must meet exacting standards. Any restriction on the press's access to criminal trials must be narrowly tailored to achieve a compelling state interest.
    - ❑ However, the press enjoys no greater access to prisons than the general public.
  - ❑ **Regulation of Broadcast Media versus Print Media**
    - ❑ Generally, the broadcast media is subject to greater regulation than the print media because of (1) the scarcity of the broadcast frequencies; and (2) the government is responsible for allocating the channels

and without government assistance some persons would not have access to the channels to express their viewpoints.

- ❑ **Regulation of New and Emerging Technologies**
  - ❑ Cable companies and programming providers are less regulated than are the broadcast media.
  - ❑ The Court has endorsed a form of intermediate scrutiny for regulations of cable companies and programming, requiring the regulation: (1) to be content-neutral; (2) to serve a substantial government interest; and (3) to be narrowly tailored to serve that interest.
  - ❑ The Court has generally been hostile to regulations of content on the Internet.
  - ❑ Regulations of content on the Internet must pass strict scrutiny else they are invalid.

Chapter 5: Freedom of Association, Political Parties, and Campaign Finance

- ❑ **Freedom of Association**
  - ❑ Generally, the First Amendment protects the right to associate, though it is not expressly stated in the Amendment.
  - ❑ The freedom of association has been incorporated against the states through the Fourteenth Amendment.
  - ❑ Infringements on the freedom must be narrowly tailored to achieve a legitimate government interest.
  - ❑ **Defining Association**
    - ❑ Generally, freedom of association does not protect a group that has discriminatory membership policies.
    - ❑ However, the freedom of association does protect a group with discriminatory membership policies if:
      - ❑ The group is an intimate association, defined as a small, private gathering, or
      - ❑ The group is an integral part of an expressive activity.
    - ❑ A local union can charge nonmembers for their share of its contribution to a national's litigation expenses if (1) the subject matter of the

litigation is something that would be chargeable if the litigation were local, and (2) the local chapter could ultimately benefit from the outcome of the national litigation.

- ❑ **The Electoral Process and Campaign Finance**
  - ❑ Generally, campaigns can be required to disclose lists of donors because of the government's substantial interests in preventing corruption and the appearance of corruption.
  - ❑ However, a minor party may refuse to comply with disclosure requirements because of the risk that the disclosure requirement could chill contributions to the party and because the party is unlikely to win at the ballot box.
  - ❑ It is unconstitutional to place expenditure limits on individuals running for office.
  - ❑ It is unconstitutional to place limits on contributions if there is no purpose for doing so.
  - ❑ Congress is prohibited from fining or jailing an association of citizens for engaging in political speech, and may not impose restrictions on disfavored speakers.
    - ❑ Corporations have a First Amendment right to make contributions to ballot initiative campaigns because commercial speech is accorded some constitutional protection because it furthers the societal interest in the free flow of commercial information.
  - ❑ The decision of *Citizens United v. Federal Election Commission* found that corporations, like individuals, have a First Amendment right to free speech.
  - ❑ In *American Tradition Partnership, Inc. v. Bullock* the Supreme Court extended the ruling in *Citizens* to the states.
  - ❑ "We the people who are sovereign" includes human beings and corporations; thus, corporations are protected by the First Amendment Freedom of Association Clause. However, the government has a justifiable interest in requiring corporations to disclose spending amounts, as such requirements do not subject corporations to danger, threats, or harassment.
  - ❑ Exacting scrutiny is the appropriate level of review when reviewing challenges to the electoral process.

- ❑ Exacting scrutiny requires a substantial relation between the disclosure requirement and a sufficiently important governmental interest.
- ❑ The strength of the government's interest must reflect the seriousness of the actual burden on the First Amendment.
- ❑ Limits on aggregate federal campaign contributions violate the First Amendment (*McCutcheon v. FEC*, 2014).
    - ❑ States can ban judicial candidates from personally soliciting campaign funds because they have a vital interest in safeguarding public confidence in the fairness and integrity of the elected judges.

Chapter 6: The Establishment Clause

- ❑ **Definition of Religion**
    - ❑ A "religion" is any deep, sincere belief that occupies a place in that person's life analogous to that of God in commonly recognized religions.
    - ❑ The Court has provided three different approaches to defining religion: First, it has attempted to outline who qualifies under the conscientious objector status; second, it has required that a belief must be sincerely held, which is subject to examination by the court; and third, it has extended this class of people to include those with non-traditional beliefs that are associated with traditional religions.
    - ❑ In determining whether a belief constitutes a religion, the courts cannot inquire into subjective aspects, such as the truth of religious views, or of the correct interpretation of matters of faith, including doctrines, tenets, and dogma.
    - ❑ When evaluating a person's sincerity, the inquiry cannot include whether a belief system is generally recognized, whether it has a certain minimum number of believers, or what constitutes the particular beliefs of the system.
- ❑ **Applicability of the Religion Clauses to the States**
    - ❑ The Court first incorporated and applied the Free Exercise Clause to the states in 1940 and applied the Establishment Clause to the states in 1947.
- ❑ **Analytical Frameworks for the Establishment Clause**
    - ❑ There are three primary frameworks used to analyze Establishment Clause cases.

- ❑ Strict separation: There is a "wall of separation" between the government and religion, and the Court should not tolerate a breach of that wall, no matter how *de minimis* the breach may be. Government should never directly support religion and cannot provide aid to individuals that indirectly benefits religion.
- ❑ Neutrality: The government should approach religion neutrally. This means that the government should neither actively aid nor actively inhibit religion. The government should keep its promotion or discouragement of religious observance, belief, or activity to a minimum.
- ❑ Accommodation: The government should accommodate religion. This framework allows for the most intermingling of state and religion. The Establishment Clause is violated only if the government establishes an official religion, coerces religious participation, or favors one religion over another. Coercion occurs only if the government requires or punishes the failure to engage in religious practice. Social pressure is not coercion.

❑ **Tests for Analyzing Establishment Clause Questions**

- ❑ The *Lemon* test consists of three prongs, all of which must be met to comply with the Establishment Clause:
  - ❑ Law must have a valid secular purpose (sometimes the Court says that the law's primary purpose must be secular);
  - ❑ Law's primary effect must neither advance nor inhibit religion; and
  - ❑ Law must not create an "excessive entanglement" between government and religion.

❑ **Other Tests Proposed but not Adopted**

- ❑ The symbolic endorsement test, espoused by Justice O'Connor in *Lynch v. Donnelly*, examines whether the challenged government act expressed government endorsement or disapproval of religion. This endorsement or disapproval can either be direct (intentional) or indirect (by effect, rather than intent). The test changes the *Lemon* test by deemphasizing the secular purpose prong and reformulating the remaining two prongs.
- ❑ The endorsement test views the challenged religious display through the eyes of a hypothetical reasonable viewer who is aware of all pertinent facts and history surrounding the display.
- ❑ The coercion test examines the coercive effect of the government action on participation in state-sponsored or state-initiated religious activity.

The coercion can be either obvious or subtle, such as through peer pressure, and the latter is more insidious because it is harder to detect. Justice Kennedy applied this test in *County of Allegheny v. ACLU* and *Lee v. Weisman*.

- ❑ **Categories of Establishment Clause Cases**
  - ❑ **School Prayer and Other State-Sanctioned Prayer or Religious Activity**
    - ❑ The Court typically applies the *Lemon* test when prayer in public schools is involved.
    - ❑ Generally, prayer in public schools is not permitted if a public school or any level of government sanctions the prayer in any way. This includes student-led nondenominational prayer that is voluntary if the school sanctioned the prayer, its organization, or its delivery. This general prohibition cannot be circumvented by permitting the students to vote on whether to have the prayer and on who shall deliver it.
  - ❑ **School Curriculum Decisions Involving Religion**
    - ❑ Through application of the *Lemon* test, the Establishment Clause prohibits the states from infusing religion into their public school curricula.
    - ❑ The states cannot condition the teaching of a scientific theory on the teaching of a competing religious theory. Furthermore, states cannot require public schools to participate in religious exercises, even if the state espouses a secular purpose or allows students and teachers to voluntarily participate.
  - ❑ **Equal Access to Public Facilities**
    - ❑ If a public facility is open to the public, then the government cannot deny a group access solely because that group is religious in nature.
  - ❑ **Prayer in Legislatures**
    - ❑ Town boards may open with prayer as long as it does not coerce participation and does not discriminate against minority faiths in determining who can offer the prayer (*Town of Greece v. Galloway*, 2014).
  - ❑ **Religious Displays on Public Property**
    - ❑ The Court permits placement of religious symbols on public property, as long as the placement does not convey symbolic endorsement of a particular religion, or endorsement of religion in general, and as long as the symbols are included among other secular and religious symbols in equal fashion.

- ❑ The Court has found ways around the Establishment Clause when dealing with the obstruction of monuments donated by private groups. This alternative is to call the display a form of government speech, which is not subject to a view-point discrimination analysis.

❑ **Official Acknowledgment of Religion**

- ❑ Official acknowledgment typically occurs when a religious display or other religious expression is made by the government or included in a governmental building.
- ❑ The Court is generally suspicious of such governmental religious displays when they are not balanced by secular displays. However, the Court generally finds no violation of the Establishment Clause if the religious displays are accompanied to an equal degree by secular displays.
- ❑ The Court distinguishes between governmental acts and independent acts by government officials, such as presidential speeches.
- ❑ If a solely religious display is intended to emphasize religious pluralism or another secular purpose, it will likely be upheld by the Court.
- ❑ The Court is generally very suspicious about religious displays and expression in the context of primary and secondary schools.
- ❑ The government cannot symbolically endorse a religion or uphold laws that solely benefit religion.

❑ **Financial Aid to Religious Institutions**

- ❑ The Court is generally suspicious of and does not permit government-based financial aid to religious primary and secondary schools. However, if the aid can be separated from the school's primary mission, and it can be provided solely by state employees, the Court may permit it. The Court feels a greater need to monitor the primary and secondary schools because of the youth and impressionability of the children, as well as the greater emphasis on religious indoctrination in those schools.
- ❑ In contrast, the Court is generally more accepting of government-based financial aid to religious colleges and universities, as well as nonscholastic institutions, because they tend to place less emphasis on indoctrination and the students are able to critically analyze and choose their own beliefs.

- ❑ **Aid to Nonscholastic Religious Organizations**
  - ❑ Tax exemptions that benefit religion are constitutional so long as they benefit other institutions, such as charitable and educational organizations

Chapter 7: Freedom of Religion: The Free Exercise Clause

- ❑ **The Free Exercise Clause**
  - ❑ The Court generally interprets this Clause as preventing the government from either punishing religious beliefs or from compelling religious beliefs. The Clause protects both the freedom to believe, which is absolute and may not be infringed, and the freedom to act, which the government has the power to regulate, if it does not unduly burden religion.
  - ❑ **Laws Discriminating against Religion**
    - ❑ Under the *Smith* test, a law is facially discriminatory if the law is not:
      - ❑ Facially neutral toward religion; and
      - ❑ Generally applicable to everyone, regardless of religion.
    - ❑ When a law facially discriminates against religion, the Court generally requires the law to pass strict scrutiny.
  - ❑ **Facially Neutral Laws**
    - ❑ A law that is enacted to remedy a social problem and that is not discriminatory toward religion may still have a discriminatory impact. Application of the *Smith* test renders a law not facially discriminatory if the law is:
      - ❑ Facially neutral toward religion; and
      - ❑ Generally applicable.
    - ❑ The Court applies a rational basis test to facially neutral laws. The Court greatly defers to the government, even if it burdens religion, because to do otherwise would allow person to nullify or escape application of the law by claiming that it conflicted with his or her religious beliefs.

- ❑ In the twentieth century, the Court began to chip away at the deference, and in early 1960, it applied strict scrutiny to facially neutral laws that burdened religion. However, in 1990, the Court returned to its early determination that government actions deserved great deference.
- ❑ Note, however, that Congress opposed returning to the rational basis test and attempted to restore strict scrutiny as the test. The Court struck down the Religious Freedom Restoration Act as applied to state and local governments because Congress had overstepped its power under the Enforcement Clause of the Fourteenth Amendment. The Court upheld the Religious Land Usage and Institutionalized Persons Act because Congress had express relied on its power under the Commerce and Taxing and Spending Clauses.
- ❑ Prisoners are protected by the Free Exercise Clause, but are subject to a lower level of scrutiny. When a prison infringes on prisoner's constitutional rights, the regulation is valid if it is reasonably related to legitimate penological interests.
- ❑ Under the Affordable Care Act, requiring closely held for-profit corporations to provide their female employees with no-cost access to contraception violated the Religious Freedom Restoration Act (*Burwell v. Hobby Lobby Stores, Inc.*, 2014).

❑ **Resolving Conflicts between the Establishment, Free Exercise, and Free Speech Clauses**

- ❑ The Establishment and Free Expression Clauses frequently conflict because they protect opposing freedoms.
- ❑ When the Establishment Clause and the Free Speech Clause conflict, the Court has protected the freedom of speech.

Index